Adopting the Older Child

Adopting the Older Child

CLAUDIA L. JEWETT

The Harvard Common Press

The Harvard Common Press
535 Albany Street
Boston, Massachusetts 02118

Printed in the United States of America.

Library of Congress Cataloging in Publication Data

Jewett, Claudia L.   1939–
    Adopting the older child.

    Bibliography: p.
    Includes index.
    1. Adoption—United States. 2. Children, Adopted
—United States—Case studies. I. Title.
HV675.J48   362.7'34   77-26973

ISBN 0-916782-08-5
ISBN 0-916782-09-3 pbk.

Cover design by Paul Bacon

Paperback edition published May 1979

20 19 18 17

To my husband, Dave,
and to our children :
Larry, Sally, Josh, Mary,
Matt, Helena, Megan,
Rachel, James, and Kristen

Contents

Introduction

Some years ago, my husband Dave and I set about on a great adventure. We decided to fulfill our dream of having a large family by adding to our three biological children some of the children who waited, the older children in need of parents. We didn't adopt out of pity, although compassion was there; we adopted because we deeply wanted a larger family and we felt that this was a good way to go about it. We didn't see adoption as a cause, although social consciousness was there; we adopted because we really like to be parents, and because we felt there was no need to reproduce ourselves again. We didn't adopt because we are noble, unusual people; we adopted in spite of our shortcomings, because we wanted each of the children who came to join us.

Through the problems we encountered, we became better problem solvers and more competent people. Through the experiences we shared with our children, we grew to be wiser and to know ourselves better. Through the excitements and the discouragements we lived with as we became a family, we became more compassionate. Through being stretched, we grew.

In the process, the size of our dream and the risks we allowed ourselves to take also grew. We don't know what the eventual outcome for all of us will be, but the daily living is good, rich, and full. It is better than we could have ever guessed it might be.

Over these years, my own experience as an adoptive parent of older children, coupled with my professional training in family counseling, has put me in the position of closely sharing this particular kind of adoption experience with a great many other families. I have worked for some time with placement agencies and social workers as they tried to find the best ways to help build families through older child adoption. And I have known a good number of children who needed families, and have felt their confusions, their loneliness, their pain.

This book grew out of these experiences. It tells the stories of five particular children of differing needs and ages and of the individual families who adopt them. None of these stories reflects any one child I have known, nor represents any particular family I have worked with. Rather these stories tell the common feelings, concerns, and problems of many families and of the older children they have adopted. Although the characters are fictional, their experiences and the ways they work out their adoptions are not.

These families are unusually fortunate in the social worker with whom they share their adoption experiences. She works in a state where a unique commitment has been made by legislators to provide adequate funds for agency staffing, training, and administration so that children can be provided with outstanding services. She is, therefore, able to do her job in ideal circumstances, unhampered by the time conflicts and the unmanageable caseloads that force most workers to perform under the pressure of a crisis-to-crisis schedule. Although her sensitivity, thoroughness, and professional training make her remarkable today, she is not atypical of the quality of personnel developed in those very few programs that adequately prepare workers and provide them the opportunity to do the kind of job that is needed. There is hope that in the future concerned people will join to demand realistic funding so that workers can better go about placing children and so that more children and families will receive the services represented in this book.

C. L. J.
Harvard, Massachusetts
September 1977

1
Who Are the Children Who Wait?

While you are reading this there are between 100,000 and 120,000 children in this country waiting for families of their own. Cut loose from their original families, never to return, adoption may be their only chance for the love, guidance, and concern that all children need in order to grow into well-adjusted adults—able to like themselves, love others, build strong marriages, and raise healthy children of their own. And yet they wait, each passing year making their chances for a permanent family slimmer. Rejected, neglected, often moving time and time again—they need a place to belong.

These children need a social welfare system to go to bat for them—to end the red tape that keeps them in limbo without a tailored plan for their survival; to provide monies to staff offices adequately so that parents can be recruited, homes studied, children placed. Each of these children needs a dedicated social worker to translate him or her from another impersonal case study into a living, breathing child. Each needs a family where the child counts, is valued, and can develop according to his or her potential. Each of these children has a story worth telling.

If all these stories of past separations, losses, and adjustments could be gathered together, it would take a large file room to house them. One could randomly open any of these master file drawers, flip through its contents, and arbitrarily pick out four of the many manila folders within—selecting one fat, dog-eared folder; one skimpy, almost untouched and easily overlooked folder; and two medium-sized folders. These files would contain few surprises to the worker or the parent with some experience in older child adoption. For others, to spread them on a table and settle down to read what lies within them is the best way to understand the children who wait.

Danny, Age 13

Clipped to the inside cover of the largest, well-handled file is a color snapshot of an alert black youngster with expressive brown eyes and a slight frown. He has medium-brown skin and a full, stylish Afro. Something about this young man is both attractive and a little challenging. The picture makes the sketchy dictated record more real, but it does not show how easily this teen-ager makes friends, how skillfully he plays soccer and street hockey, how enthusiastically he fills spare time listening to the latest rock music and avoids his current situation by dreaming about playing a guitar in his own band.

According to the recorded information, Danny spent his early years with parents from whom he received little care and less attention. Both of his parents had serious drinking problems; as a result, Danny's father was often unemployed. When Danny was eight a complaint was lodged against his parents by the school, and he was found to be both malnourished and severely neglected. Danny was removed from his family and placed in a foster home by the children's protective agency. Although attempts were made to aid his birth parents, conditions did not show much change.

The next few entries show that Danny seemed to get along with the foster family. But after two years his foster father was transferred to another state; Danny was not included in the family plans. His second foster family had just begun to seem comfortable to Danny when his foster mother broke her hip and Danny had to move again.

Danny is currently living in a foster home where there are a great many children. No one pays much attention to Danny or to what he thinks and feels and does. He comes and goes as he pleases. Although his intelligence tests show him to be of average ability and he is not a discipline problem, Danny is falling behind in school. He seems to be giving up on himself academically.

Like those of many other waiting children, Danny's problems began because he was born into a family so troubled by chronic illness, unemployment, and poverty that it was unable to provide for his needs. Frequently these homes are headed by parents who suffer from their own unhappy pasts, whose childhoods lacked the care and love that would have better enabled them to be nurturing parents.

Taken into care by the court system, children like Danny sometimes go into foster homes until the original family can be rehabilitated or another permanent plan can be made for them. About half of the older children subsequently freed for adoption become permanent, legal members of their foster families —which attests to the love, caring, and commitment so often evident in foster parents. Unfortunately there are always more children needing foster care than there are good foster homes available. Because children usually need foster placement suddenly, workers rarely have the luxury of matching a child's particular needs to the home most able to help. And often the child's needs remain unmet.

Also, because foster care is intended to be temporary, foster parents are often reluctant to form any deep emotional bonds with the child. As Goldstein, Freud, and Solnit (1973) point out, they lack the foundation of parental tolerance, endurance, and devotion—the knowledge that they are "the undisputed sole possessor of the child and the supreme arbiter of his fate. What is left, apart from the conscientious fulfillment of a task once taken over, is the appeal made by a helpless immature being on the mature adult's concern." And though this can be counted on in many instances, understandably enough it is present more often for the infant and very young child. Because the older child is less helpless and more troublesome, this child often seems less appealing. "The emotional bonds of the adults to the children will be loose enough to be broken whenever external circumstances make the presence of the foster child in the home inconvenient and irksome," and therefore foster placements frequently break down (Goldstein, Freud, and Solnit 1973, pp. 25, 26). As a result, there is a continual shifting of children like Danny.

Many of the children who are moved respond like Danny has. After each loss — of a home, a familiar neighborhood, and people he was fond of — Danny has acted increasingly hard and tough, as if to show that he could take being moved around, as if he didn't need *anyone*. Danny's aloofness and his apparent toughness intimidate some people; others are able to see through to the needful, frightened young boy inside.

Because Danny is a black teen-ager from an unstable background, the odds are against him when it comes to finding permanent parents. Few people are willing to tackle the problems of a child as old as Danny. They fear that a child so far away from his early formative years is beyond help, that his personality and his values are permanently set.

And yet, those same people see their own growth, change, and maturation as an ongoing process. They don't feel that they stopped changing at two, or five, or ten, or twenty. They can remember how much they rearranged their own thinking and values in their teen-age years and the years since. Is it fair then to assume that Danny will not also be able to change, especially if his life conditions change?

Many experts on child behavior believe that although Danny may resist change he has the capacity to grow. He is not too fixed, he is not too old, he is not too damaged. Michael Rutter, who did several studies on severely deprived children, says: "It is frequently thought that the infancy period has a special significance in development so that environmental influences in early life have an overriding effect on what happens to the child regardless of later experiences. This claim has been disputed in several reviews and actually there is no evidence that environmental factors can only have a decisive influence in early childhood" (Rutter 1972, p. 58).

No child can be protected from anxiety and trauma in his life. It is how he deals with what happens to him, what kind of support and help he gets, that determines how his personality will be affected.

Alfred Kadushin (1971), who studied 95 families who had adopted children ages five to twelve, found that, once the adjustment was over, the age of the child when he entered his adoptive family did not make a difference or impede the successful outcome of the adoption. Sula Wolff, a recognized authority on the impact of stress on children, says: "All children who need to be looked after outside their own homes, for whatever reason, are children at risk. All have experienced unusual stresses and many are disturbed. The people who adopt them are in a unique position to prevent life crises from becoming pathogenic, to prevent separation experiences from developing into deprivation, to provide the kind of upbringing for each child that will make good his past deficiencies" (Wolff 1969, p. 225).

Frequently one of the most gratifying experiences for parents of older displaced children is sharing and guiding this change. A child's resilience, his ability to be healed and to recover lost ground, is often astonishing. The normal parental excitement that comes when children master a new skill, integrate a new concept, or solidify their values is heightened with these children, who have had so much against their making it in life at all.

Gena and Tommy, Ages 11 and 7

One of the medium-sized folders selected from our fictitious file contains the story of Gena, eleven, and Tommy, seven — brother and sister. Their current worker describes them like this:

> An attractive pair of children with ash blond hair and blue eyes, Gena and Tommy are looking for a home together.
> Gena is a very verbal child, bright and imaginative. Constantly

on the go, Gena likes everybody. Since she and Tommy were abandoned by their mother four years ago, Gena has shown a deep need to feel loved and wanted. She seems starved for attention. She has looked out for Tommy for a long time and she feels the responsibility of giving him his only sense of family. Gena is inclined to be overprotective of her younger brother, not giving him the chance to do things for himself. She seems to need to feel that he depends on her. She is frequently critical and bossy with him.

Although Gena lacks some of the basic academic skills, she is intelligent and eager to learn. She is currently attending the sixth grade.

Tommy is a likable, handsome boy who is quite dependent on his older sister.

He is well coordinated and loves to ride his bike. In school, he is eager to learn. With praise and encouragement he does well, but he gets frustrated and panicky if given too many choices. Because he is so anxious to please, he overreacts when he fears that he will not measure up, giving up on tasks too easily. He is also reluctant to try new things, which gets in the way of his academic performance.

Tommy is a sensitive boy who cries easily and seems very young for his age. He has frequent bad dreams and is afraid of the dark.

Sometimes children like Gena and Tommy have never known adults who felt affection for them. Many show an enormous need to be noticed, to be needed, to be loved. Their hunger for someone who cares is constant. Unable to understand the life pressures and problems of their parents, these children often believe themselves to be the cause of their rejection. They feel that they must be such bad children that even their own parents couldn't love them.

Children like Gena and Tommy frequently feel that if they could only be different, be better, things would improve. They can't allow themselves to make mistakes, to be wrong. Like Gena's, their feelings of worthlessness sometimes cause them to reach out indiscriminately to anyone for reassurance. Sometimes, as in Tommy's case, these same fears and feelings cause them to become unsure and fearful.

What will happen to Gena and Tommy?

Maggie, Age 8

Although their files are very much the same size, the contrast between Gena and Maggie is striking. The description of Maggie reads: "A very shy, quiet child, usually well behaved and undemanding, Maggie can seem hostile at times. She finds it hard to trust people." The accompanying picture shows a strikingly attractive, feminine little girl with delicate features, a mass of curls, and large, wide-spaced eyes.

Maggie's original home was broken by divorce and neither of her parents was able or willing to provide a home for her. Maggie spent some time moving from one relative to another before coming into the care of an agency. Unlike Gena, who reaches out, Maggie handles her sense of worthlessness, of failure, by turning inward. Much of Maggie's hostility and distrust stems from her many rejections in the past by adults who failed to give her a permanent home. She has come to believe that life will always hold more of the same: if she lets herself want—to stay, to love and be loved, to belong—she is only opening herself up again to more painful loss, disappointment, and sadness. So she denies her real need and seems unfeeling, uncaring. Maggie's foster mother does not like her and would like to have Maggie removed from her home. She complains that Maggie is a cold, unresponsive child and she is intolerant of the problem that Maggie has with bedwetting.

Some of the children who wait are eager for parents; many of them, though, are like Maggie, challenging parents to convince them that a new family is different and safe. These children frequently act in a manner that says, "Who needs you?" They are likely to compare new parents unfavorably with other adults in their past, outwardly rejecting the love offered, the way of life, the discipline, and the people that their new parents love.

If Maggie is adopted, she will probably go into a new family unsure if she wants to bother to know these adoptive parents, let alone to love them. She will find it hard to believe that parents *can* love a child like her, and that it is safe and pleasant to love them back. She will not be able to meet them halfway. Only after a long while, with constant love and under-standing from parents, will she let herself trust; it will be even longer before she can let herself risk enough to love again. Maggie needs parents who are able to keep giving even when they receive little in return, who are secure enough not to feel personally rejected, who can curb their own impatience and trust that the waiting will pay off. Frequent moves will have taken their emotional toll, and temporary behavior problems — bedwetting, temper tantrums, anxieties, lying — may be expected.

A green elementary school report card shows Maggie to be a grade behind in school. In the individual comments at the bottom Maggie's teacher writes that Maggie is a daydreamer, preoccupied in the classroom and inclined to be slow about finishing her work.

Part of the difficulty for children who are deprived of parental care is that their development is almost always retarded — physically, intellectually, and socially (Bowlby 1965, p. 21). Like Maggie, many of these children perform much more poorly than their classmates. They are behind in general knowledge, reading, arithmetic, and in the ability to express themselves in conversation. They are also short on concentration; their teachers describe them as messy, slapdash, or careless. Many of the children are like Tommy, quite immature for their ages. By the time they are seven, propor-tionately more children who have been in foster care are short in height and underweight for their ages. In comparison with their classmates they appear to have poor control of their hands when writing, drawing, or buttoning up their coats; they are fidgety; they tend to have poor physical coordination in running, jumping, or throwing balls; they are clumsy; and they are hardly ever still. Their teachers describe them as less attractive than other children; one in five is said to look scruffy or very dirty, and one in ten underfed (Pringle 1975, pp. 131–133).

Can a family be found for Maggie?

Joey, Age 10

Joey's file has almost no information in it. Much of his time in care he has not had a worker assigned him, and there are gaps of several years between entries. The early entries establish that Joey was born to a young, immature unwed mother who cared for him during parts of the first fifteen months of his life. She seems to have been somewhat erratic in her handling of him — wanting him around for short periods of time and then farming him out to neighbors to be minded until she felt like taking him on again. Eventually she put Joey into a state-licensed foster home, where the foster mother pointed out that Joey's physical and verbal development were both quite slow.

The next entry, several years later, reports that at five Joey still showed somewhat slow development, but that he seemed much closer to average than in the previous report. He was no longer assumed to be intellectually handicapped. His worker did not refer him for adoption because he felt that the boy's history of slowness and his "advanced" age ruled him ineligible.

Now Joey has a new worker. She describes him as "a freckle-faced, enthusiastic ten-year-old boy, who can succeed in most of what he tries to do but who has a poor self image. Joey is rather impulsive and gets into jams because he hasn't thought his actions or ideas through. He is easily frustrated. His foster mother has called him 'a likable boy with a short fuse.' When things don't go smoothly for him he has temper tantrums. Lately these have been coming more frequently."

Joey is one grade behind in school and is receiving extra help for reading and for math. The plan at this time is to try to locate an adoptive family for him.

The impulsiveness, quick anger, and easy frustration that are part of Joey's makeup are not uncommon traits in the children needing parents. Many of them have not learned to wait, to try again, to plan ahead, to work their problems out. Lacking a sense of personal competence and control, they suffer from low self-esteem. Sometimes they set impossible goals for themselves; at other times they see themselves as perpetual failures. When they do succeed, they tend to devalue their successes by demeaning anything that they can do well. In this way they perpetuate their cycle of low self-esteem.

Danny, Gena and Tommy, Maggie, Joey. What each of these children needs is a permanent, caring family,

> . . . responsible for and capable of providing the child on a continuing basis with an environment . . . [where] the child's body [can be] tended, nourished, and protected. . . . He needs help in understanding and organizing his sensations and perceptions. He needs people to love, receive affection from, and to serve as safe targets for his infantile anger and aggression. He needs assistance from the adults in curbing and modifying his primitive drives (sex and aggression). He needs patterns for identification provided by the parents, to build up a functioning moral conscience. As much as anything else, he needs to be accepted, valued, and wanted as a member of the family unit (Goldstein, Freud, and Solnit 1973, pp. 13-14).

It will be too bad if these children are once again filed away in some forgotten drawer where they remain alone, unwanted, hopeless. Once we have looked into their lives it is hard to turn away from Danny, Gena and Tommy, Maggie, and Joey.

2
Making the Decision to Adopt an Older Child

The outlook for waiting older children was very bleak at the beginning of the 1970s. Only 4 percent of the children adopted in 1971 were over five years of age. But by the mid-1970s, older children had a much better chance for adoption. How do people come to decide to add one of these children to their family?

Jack and Maureen Reilly

It is a warm Sunday afternoon in late summer. Jack and Maureen Reilly sit on the front steps of their apartment building, talking. This has been quite a year for the Reillys, and they are just beginning to regain some sense of ease and direction. A young Catholic couple in their late twenties, Maureen and Jack have been trying unsuccessfully for most of their five years of marriage to start a family. Last spring they went to a highly regarded fertility specialist to investigate their situation, to find out where their difficulty lay and what they could do about it. After undergoing a thorough battery of tests, the Reillys were told that Jack was infertile and that they would never be able to have the baby that each of them wants so badly.

Jack had a rough time accepting the diagnosis. Somehow he felt that his masculinity was in question, that he was not a full man. He worried about how Maureen would feel. Would she still lovingly accept him as her husband? Maureen did her best to reassure him that nothing had changed between them. She did her crying privately so that Jack would not be hurt. Inwardly, both Reillys felt a great deal of anger. Why had this happened to them? They would be wonderful parents, much better able to care for a baby than people that they knew who seemed to conceive a child a year. Why had they been singled out?

Even in today's society, in which childbearing has become more of a personal choice and it is not so automatically assumed that every couple will choose to have children, little is done to prepare couples like Jack and Maureen for the possibility that they might not be *able* to have children. Most boys and girls still grow up hearing, "When you grow up and have children . . . ." Some, with liberated parents, may hear, "When you grow up, if you decide to have children . . . ." But almost no one hears, "When you grow up, if you *can* have children . . . ." A diagnosis of untreatable infertility is a cruel blow — to one's self-esteem, sense of health, sexuality, feelings of control, and especially to one's plans for the future.

By early summer Jack was more resigned to their situation and Maureen began talking about the possibility of adopting a baby. After they thought about it for a while they both decided that this was a good solution for them, so Maureen began to call the adoption agencies in their large city, hoping to get their names on a placement list so that they might start their family. Although they assumed that they might have to wait for their baby, they were not at all prepared for the response that they received from agency personnel. No one would put their names on a list for a baby; no one would talk to them; one woman even laughed and asked them where they had been the last several years. There were no babies, she said—not in this city, not in this state, perhaps not in this country.

Because so many unwanted pregnancies end in abortion, and because there has been a great increase in the number of unwed mothers who choose to keep their babies at a time when more and more couples seek to adopt, there has been a sharp decrease in the number of babies available for the couples who want them. Some agencies still place infants with couples willing to wait several years. Other agencies will not even consider doing a home study on a couple desiring a normal white infant. As a result of the shortage of available babies, infertile couples who might first think to become parents by adopting a young child must often rethink their plans.

There are really three lawful options for Jack and Maureen —they can decide to remain childless, they can adopt a baby from overseas, or they can consider an older or handicapped child. There is no question for the Reillys about the first option; they definitely want children. They have given serious consideration to adopting from overseas, but they are concerned about several things—the red tape, the expense, and the problems they feel they might incur in their community and in their family if they tried to raise a child of another race. Now they are looking into their feelings about starting their family not with a baby but with an older child.

Maureen feels some reluctance to let go of the chance to cuddle a helpless, trusting bundle of little baby. All those pictures in her head—kneeling down, arms outstretched, for those first uncertain steps; pushing a carriage or a stroller occupied by the wondering eyes of a little one exploring the world; singing a baby to sleep—an older child would have had those experiences with someone else. On the other hand, though Jack finds infants appealing, the kinds of things he is really looking forward to doing with his child mostly involve an older youngster.

The biggest question the Reillys are dealing with is whether they could love a school-age child as much as they would have loved a child who came to them as a baby or a toddler. Maybe an older child would never seem like their own because too much of his life, his personality, and his identity would be strange to them.

As they sit sipping iced tea, they watch the neighborhood children playing kickball in the park across the street. Maureen and Jack try to imagine what it would be like to suddenly be the parents of one of those children. There are some of them that would irritate, and others that the Reillys could take on with no hesitation. What if they could find a child that they took to instantly, that they really liked for his already developed personality?

In spite of the fact that older child adoption is relatively new, people tend to have strong ideas as to how it works out. There are many inconsistencies and contradictions among commonly held opinions. The Reillys are face to face with one such set of opposites: "You'll never love them like your own" versus "It will be love at first sight." The truth in these two opposing views lies somewhere in between. Jack and Maureen may love the idea of having the child; they may feel a strong emotional pull to a child or to his picture; they may love the hope that they have for their relationship with a youngster; but they won't love an older child at first sight, or at second, or at third. But as surely as they grew to love one another, so too can they grow to love an older child, should they decide to adopt one.

Parents who have both biological and older adopted children can be most reassuring in this regard. My own experience with our family totally convinces me that in time it makes no difference how old the child was when he arrived, or whether the child came from my body or from an agency. The love I feel for the children who came to us at thirteen, fourteen, and seventeen is in no way less strong than the love I feel for the children who came to us at the younger ages of two, five, ten, and eleven. The love I feel for our adopted children is in no way less strong than the love I feel for the three children in our family who were born to us. It just doesn't make any difference. It is the caring and sharing that count — love is not prevented by the things and the time that you haven't shared.

On Monday, Jack's mind is on the weekend's discussion as he fights the evening traffic on his way home from work. He wishes he and Maureen knew someone who had adopted an older child to help them sort out fact from fiction, to help them look at the pros and cons. While he idles his engine at a red light, an announcement on the local news and music station catches his attention. Reaching over quickly, he turns up the radio to see if he heard it right. Yes, there is a meeting *tonight* at one of the area high schools for people interested in being parents for special needs children. "Hey," he thinks, "just exactly the thing." If only he can get home in time for him and Maureen to make the meeting, maybe they'll have a chance to get some of their questions answered.

The meeting is fascinating. A little out of breath from their rushed dinner and departure, the Reillys arrive and grab two of the seats down front. Most of the room is full. They are surprised that there are so many other people interested.

Following an introduction by representatives of several agencies, the lights are dimmed and slides are shown of some of the children in need of parents. They aren't babies, but Maureen finds herself responding to the appeal of several of the children. All of a sudden the possibilities of adopting an older child seem much more exciting. Maureen can hear Jack chuckling under his breath from the seat next to her in the darkened room, as some of the various children are shown. He's feeling the same way, too.

After the pictures, the lights are turned back on and a social worker leads a panel discussion by three couples who have adopted children similar to the ones in the slides. None of the parents makes the task seem easy as they share some of the problems and difficulties they experienced. They have had some rough adjustments. But they are all so positive about their children now. Listening to the panel, Maureen is a little over-whelmed. The parents all sound so calm, logical, patient, and wise. Maureen wonders if those parents ever get unreasonably angry, or feel too tired to cope, or doubt the wisdom of their decision. Knowing how she sometimes responds to her younger brothers and sisters when she takes care of them, she feels a pang of concern. Those kids are not "troubled" children, but they can exasperate her until she yells at them. What would she do with a child with a real problem? Maybe people who adopt older children need to be less easily frustrated and more able to tolerate difficult situations than she is.

There is little question that people who adopt a troubled child find being parents to that child a challenge. But it's important for Maureen to remember that while most parents do their best and many do wisely and well, no one always knows the right thing to do or is able to do it all the time. Real children call forth human responses. Like the children, their parents will have good and not so good days; giving and selfish days; wise and tolerant moments and impatient and crabby ones. But parents who expect to make occasional mistakes and try to learn from them; who can love a child even when he infuriates or stumps them; who can face up to problems and work them out or get help if they need to, are what the waiting children need. Maureen need not worry that these children need perfect parents.

While the Reillys are thinking about adopting an older child, Joey's foster father talks on the phone, his burly frame leaning against the kitchen door jamb, a cup of coffee in his hand. His wife calls out the kitchen window, "Dinner, you guys," and children of various sizes begin to pour in through the back door. As Joey runs in from the front room he jostles his foster father, sending a dark stain of coffee down the front of the man's shirt. There is a frozen moment, an expletive, a desperate dash. Quick as he is, Joey is not fast enough to evade the viselike grip on his thin arm. In a methodical fashion the foster father begins to hit Joey on the head, face, and ears with the heavy telephone directory he has taken from the table. Joey struggles to protect himself. There will be no mention of this episode to Joey's social worker when she next visits, just as there has been no mention of similar situations in the past. Receiving the foster mother's assurances that all is well, the social worker will never suspect that there might be some connection between the tenseness in Joey and the foster father whom she has never met.

Dick and Ellen Lambert

The Lamberts also attended a recruitment meeting to get more information on adopting an older child. Older than the Reillys, in their late thirties, Dick and Ellen have postponed doing anything about adoption although they have known for some time that they are unable to have children. Both of them have put considerable energy into their professional lives. Dick is a mechanical engineer and Ellen is a buyer for a large department store. Now they are well established in their work. Although they have a fine marriage and a sizable income, and enjoy each other and the things that they do together, they feel that they are missing out. The sailing and the skiing that they love fill much of their time, but they would really like to have a child to nurture, to care for, to share their interests with. Ellen thinks that Dick would be a great father; he likes children, and the kids in their neighborhood are crazy about him. Dick feels that any child would be lucky to have a mother as talented and caring as Ellen. Both the Lamberts feel that an older child would fit into their lives more smoothly than a baby. Even if they could adopt a baby, their stage in life doesn't make them eager to take on diapers and midnight feedings.

There are many couples like Dick and Ellen Lambert — couples who have postponed parenthood while they developed their individual careers, or who have tried to conceive a child for many years without success. When the time comes that they decide to adopt, these couples frequently want a child similar in age to the children of their friends. They do not look forward to being tied down to caring for an infant. These more mature couples often look toward older children to adopt.

Dick's and Ellen's professional associates react with disbelief. They don't understand why the Lamberts would alter their enviable life style, risk a change in their good relationship. They can't see how Dick and Ellen would consider an older child when they have no experience being parents. Most of them think the Lamberts would be wiser either to start out with a baby or to leave well enough alone. One of Ellen's coworkers asked her what she was going to do if she got a child and then found out that she didn't like being a mother.

Like many couples thinking through the decision to adopt an older child, the Lamberts find it hard to be sure of their choice, and their friends are very discouraging. Some days it seems to Dick and Ellen that the thing to do is to go ahead. They know they want a child and they find the idea of an older child exciting. Other days they feel confused, uncertain, and a little bit scared. There are no guarantees. No one can tell them what they are opening themselves up to, what the outcome of this gamble will be. What if they are not up to the task? What if they make the wrong decision? What if they hurt some needful child?

Dick and Ellen need to take some time to think about what it is they want to give a child, and what it is they want from a child. They need to remember that children aren't always cute or on their good behavior. Real children get tired, dirty, and upset; they whine and demand and argue; they misbehave and become unhappy and respond to pressure in different ways. Are the Lamberts being realistic about the demands of being parents as well as the joys? Perhaps they should spend more time with their friends and their friends' children to make sure that this is the type of life they want.

As time goes by the inner pull to go ahead and adopt becomes stronger to both Dick and Ellen. Somewhere out there a child is waiting to share a life with them. That child needs them; they want him. Maybe it will be a terrible mistake, but maybe it will be a wonderful experience for them and for that unknown child.

When our family first seriously weighed the decision to adopt an older child, we found it very difficult to get much helpful information. We wanted our decision to be a careful one, but we could not find anyone who had adopted this way before and could tell us what it was like, nor much to read that was useful. Our friends and family were so discouraging that we soon realized what we wanted to do was thought by many to be a dangerous undertaking.

Dave, my husband, finally drew the analogy that helped us the most. What we were talking about was new, untried by anyone we knew. Like the early settlers who decided to sell the farm and go West, we would be giving up the known and gambling on the unknown. Although we wouldn't be crossing a hostile wilderness, there would undoubtedly be dangers and risks involved. No one could tell us what was in store for us. But at the end of the journey there was great promise for something that we deeply wanted to have.

In the end, we decided to take our chances, to set out on the adventure. We weren't at all sure that we were doing the right thing. And we were certain that we weren't doing the easy thing. But we were doing what we wanted to do; we were giving our dream a chance.

It is perfectly normal for the Lamberts to have mood swings from confidence or excitement to concern or panic. By looking at themselves and at their feelings about adopting an older child they are just getting ready to explore the idea with an agency. The good agency will not expect them to come with a final commitment to adopt; rather, the agency is there to help settle any additional questions and concerns that the Lamberts might have about adoption in general and older child adoption in particular. There is no need to be positively certain that this kind of adoption is for them before they start the process.

It is the end of a busy day of shopping in Gena's and Tommy's foster home. The children have rushed through supper to have time to model their new school clothes for their appreciative foster father. The children are complimented on how nice they look. The girl shows how new socks just match her new outfit; the boy, how fast the new sneakers make his feet run. Warm feelings of concern and fondness fill the air.

After the new garments are safely put away and the children are asleep, the foster mother tells her husband that she has had a call from the new worker assigned to find Gena and Tommy an adoptive family and help them make a permanent move. The worker will be beginning her visits soon. "Well, we've been through this with other kids, Mary. We know that it is the best thing." "I know, Jim, but I keep thinking about all those smug, self-righteous women who tell me, 'I could never be a foster parent. I would just love the children too much to ever be able to let them go.' What do they know about kids who need a good place to stay? Kids that have to move on? It makes me so mad!" The pain of parting is evident in her voice. Holding her close, her husband feels her tears on his neck. He too envisions the emptiness that will fill the house, the sadness when the children move on. He tries hard to hang onto the conviction that adoption by a younger couple holds the promise of the best life for the two youngsters asleep upstairs.

Bob and Linda Allen

The Allens know nothing about Danny, Maggie, Gena and Tommy, or Joey; but they also are considering adding an older child to their family. Bob and Linda are very concerned with the crowded conditions and shortages caused by overpopulation and mismanaged natural resources. Three years ago, Bob quit his job as a marketing analyst and he and Linda left their suburban home to move with their children, Julie and Mark, to an old farm in the western part of their state. They have reclaimed much of the fertile land from the brush that had threatened to choke it, and now have a productive organic farm. They supplement their income with a small antiques business, and keep their expenses down by living as much as possible off their own land. Most of what goes on the Allens' table is a result of their work together on their garden. They heat their house almost entirely with wood cut from their own trees. It is a demanding life, but Bob and Linda find it remarkably satisfying. The primary thing that they feel lacking is another child. Julie, twelve, and Mark, eight, bring them a great deal of pleasure but Linda has always wanted a larger family.

Lately, Bob and Linda have been giving the thought of adopting a child to expand their family a lot of consideration. Because they are already parents, the Allens know that they like to take care of children. How much trouble could one more child be? Any child coming into a new family, of course, would be disturbed by the move at first. It is not hard to imagine how terribly upset *their* children would be if they were moved into a strange family. But the Allens feel sure that the problems arising from the move would be ironed out in time as the new child came to feel at home with them.

A growing concern about rapidly increasing global population and rapidly diminishing natural resources has caused many parents to choose to limit their own biological reproduction and to look instead to adoption as a way to complete their families. These parents, who are not concerned with infertility, differ from the traditional adopting family. Frequently they are experienced parents already, and often are more flexible about the type of child that they might adopt. More realistic about children and childrearing, they often push agencies to look at their adoption practices and at the children who have previously been considered unadoptable.

The important thing that the Allens should consider is whether they truly want another person in their family. What they are talking about doing is taking on another personality with needs of his own, ideas of his own, talents of his own. This child will not be a demonstration of social concern; he will be a real individual. Do they really want another child for himself, to work for and worry about, to help and to love?

Bob Allen feels that he and Linda could be excellent prospects for an older child placement. They know that another child coming into their family from a different background not only will hold different opinions and outlooks, but will have different daily habits and ways of relating to people. But the Allens hold no preconceived expectations for either Julie or Mark. They are committed to the idea that everyone should live his life in the way that brings him the most satisfaction and that is his best contribution to others. One of the things they want to do for another child is to give him the room and encouragement to find out who he is, what he has to give. They would not try to fit another child into a mold.

Linda Allen feels that she is a fairly tolerant mother, not easily upset by the demands of her children or the way they invade her living space. Always attracted to the idea of a large family, Linda is becoming increasingly excited about the prospect of having one more child to talk to, to play with, to enjoy. She feels that her calm nature and her genuine acceptance of children and their intense feelings are in her favor.

Linda's ability to accept strong feelings will be important if the Allens decide to adopt an older child. Many of these children come into their new families filled with pain and grief from the happenings in their pasts. Many of them respond to life with deep, built-up anger. They need strong parents who can accept them and their feelings, parents who can live with the negative feelings as they come out, and who can wait for the more pleasant ones.

Bob and Linda have spent quite some time discussing what the impact of another child — particularly a troubled child — will be on them and on Julie and Mark. They have tried to talk to their children realistically about what might happen if they were to bring an older child into their family. Both Julie and Mark are enthusiastic about having another brother or sister. Although their parents have pointed out to them that it would mean having to share with one more person, the children still think that it would be fun. Julie would love to have a little sister to confide in, to play with, to share her room. She imagines that this sister will enjoy the things that she enjoys, dream the same dreams. Mark strongly disagrees with Julie's plan. He feels the family has enough girls now. What they need is another boy! He too finds it difficult to think about how he might be affected unpleasantly.

It is not uncommon for families to find it difficult to get a realistic reaction from their other children as to how they might feel about the arrival of a new child. Basically, parents have to make the decision for their children, and for their family, as wisely as they can. Bob and Linda can try to help Julie and Mark understand the possible negatives by pointing out that they might adopt a child who did not like any of them for some time, who missed his foster parents and foster brothers and sisters, who did not like being at their house. The new brother or sister might be selfish, jealous, demanding. Their smoothly running family could change drastically. But it is important also to reassure their children that problems can be worked out. Building a family this way can be hard work, but it is worth it.

Because Bob and Linda have had the experience of unsettling their children once before, with the move to the farm, they are in a good position to draw analogies. "Remember how we all thought that living on a farm would be a picnic every day and then we learned about weeds?" They are also in a good position because they have seen their children adjust to change, handle a strange situation, and weather the experience just fine. They may be less worried than many families that the experience could cause a permanent setback to their present children if they adopt an older child with problems.

Maggie lies woodenly on her bed, her arms wrapped around the pillow she holds on her chest, her eyes fixed on some invisible point on the ceiling. If she concentrates, she can just manage to ignore the indignant grumblings from the woman on her hands and knees, pulling the soiled sheets from the back of her closet. A familiar smell of stale urine fills the room. "You filthy, sneaking pig. I don't know what I'm supposed to do with a child like you. You're big enough not to be wetting your bed like a baby. I ought to hang these sheets out your window. Then maybe you'd stop this nonsense."

Tony and Beth DeSando

It is one-thirty in the morning and Tony and Beth DeSando are sitting in their living room, talking. Between them on the couch is the object of conversation, a newspaper article. In it is a picture of Danny and a write-up about him. The DeSandos are sorting out their feelings about adding this attractive but troubled young man to their family of three children — Sam, eleven; Gillian, nine; and Adam, six.

Although the DeSandos had not given previous thought to adopting a teen-ager, they have been very active with children of that age. Remembering his own tough years growing up on the streets in a black-Hispanic neighborhood, Tony DeSando feels close to the problems he and Beth see as the advisers to their church's junior-high group. Both of them are sensitive people who care deeply about the troubles that black teen-agers can get themselves into during their turbulent growing-up years.

Beth and Tony feel a strong pull to Danny. They are excited and a little bit scared about the possibilities of opening their family up to him and they are trying to think realistically about the problems such a step might create. They have two immediate concerns — could Danny fit into their family, and what would be the effect of his coming on the children they already have?

Tony DeSando is having doubts whether a child of Danny's age could handle becoming a part of a family at the same time that most teen-agers are working out ways to move away from their families, to find their own lives. He wonders if Danny could blend in, could learn to be a real member of their family.

Much of the answer to his question lies with Danny. Some teen-agers are so hardened to being alone that they are not able to fit into a family setting. Other teens are still "soft" and open inside to making family relationships. Danny will become a real family member only if he chooses to and is able to. The fact that he has close friends shows that Danny has learned to give and take with people and to make relationships; both skills will help him become integrated into an adopting family. It may be hard for Danny and for an adopting family as he fights through his conflicts about being independent versus belonging; but the chances are good that after his initial distrust is overcome, he will adapt and will take real pleasure in being part of a family.

Beth herself grew up in a large, loving black family; she expects that even if Danny were slow to accept them as his parents, his feeling would come if they treated him like their son. Even if he resisted their caring, he would have parents to be there if and when he needed them, a family to launch himself from as he entered his older teen-age years. She is more concerned about how adopting Danny would affect Sam, Gillian, and Adam. Sam has always been the oldest child in his family. Would he feel that he had lost his value, his niche? Would he resent Danny as an intruder? What if Danny's disturbed behavior were contagious? Danny has given up on himself in school, the article says. Is Sam likely to follow his example? Will Sam and Gillian and Adam be cheated of the normal childhood they deserve by asking them to share their parents, their home, the rest of their lives with a stranger? And will Danny himself feel cheated and jealous because the other children have had an easier time in their lives?

Many parents are like the DeSandos, worried about possible contagion of behavior and contamination of thinking in their children if they add a child as old as Danny. Indeed, the addition of any other person to the family does frequently cause temporary upsets and backsliding among the children already there. But it is far more likely in the long run that Danny will "catch" behavior from his new brothers and sisters than that they will pick up permanent bad habits and attitudes from him.

The DeSandos would be wise to talk with their children and find out how they would feel about adding Danny to their family. Sam may be able to clearly tell them his reaction to the idea of having someone else be the oldest brother in the family —whether he finds it disturbing, and needs reassurance that he is loved and admired for the unique, special person he is and not for his position in the family; or whether he responds to the idea with relief at no longer always having to break the way or set the example for the others. Both reactions are common.

If they are to have a new teen-aged brother, Gillian and Adam will also have reactions to take into consideration. One that is common among young children is concern about why there are children without parents. It makes them feel vulnerable, as if something might happen to their own parents. They need to be helped to understand the pressures upon some parents that make it difficult to care for their children, and reassured that their own parents are old enough to look after them, are not contemplating divorce, and will make sure that the family stays together in case of a calamity.

Essentially, if the DeSandos become more sure of their own desire and ability to be parents to Danny, any uncertain effects upon their children will pass. In our own family we have found that adding children older than our oldest, putting children into the middle, and adding one at the end of the family did cause temporary confusion and sometimes discord as our children sorted out where they belonged in the family cluster. We have never found that this was a long-lived problem.

We have found that our children gained from the additions, even when the adjustments were very turbulent and personality clashes strong. Much of this is due to our own conviction that love would come and grow, and that things could work out. The knowledge that Mommy and Daddy believed that things would get better seemed to protect our children. With each adoption, our children gain another person to give to, to take from; one more person who is interested in them, who cares. In the end, there is little resentment for the difficult times; each child has expressed a great deal of personal satisfaction for his or her part in making our family into a whole, loving unit.

The real decision about adopting an older child boils down to two questions: *Do I think I can do it?* and *Do I want to try?* If the Reillys, the Lamberts, the Allens, and the DeSandos find an affirmative answer within themselves, the adoption of an older child can be richness within their means. Meanwhile, Danny, Maggie, Gena and Tommy, and Joey are waiting.

3
The Home Study

Finding an Agency

While the children wait, steps are being taken that will perhaps culminate in the creation of new families. Today is the beginning for the Reillys. Their decision is firm; Maureen intends to call the state agency on her lunch hour and find out what she and Jack have to do to adopt an older child. All the way to work on the crowded subway she has been rehearsing what she will say. She is feeling both excited and a little apprehensive. What if the agency is discouraging? She and Jack have wondered how long it will be before they will know if they will be allowed to adopt. What if the agency doesn't like them?

Although Maureen is understandably nervous about this initial contact, it is extremely important for her to keep in mind that when the Reillys begin working with an agency, they are purchasing a service. Whether they go to a private agency and pay the fees directly or whether they go to the public welfare unit, where the services they receive are provided from the taxes they have paid, they are paying consumers. They need to select an agency that will do a satisfying job for them, and not allow themselves to become so awed by the agency's power to give or deny them a child that they do not get the information from the agency that they should have.

Among the questions that Maureen needs to ask before the Reillys make a decision on a particular agency are "What type of child does this agency usually place?" "How much experience has this agency had placing older children?" "How many older children did it place during the last year?" It is frequently safer to work with an agency to whom older child adoption is a common practice. Obviously, the number of children placed is less important than how good a job of placement is done. But an agency with a good deal of experience placing older children and working with their special problems will probably have improved its procedures over time.

At her desk, Maureen finds it hard to concentrate on her typing. She can't decide whether she wishes the hands on the large clock on the wall would move faster so she can get the call over with or slower to give her time to get ready. At lunchtime, instead of heading for the cafeteria where she usually eats with friends, she lags behind hoping to find the public phone booth unoccupied. Settling herself in the booth she nervously drops her dime into the slot and dials the number of her state's adoption unit. She waits for what seems a very long time while the phone rings and rings. About the time she decides that the office must be closed, a secretary answers. Maureen gives her name and explains that she and her husband are interested in adopting an older child. The secretary seems pleasant and businesslike. She tells Maureen that there is to be an information meeting in the next month and that she will put the Reillys' names on the list so that they can come and find out more about how the agency works and about the children they have waiting for placement. (Maureen is lucky to have called an agency able to meet the inquiries of its clients so quickly. More frequently, understaffing causes a delay of months before the process can begin.)

When Maureen asks about the type and number of children that the agency usually places, she gets a partial answer from the secretary, who explains that she is new but promises that the Reillys will be able to get answers to any of their questions at the upcoming meeting. Satisfied, Maureen hangs up the phone. The Reillys are on their way.

Beth and Tony DeSando have decided that they are seriously interested in Danny. The newspaper clipping lists the telephone number of the state Adoption Resource Exchange so Beth calls that number, expresses interest in Danny, and asks what they would have to do to adopt him. The person answering the phone shows warm understanding of the appeal Danny has for Beth and Tony. She explains that they have not called an adoption agency but a referral service, which serves agencies and children by matching children with families already studied. The first step in the process is a completed home study. Danny, she says, has been listed by the state agency; if the DeSandos would like they could call his agency to see about starting a study.

An adoption resource exchange is a good place to begin the adoption process. Sometimes it can be useful in locating an adoption agency for the type of child a couple is considering. It is usually able to tell couples which agencies near them are actively placing older children, and often it will also know if there is a waiting list for those who want home studies done by these agencies. The adoption resource exchange will also be able to give couples the address of their local adoptive parents group or the name of someone who has adopted a child similar to the child they are considering, so that they can talk to another parent and get more information about older child adoption.

When Beth calls the state agency she and Tony are also invited to attend the information meeting. The person answering the phone says that although it is unusual for them to have a particular child in mind so early, perhaps Danny will prove to be the right child for them. She promises to mention their call and their interest in Danny to his worker, but cautions them not to count on taking Danny home, explaining that there may be other couples already approved by the agency who are interested in him. Sensing Beth's disappointment, she adds that the agency has many children like Danny and that even if things do not work out with him there will most definitely be other children with a similar need.

Dick and Ellen Lambert, on the other hand, begin to look for an agency in a different way. At the meeting they attended on adopting special needs children, they picked up a pamphlet about their state adoptive parents'. group. Ellen had a good talk with the local chairperson over the telephone and the Lamberts were invited to a potluck supper to meet some other members of the group. Over dinner, Dick and Ellen are now talking to several couples who have adopted older children to sound them out on how they felt about the agencies they used, and to get a better idea of what to expect from the home study.

In a number of ways, an adoptive parents' group can be a valuable resource for prospective parents. The Lamberts can ask these families whether they were satisfied with the agency's outlook and placement procedures. They can find out if these couples would recommend their agency or if there is another place that they think is better. Another adoptive parent is often a good guide to the quality of service provided. The Lamberts may find disagreement about a given agency among parents who had contrasting experiences with different workers. In adoption workers, as in all professions, there is a variety of ability, and parents may form strongly differing opinions.

By the time the Lamberts have finished dinner and are having coffee and dessert, they are feeling interested in one private agency in particular. Tomorrow Ellen will call and try to get answers to some of her questions so the Lamberts can get things started.

Ellen begins her call in the morning by asking for some information. She is worried that the agency may feel that she and Dick are too old to be beginning a family. Having heard that religious matching is sometimes important, she is wondering if she and Dick will find their different religious backgrounds a problem in any way. (Depending on the agency and on geographical location, religion may make a difference in getting a child.) The secretary refers Ellen to an "intake" worker, who is on call to answer questions and speak to new clients for that day. This worker explains that the agency does not have fixed requirements for adoption—neither age nor religious background will present any problem. Rather, the agency's major interest is in finding families for children without parents. She explains that this agency's procedure is to begin with a four-week series of meetings in which prospective parents find out about the type of children in care and learn what it would be like to adopt one. The agency does not ask parents to submit an application to adopt until this set of meetings is completed, feeling that couples who decide not to go ahead may find it easier to select themselves out of the process if no formal procedure has begun. If a couple needs time to be sure of its decision, or decides not to pursue an adoption right away, it is always welcome to return to the agency in the future. This way the couple is encouraged to help decide whether the two of them really want to be parents to an older adopted child; they can feel comfortable sharing any hesitations with the agency without prejudicing the agency's judgment of them as prospective adoptive parents.

The worker tells Ellen when the next series will begin. Ellen hangs up the phone feeling relieved and excited.

The Allens also are in the process of starting up with an agency. Bob and Linda have selected a small private agency in a nearby city, primarily for its convenience—all the other agencies are a considerable drive from their rural home. Their initial call was put through directly to an adoption worker who seemed pleased to hear from them and to answer their questions. She told them that although this agency had only a few children available for adoption, it would be happy to study the Allens and then help them to locate an appropriate child from another agency.

Bob and Linda need to inquire how the agency intends to go about locating their child. Will they be using an adoption resource exchange such as the one that publicized Danny's case, or a national registry of available children? How much additional time do they expect this procedure to add to the time the Allens will wait? Have they found this to be successful for other families? Will the Allens be expected to travel a long distance?

Exchanges can work well. Any agency with a child in its care for whom there is not an in-agency family may register that child with the regional, state, or national adoption exchange. Likewise, any agency that approves a couple for adoption but does not have a suitable child available, can register the couple. The exchange is then able to refer children from one area to agencies in another, providing a sometimes large pool of waiting children and parents who need only to be matched up and presented to each other. There can be problems with this kind of program, however. If there is no local state adoption exchange and a national registry is used, the procedure tends to be lengthy and distances traveled may be great. If the state is one with an active public agency of its own, fewer children may be referred to the state adoption exchange and the children in the available pool may be youngsters who are considered more difficult to place because of their advanced age, physical and/or emotional handicaps, or minority race.

Bob and Linda Allen also have some concern about what the agency they have called will charge them for its services. Their income, though adequate for their own needs, does not allow for many extras, and money is tight. The worker reassures them that something can be worked out; fees are charged on a sliding scale by many agencies according to what a couple is able to afford. She also tells them that should they decide to adopt a child with a medical handicap who needs expensive care, or if they have difficulty affording another child, state monies are available and a subsidized adoption could be applied for. (This is true of a number of states at this time, but not all.) The Allens readily make an appointment with the worker to come in and begin their process of adoption.

Agency fees are highly variable. Agencies may be privately endowed, religiously supported, and/or supported by the United Fund. Some private agencies charge no fees for couples adopting difficult-to-place children. Some agencies charge according to ability to pay. Public agencies usually charge only a dollar or two for a copy of the amended birth certificate at the time the adoption is made final; their other services are supported by tax monies. Any couple that wants to adopt an older child should be able to find an agency that it can afford.

The Reillys, the DeSandos, the Lamberts, the Allens: all are now on their way toward a wanted child, having found an agency that they feel will meet their needs and with whom they feel they can work. Because other questions will come up during the adoption process, it is wise for them to have located agencies where questions are answered and where the staff feels comfortable with couples who are question askers.

Spaulding for Children, a Michigan agency that has specialized since 1968 in placing older and handicapped children, describes how an agency can function as effectively as it does. Any agency placing children would do well to imitate its approach and high standard of service. Here is what Spaulding for Children has to say about placement services:

> It is important that the agency image be an open and honest one and that the staff be friendly, enthusiastic social workers interested in children and eager and able to talk with all kinds of people about caring for children. Without that kind of atmosphere, success is impossible. But the public image must be affirmed by the private performance. The person answering the telephone must be warm and helpful. Letters must be promptly answered and the responses appropriate. Meetings must be comfortable and thoughtfully scheduled. Appointments must be a mutual convenience. The process must be streamlined, the paperwork minimized. Contacts between worker and family should result in more understanding of adoption, of experiences typical to families who have already adopted older or handicapped youngsters, of one another's assets and liabilities. Experienced adopters should be included in the process. They not only convey more believable information, they also can advise the applicant family about the services of the agency, the dependability of staff, the routine details the social worker may have forgotten or never learned.
>
> Supportive services throughout the placement process and well beyond must be freely offered, the certainty of some problems of adjustment accepted. There should be a *shared* responsibility for the placement of a child. By eliminating as much as possible of traditional "game-playing" of adoption (if they answer an appropriate question with an appropriate answer enough times in succession, they are rewarded with a child), we try to reach a

position where mature people, having learned a great deal about themselves and the children available for adoption, make a decision to proceed into placement with the assistance of an agency they trust. Sweeping away our preconceived notions of a typical "acceptable" family is imperative. The new families coming to us should be old, young, and in-between. They should have comfortable incomes or be barely managing. They may have different levels of motivation; they may be well educated or semi-literate. Their only common trait must be the capacity to care for a child not born to them.

As the process begins, Maggie turns nine, making her one year less attractive to waiting couples. At her place at the breakfast table is a card to mark the day. Before she leaves for school, she stands it proudly on her dresser to admire the bright colors, the warm sentiment. In her classroom she sneaks glances at her name written in large letters under the day's date, pointing her out as a "birthday girl." When it is time for "show and tell" Louisa monopolizes the conversation with an animated discussion of the party her mother is planning for her birthday the following Tuesday. She is counting on a new bike and a cake that looks like Raggedy Ann. Turning her attention to Maggie she asks, "What are you getting for your birthday?" "I dunno," Maggie mumbles. "It's a surprise."

Walking home, her feet scuffing the piles of bright leaves, Maggie knows that there will be no presents, no party, no cake for her. At home, she walks slowly up the stairs to her bedroom. The card which seemed so attractive this morning now looks forlorn. Opening the top drawer of her dresser, she deliberately crams the card into the back, pushing it behind the pile of carefully rolled socks. Later her foster mother will pull it out, crumpled and askew, and wonder again what makes Maggie such a careless child.

The Home-Study Process

It is ten o'clock on a bright, clear Thursday morning. There is a hint of fall in the air. Maureen and Jack Reilly have just entered the conference room at their state agency where the initial information meeting is to be held. They sit down at the large square table and wait as other couples find their places and settle themselves. The DeSandos, whom they do not know, are already there. Although the receptionist who showed them into this meeting place and the other agency personnel they have met seemed very pleasant, there is real tension in the room. Some waiting couples start tentative conversations with their neighbors; others sit quietly, some openly sizing up the competition. The atmosphere seems charged.

Two social workers begin the meeting, introducing themselves and asking each couple to tell the group who they are and what type of child they are interested in adopting. They show some slides of waiting children and talk about the kinds of children that the agency has available for adoption. The costs, requirements, and restrictions, and the methods and time involved in the home study and placement are explained. In this agency, as in many, couples wishing to adopt older children will be studied in a group. There are to be a number of mandatory group meetings where issues can be raised and dealt with, and information can be shared. At the end of these group meetings, each couple will be assigned to their own worker, who will meet with them several times to assess them and to help them assess their feelings and worries and decide what type of child they are interested in adopting.

Many agencies are now using group meetings as a part of their home study. It is both an economical and an effective way to work. Instead of being limited to their personal concerns and ideas and those of their particular social worker, couples are exposed to a far greater pool of questions and ideas. They are likely to share ideas that would not have come up for them in an individual study. Workers also get to know couples in a different way as they interact with people who are not agency personnel. It is easier to see what kinds of people a couple can relate to, how they handle new ideas, how they deal with differences of opinion, and where they need to give more thought — all things that can help a worker make a better placement, one that is in the couple's best interests.

The workers running the information meeting explain that

at the close today, applications for a home study will be passed out; couples may fill out these applications when they feel ready to begin their home-study process. The applications also include a list of documents that will be necessary for a child to be placed.

It is a good idea, once couples are strong in their determination to adopt and submit their home-study applications, for them to begin accumulating the necessary documents. They will most likely need certified copies of their own birth certificates and their marriage certificate (unless the applicant is a single parent). They will also need to have a medical examination by their doctor or clinic, and a statement that their health will not prevent them from caring for a child. Undoubtedly the application will request several personal references. The earlier that couples complete this part of the paperwork, the less likely that it will hold them up later in the adoption procedure.

Jack Reilly expresses concern at this meeting about the problems these children have. Will he and Maureen have enough experience to help a troubled child? Jack feels that having two loving parents is a large part of the cure for these children, but he is not sure he knows what else he will need to do. How can he find out? Will the agency help them?

This is a good question, for it is important in selecting an agency to have some idea what kinds of pre-placement and post-placement services are provided. Does this agency have courses in childrearing techniques available to prospective adopters? Does it have post-placement support groups of adopting parents, where couples can come together and share their problems in the adjustment to their new child?

Another concern that should be investigated at this meeting is the length of time couples can expect to wait for a home study after they submit their applications. If there is a long waiting list, it may be wise to call a second agency and get on its waiting list also. It is against agencies' policies to study a couple that is already working with another agency, and it is also a waste of agency time. But there is no reason why couples cannot be on more than one list during the waiting period, before they have begun a study.

Following the meeting both the DeSandos and the Reillys filled out and returned their home-study applications promptly. Soon they were contacted and meetings were scheduled for their home-study group.

The Lamberts have attended the four educational meetings sponsored by their agency. They found these meetings to be helpful and interesting. At one meeting parents who had adopted an older child talked about the experience — in what ways it was difficult, how they feel about it now. At another, a child psychologist talked about some of the difficulties children have when they lose parents, how it makes them feel about themselves, and how they are likely to react to being moved again into an adoptive home. The couples also were able to experience how they might feel about a child's acting out and how they might handle it, through playing out different situations where they took the roles of both parents and newly adopted children. At the end of the educational series, the Lamberts were even more sure of their decision to adopt; they began to meet with their own caseworker, to share information about themselves and what they expect from this kind of adoption, and to look at the type of child who might best fit into their home.

Bob and Linda Allen's small agency does not run group studies but assigns clients to an individual worker from the beginning. They will be having four to six meetings with their worker: first, to get to know each other and to look at why the Allens are interested in adopting a child; second, for Bob and Linda each to have a chance to talk with their worker privately about themselves, their feelings about adoption, and their marriage; third, to come together and talk over any additional issues that they or the worker feel need to be discussed; and finally, to discover what particular type of child they want to adopt. It is this agency's policy, as is usual, for the worker to hold one of these meetings, usually the next to last, in the Allens' home.

The home visit is not something that Bob and Linda need feel apprehensive about. The worker does not come to judge their decor or make a "white glove" inspection. If she were to discover some unacceptable conditions — such as no running water or obvious filth — there might be difficulty. But the worker probably has two primary goals: to meet the Allen children and to see how the family relates together so that she may get a better feel for what type of child would fit in; and to give the Allens a chance to talk with her when they are on their familiar home ground, because some couples find it difficult to be themselves in an agency office.

It is half-way through the first marking period in Danny's junior high school. At the close of the day he wanders in, grabs something to eat, and drops onto the counter four light green warning slips pointing out that he is doing unsatisfactory work in all his major classes. Ignoring his foster mother's tirade about his dumbness and the irritation he is to her, Danny is out the door to join his friends, who think the situation a big joke. Two of the slips request the foster mother to call for a meeting with Danny's teachers to discuss his work, but she has no intention of calling. What do the teachers think? That she has nothing better to do than to waste her time on that no-good kid?

Assessing Candidates for Older Child Adoption

The different agencies with their different styles of home studies are all looking for essentially the same things. They want to assess each applicant's personal emotional stability and motives for adoption. If the couple is infertile, the agency will want to determine how the partners have dealt with their infertility. Have they tried to resolve their problem medically? Have they worked through their feelings of guilt or anger or decreased self-worth?

Because each of the waiting children has lost at least one set of parents, his birth parents, agencies do their best to make sure that he will not lose another. Therefore, they need to know how sound the applicants' marriage is and whether the couple is in good physical health. Agencies also spend some time assessing applicants' abilities to love and accept a child not born to them. Does the couple see adoption as a second-best way to have children? The agency will be interested in the feelings and ideas that adopting couples have about the biological parents of an adopted child. Are they sensitive to the pressures and problems that cause parents to relinquish, neglect, or abuse their children? How will they answer their adopted child's questions about why his first parents gave him up? Can they help their child understand negative experiences like neglect, abuse, abandonment? How does the couple feel about foster care? Why do they think people take in foster children? Could they allow their new child to keep in touch with his foster parents?

The agency will want to know how the prospective parents feel about raising children. What are their rules about behavior? About religion? The agency will want to discuss issues surrounding needs of children, needs of parents, discipline, guidance, and expectations.

In addition to the usual considerations given to adoption applicants, workers who are studying candidates for older child placements are wise to look for the following characteristics:

1. *Do these people like themselves?* Living with a child who has had many negative experiences in his life can be quite erosive. Many of these children do not like themselves. They tend to dump their discomfort on others, sometimes being very critical and uncooperative. They may bombard their new parents with uncomplimentary comments at the same time that they are being the chief source of irritation and problems in the family. The worry and fatigue of living with this criticism, and the constant problem solving, wear people down. Parents sometimes compound this fatigue by harboring the feeling that they should be able to solve in a short period all the problems their son or daughter has accumulated in other places during his or her whole lifetime. It takes parents with a good sense of personal self-esteem to let their children heal slowly, to handle the hard times, to continue to like themselves and their child even when things are difficult.

2. *How does this couple handle heated situations? What do they do about conflict, differences of outlook and opinion?* Most often, couples react to stressful confrontations with an upset

older child similarly to the way they handle marital disagreements. Workers can often get a feeling for a particular family's "conflict dynamics" by asking a couple to share the events in their last major or minor disagreement. This often gives a caseworker an idea of how the couple talk about their feelings, good and bad; how they solve problems; how sensitive they are to their own needs and the needs of others when things are tense. Couples need to be open with the worker, who undoubtedly understands that all people who live together have disagreements, some of them heated, and needs to know how to select a combination of child and family that complement rather than harm each other when things are rough.

In addition, the worker should try to determine whether this couple feels that disagreements and differences must always be resolved. Parents who do not need perfect agreement within their family, but who can feel comfortable looking for a compromise or who can allow for differences of opinion where neither side wins or gives in, seem to create a sense of reasonableness and respect that often helps moved children learn a more flexible approach to handling interpersonal stress. Many of these children have learned that life is a series of win-or-lose confrontations. Such children are frequently more able to look for compromises with parents who do not make differences of thought into an issue of control.

3. *What are this couple's expectations from an older adopted child?* It is important to find parents who are both optimistic about an older adopted child's ability to overcome problems, and realistic about how slowly this process may take place. These parents need to be able to make plans for their family and for their child, but also to be flexible if those plans do not turn out as expected. They should be firm in their decision to adopt an older child. It is also necessary that they have realistic expectations of performance for the age and type of child they are considering.

4. *Has this couple had any major problems to overcome in the past?* Families who adopt older children often have periods when everything seems to be a drain, when nothing seems to be

going right. They need confidence in their ability to weather the hard times, confidence that is frequently the result of having managed difficult periods before. A sense of humor — the ability to laugh at oneself — is often a real asset, too. And assessment should be made of the couple's ability to handle the frustration and confusion that any parent encounters.

5. *Does this couple take verbal responsibility for their own actions, feelings, and ideas?* Do they communicate clearly and honestly? Do they face the truth? Many of the older children who are placed for adoption use denial, displacement, or lying to avoid taking responsibility for their choices and actions. Parents who communicate their own involvement and feelings seem best able to help these children become more accountable so that they can improve in their areas of difficulty. The best way to learn to be an honest, responsible adult is to live with adults who act honestly and responsibly.

6. *Can this couple recognize and meet their child's need for dependency and at the same time help him develop tools for growing up?* Because so many of these children have had their previous needs for dependency and gratification unfilled, they are quite often overly dependent, needing to recover from past neglect. They need parents who are comfortable giving them time to meet these needs, but who also will encourage their children to grow, to become capable, independent adults. These children need parents who not only can say "We love you," but who also send the message "We trust you will be able in time to do things on your own." They need parents who can let them make many of their own choices and solve many of their own problems, as well as protecting and caring for them. In this way they can come to see themselves as being able to grow into capable adults.

7. *How well does this couple do on the Forbes scale for predicting successful placement?* Dr. Lorna Forbes has established the following family characteristics as indicative of successful older child placements:

    1. The ability to work with the agency.

2. The ability to express tenderness.
3. The ability to arbitrate.
4. The ability to be tolerant.
5. The ability to live non-isolated lives, to have other relationships and interests beyond the family.
6. The ability to be resilient.
7. A healthy ego, enabling them to defer gratification.
8. A life style reciprocal to that of the child to be placed.

She finds couples with only a limited number of these characteristics to be "high-risk."

Different couples applying for adoption will have different blends of all these traits. It is not essential for each couple to meet every specification, but the more potential they have to do so, the better their chances for successfully adopting an older child, weathering the stormy times, and coming through in a way that is good for everyone.

As Gena dances around, her foster mother gives one more try to straighten the collar which is caught awry in the top of her sweater. Gena is bubbling over about the new friend in her class. Arriving at school, she seeks her out, eventually finding her in the corner of the playground, part of a tight knot of girls whispering and giggling, their heads together, their backs to Gena. "Come on, Sally, let's play," she calls. "I'm not playing with you, Gena. My mother says you're nothing but a state kid." "So what," Gena responds. "I didn't want to be your friend anyway. You're nothing but a big dummy!"

Snags in the Approval Process

Things are not going smoothly for the Allens in their home study. Somehow, they seem to have gotten off on the wrong foot with their social worker, although they are not quite sure why. The worker has seen the two of them together and each of them separately. She has not deliberately made things stressful, but Bob and Linda each have the sense that she doesn't quite like them, that for some reason they are not getting through. Today, as they meet there is once again that sense of coolness and disapproval. Finally Bob finds he can't even concentrate on the questions she is asking. Apprehensively he wonders if the agency is going to turn them down. He tries to wait for a good opening but ends up blurting out that he feels they have to stop talking about the adoption temporarily and talk about how things are going in the home study. He explains that he is feeling a growing sense of strain among the three of them and he wonders what the problem is. The worker flinches and stiffens, then consciously relaxes herself. Thinking aloud, she tries to be open with the Allens. She is certainly not bothered by their way of life. As far as she is concerned, the move to the farm is positive; it shows her that this family can accommodate themselves well to a new experience and learn to make it work. But she is uncertain how much of their decision to adopt comes from a desire to have another child, and how much of it come from their need to make a strong social statement about over-population.

As the three adults in the small crowded office try to talk openly, Bob, Linda, and the worker are all conscious of how difficult it is to distill feelings accurately into words. Bob and Linda both speak with conviction; they don't feel they will be parents of a "cause," they insist, they want a *child*. Out of the discussion grows the sense that the worker is not trying to be difficult but rather is committed to making a good placement. In the end, the worker agrees to visit the farm and to spend some time with the Allens and their children, to try to get a better understanding of them as people and as parents.

Although Bob and Linda are understandably nervous during the subsequent home visit, by the time the afternoon is over the worker seems much more relaxed with them. When they talk there is the feeling that a door has been opened. By the end of the home study, her hesitations resolved, the worker recommends that Bob and Linda be approved for adoption.

There are several important points raised by what happened to the Allens. First is the way they handled their concern that they were being misunderstood and might not be approved. Because they were able to talk with their worker about this feeling, and because she was open and willing to be direct with them about the source of difficulty in her mind, they were not just written off and things proceeded well. Sometimes, however, couples are hesitant to do what the Allens did. Afraid to anger their social worker, they do not share their feeling that things are not going well. When this happens it is important for the couple under home study to remember that they are purchasing a service, and to act in such a way that good service is provided them. If a couple is unable to work things through with one worker, a request for another worker may be made. Or the couple may want to request a conference with the worker's supervisor, in hopes that things can be ironed out. If the couple has initially tried unsuccessfully to talk directly with their worker, neither of these approaches is usually held against them. If after trying to work through a snag in the home study there is no resolution, and the couple still feel strongly that they want to pursue an adoption, they should not hesitate to go to another agency.

It is also important for a worker to be sensitive to her own personal biases, taking a close look to see if there are common situations for which she has no rationale but that make her hesitant to approve applicants. The Allens may have given their worker genuine cause to be hesitant about them, but she may also have approached them with unfair preconceptions about their particular motivation and way of life. Workers often hold common biases: the "rightness" of families of middle-class backgrounds and values; an unconscious rejection of very obese clients; hesitation about accepting mothers (more than fathers) with longstanding medical problems even if the attending physician feels his patient able to be a good parent; the sense that a safe placement is one where there are experienced parents with a not-too-large family, and where the new child assumes the position of "youngest."

By the time the Reillys, the Lamberts, the Allens, and the DeSandos are approved, they should be able to evaluate whether they have had a good home study. They should have a better idea who they are, how they work as individuals and as a family, what they want from life and from their children. They should have grown in understanding the children who wait, what it means to be parents to them, and how they feel about taking part in this kind of adoption. Frequently they will have faced down some of their half-buried notions about adoption in general and older child adoption in particular. They should have found their worker honest with them, and found their own honesty with her not a detriment. By the time the home study ends they should be able to help their worker realistically decide what types of children they do and do not want to consider adopting.

Time is passing, the winter coming on. Although it is early evening the cafeteria in the junior high school is ablaze with light. Dressed in his careful best, Danny stands somewhat apart from the group of boys and parents waiting for the fall athletic banquet. At a signal from one of the coaches, the crowd excitedly pours into the room, each youngster trying to introduce his parents and to find the place card that marks their spot for supper. Danny slips into his place quietly removing the brightly printed card with his foster mother's name. The food is good; the company shares the closeness of those who have played hard and well together. There is hearty laughter during the after-supper speeches in which the coaches kiddingly point out some of the more amusing incidents during the season. The trophies lined up in front of the cc ιches shine tantalizingly. At the end of the evening Danny heads up to the stage, to thunderous applause, to receive the soccer trophy as "most valuable player." Dropped off at his house later, Danny goes up the dark front stairs. The house is absolutely silent. Everyone is asleep. Danny lies awake in bed, filled with excitement over his prize, hearing again the whistles, shouts, and congratulations from his friends. Why does he feel so lonely?

What Kind of a Child?

Although sometimes workers and parents are reluctant to admit that not every family can adopt any child, it is important for them to overcome that hesitation and to talk concretely about the kind of child seemingly best suited to a given family. This is not to say that all issues, behaviors, and types of children must be examined, and the couple's feelings about them spelled out. Rather, there should be a mutual assessment of a family's strengths and weaknesses in its ability to raise various kinds of children, and a clear statement from the approved couple of their hopes for and their limits regarding the child who will come to them. Here are some of the things that can be looked at, so that when the time comes, a child can be selected that will best fit:

1. Describe the type of child toward whom you have the most positive feeling. What does this child look like? How does the child respond? Is its response affectionate, self-reliant, inquisitive, trusting, bright, independent, dependent, grateful? What kinds of activities can you visualize yourself engaged in with this child? Is there a particular age you enjoy most? Why?

2. Describe the type of child toward whom you have the least positive feeling. What does this child look like? How does this child respond? What kinds of problems can you envision with this child? Is there a particular age you enjoy least? Why?

3. How do you express affection?

4. What rules do you have in your house for children?

5. What kinds of children intimidate you?

6. What kinds of behavior do you feel unable or unwilling to accept—defiance, destructiveness, aggression, withdrawal, sullenness, immaturity? How do you define each of these behaviors? How is your tolerance limited?

7. What kinds of handicaps could you accept?

8. What do you feel might make your placement succeed? Fail?

9. Could you turn down a child you felt uneasy about?

The DeSandos are still interested in Danny, who has yet to be placed. Their worker is making arrangements for them to meet with Danny's worker, to share information and to see if Danny might fit into the DeSandos' family; but Danny's worker is on vacation and it may be a while before such a meeting can take place.

The Reillys' worker is exploring with them whether they might consider taking a younger child with a mental or physical problem. He uses the guidelines presented by Joan McNamara in an anthology called *Adopting Children with Special Needs* (Kravik 1975), available through the North American Council on Adoptable Children. If the following statements apply to you, it says, you have a good start in considering adoption of a child with special needs:

- You like children and enjoy the challenge of raising a family. If you are not a parent already, you may have had other kinds of exposure to children through volunteer work, teaching, or your own extended family, that have given you an insight into the daily realities of being a parent.
- You are a flexible person. You usually deal with frustration with patience and are open to changes in your expectations and life style.
- You are able to view people for what they *can* accomplish, not what they cannot, and value them according to their own potentials.
- You have had contact with people who have handicapping conditions.

On the other hand, the book says, if the following statements apply to you, then you may need more time before you are ready to approach adoption of a child with special needs:

- You see adoption of a child with special needs as a charitable gesture, because you feel sorry for or pity a child, or feel a duty towards him.
- You think such adoption is exciting, romantic, or a good way to make a public or personal statement.
- You feel that you couldn't raise an "ordinary" or "normal" child.
- A child with special needs is second choice for you; the waiting time for children you would prefer is too long or there aren't any of the kind you really want.

- You place a high value on achievement and success, and have set kinds of goals for your children's futures.
- You view yourself as a person who does not react well to change and stress.
- Your chosen life style is set and the adoption of a child with special needs would disrupt the activities that are important to you.

If you see yourself in the statements above, according to *Adopting Children with Special Needs,* it doesn't mean that you can't adopt; but perhaps you should carefully examine your motivations and feelings, your attitudes and way of life, to find out what you really feel a child can give to your family and what you can give in turn to a child.

The same book also includes a good discussion of the more common types of physical and mental difficulties found in the children waiting for adoption. The adoption of a child with special needs requires adopting parents to make an affirmative choice, a choice to love and accept the child as he is. Parents have to prepare themselves to deal with the child and the child's problems, just as do birth parents of children born with disabilities. Many times adoptive parents are more easily able to help children with mental or physical handicaps, because as they deal with the child's pain and the impact of his problem on his self-esteem, they are not also struggling with their own guilt about having given birth to a child with a handicap. Parents who adopt handicapped children may have to cope with hospitals, surgery, injections, special schooling, medication schedules, sheltered workshops, or painful therapy. It will change their lives in some definite and final ways. Budgets, housing, scheduling, and time allotment are all likely to be altered. (They should not hesitate to check with their agency to see if they are eligible for financial aid from their state.) But parents who make the decision to adopt these children can find it fulfilling, humbling, and beautiful.

The Reillys' worker also encourages them to consider other kinds of special situations that make children wait a long time for placement—emotional difficulties, the need to be adopted with a sibling, being a teen-ager.

In the end Maureen and Jack decide that they are interested in adopting a school-age daughter. They do not want a child over twelve, feeling it would be hard to begin their parental experience with a teen-ager. The Reillys feel anxious about adopting a child who "acts out" with temper tantrums or the like, because they live in an apartment building where such a child might become a general nuisance; on the other hand, they feel they would not be threatened by a withdrawn, nonverbal youngster. They would like a child to do things with, like going to museums and to the zoo. Maureen is eager to share her own enjoyment of homemaking skills—cooking and sewing—with her new daughter. The Reillys would prefer a child that could attend regular classes in school and would probably be able to graduate from high school.

In the course of their home study the Lamberts discover that they are leaning strongly towards a son, although they are willing to consider a girl. They would like it if their son could share in their enjoyment of skiing and sailing. They are turned off by overly fat children. Although they are not bothered by the thought of a child with a learning disability that might necessitate special education classes, they do not feel that they could take on a retarded child. They are willing to travel out of state, if necessary, to adopt their child.

The Allens are feeling very flexible. They have decided that they are not interested in adopting a child with a handicap, but they have no preference as to whether the child is a boy or a girl. They don't feel strongly about age; they just want a child that falls somewhere between their two biological children. They do not want to adopt a child older than twelve-year-old Julie. They are leaving a lot of the decision up to the worker, hoping she will find a youngster who will fit in nicely with their other children and benefit from their style of family living.

Before the close of the final visit the workers dealing with each of these families should tell them how an appropriate child will be located, the kind of child being considered, and how the adoption proceeds from here. Their workers should also explain a little about "matching," how a child is presented to a family, and the placement procedure used by their particular agency. The legal aspects of guardianship and making the adoption final may need to be gone into. With the home study completed, and the matching process started, now the waiting begins.

4
Pre-Adoption Preliminaries for Parents and Workers

The Waiting Period

It has been three weeks since the Reillys were notified that they have been officially approved to adopt. Shopping downtown, Maureen chuckles to herself. She is tickled because her search for green towels to match a new shower curtain has led her to the preteen girls' department to look at jerseys and skirts and sweaters. What fun to think about her expected daughter: will she look smart in this tailored outfit or will she be more the frilly type? Will she be a size eight or ten or twelve? Will she look better in this bright red or this soft yellow? Maybe instead of buying her clothing ready-made, Maureen would rather sew for her at home. Fingering fabrics and looking at the current styles for school-age children, Maureen watches other mothers and daughters shopping together. Eavesdropping on their conversations, she scans their faces, wishing she could find some excuse to tell them about her expected daughter. Later, as she walks through the furniture department on her way to get some lunch, Maureen finds herself stopped at the floor model of a little girl's bedroom. Her head cocked to one side she visualizes a child, hair curtaining her face, busily at work at a project on the attractive desk. She wonders whether her awaited daughter would like the white finish or the maple better. The prices seem quite reasonable; maybe she and Jack should come in together next week and look at this set.

On the way home, Maureen strikes up a conversation with a little girl sitting beside her on the rumbling subway. They talk about school and Girl Scouts and dancing lessons. When the child and her older sister get off at their stop, Maureen leans back, her eyes closed, thinking about all the children she has seen today. Where once it was pregnant women who caught her attention, she is now seeing more girlchildren than she ever noticed before, and finding them fascinating.

Maureen is engaged in what is sometimes referred to a "pre-adoptive pregnancy." She is preparing herself for her awaited daughter. Jack is feeling "pregnant," too. Although he has always been conscientious about his work, like many expectant fathers he is now putting in even more effort. He would really like to get that raise; after all, there will be only one salary now, and one more person to feed and clothe.

It is a special time for the Reillys, filled with joyous anticipation. Their dreaming and their excited planning will lead to the making of space in a marriage, in two hearts, and in their home for another person. From these dreams will come some concrete ideas about where the new child will sleep, how the changed schedule with the extra cooking and laundry will be handled. There are things to be done—provisions need to be made for a school, a good sensitive pediatrician, a reliable babysitter.

Maureen and Jack wisely spend time talking together, making plans for their child. They are using this waiting period to think about ways to help an unsettled youngster feel at home, wanted, and safe. They have been thinking about ground rules for their new daughter. How do they feel about bedtime, about the amount and kind of television she should watch, about the use of slang or swearing, about an allowance and chores? They have talked about how having a third person in their family might affect their marriage.

One of the very useful things that the Reillys can do is to spend some of these conversations talking through a careful list of expectations. They can talk about what they expect from themselves and from each other as parents to their new child. They can weed out unrealistic or unnecessary objectives. Maureen, for example, feels that it is really important for a child to have a hot breakfast each morning, while Jack feels that it doesn't make a difference what a child eats as long as her mother serves it lovingly. They can provide a balance to each other and see where they feel differently about being good parents.

Waiting parents are wise to discuss openly their dreams and fears and plans for their coming child. What do they expect from him or her as a person? As a son or daughter? As a brother or sister? As a member of their family? Are these expectations realistic? Which ones are important and which don't particularly matter? Those couples who already have children should discuss their expectations for their present children in relation to the new child.

As the weeks pass, there is still no word from the agency. There is less and less for Jack and Maureen to do and talk about, fewer plans to make. They could paint the bedroom, but how can they decide on a color when they don't have any idea as to their daughter's preference? Jack's boss is pushing him to decide when he wants to take his vacation. When Jack tries to discuss it with Maureen, they end up snapping at each other. How are they supposed to know when they should schedule vacations? Should they go ahead and use up their time, or wait and take it after their daughter arrives? Why doesn't their worker call? Has she forgotten them?

Along with the euphoria of the "pre-adoptive pregnancy" go the "waiting blues." Caught in between stages, parents find it difficult to go forward or to make any plan. Many have frequent bouts of frustration and anger. What kinds of commitments can they make to new projects or other people, when they don't have any sense of how long it will be before they will need to direct their efforts to helping their new child feel at home? Workers hesitate to make any predictions about the length of waiting; they visualize irate couples, calling them up on the appointed day and making them the brunt of their frustration and anger if a child has not been found.

Frequently the telephone becomes the focal point for waiting couples—each time it rings there is the possibility that it is their worker with some news. It is also their best means of keeping in touch with the agency, inquiring about progress, reassuring themselves that they have not been overlooked. Hesitant to appear a nuisance, waiting couples often fabricate excuses to call, finding reassurance just in hearing the worker at the other end of the line. Some couples go so far as to make a schedule allowing themselves one call every three, four, or five weeks. In this situation it is best for the worker to take the initiative and call waiting couples monthly. If demands on her time rule this out, she should spell out clearly how she feels about being called—what is understandable, what is too much? If the worker does not specify this, parents at the time of approval may want to inquire as to how their worker prefers them to keep in contact.

In overseas adoptions there is an additional kind of difficult waiting. Not only must a suitable child be found, but there are even more procedures and red tape to go through before the child, already introduced to his new parents by description and a photograph, steps off the plane and becomes a reality. Parents involved in this kind of adoption frequently develop a mailbox neurosis—it is the high point of their day to see if the postman has brought word of their child. Parents adopting overseas can usefully fill some of their waiting time by finding someone from their expected child's country to help them better understand the cultural adjustments that he will be making. Some parents choose to focus on the language difference—learning phrases and words in their child's language or getting someone to make a greeting tape explaining to the child what is happening so he is not so frightened at the airport. An excellent source of preparatory materials for couples adopting Asian children are the information packets available from Holt Adoption Program (P.O. Box 2880, Eugene, Oregon 97402), from O.U.R.S., Inc. (3148 Humbolt Avenue South, Minneapolis, Minnesota 55408), and from *The Children* by Jan de Hartog (1969), which describes his family's adjustment to the arrival of two preschool Korean daughters.

Like the Reillys, the Lamberts are finding the waiting period hard. Ellen listens to her car radio most mornings as she drives to work. Lately there has been a frequent short broadcast appeal for people to adopt waiting children. Today, as she stops at a red light, she hears the message one more time. *"There are two thousand children in this state without families of their own. All they need is someone who cares, someone who can find a place in his or her heart and home for a waiting child. You are their hope — their chance. Do you have room for one more? If you are interested in becoming a parent for one of these children call the state Adoption Resource Exchange at 427-1985 for more information."*

Ellen has come to hate this advertisement. Two thousand children, are there? All she and Dick want is just one of them. What is taking so long? She wonders where their child is, if he is being loved and well cared for. What is he doing?

Ellen has called her social worker who has assured her that the Lamberts *are* being considered for the children that the agency has to place and they are also registered with the Adoption Resource Exchange. Try to be patient, their worker counsels; sometimes these things just take time.

The best source of support to Dick and Ellen in their adoption process has been their local adoptive parents group. Somehow, getting together monthly to talk to other parents who have been through it helps. These parents reassure the Lamberts that as soon as they hear about *their* child they will not resent the waiting. Most parents have the sense that the wait was worth it — that any other child would not have been as right as the one they got. The Lamberts find that there is something reassuring about meeting with other parents who have actually gotten a child from the system. "It happened for them; it will happen for us," they say to themselves.

Establishing this kind of a ready, caring support group is very useful. The parents' group can help Dick and Ellen not only while they are waiting, but also after their son or daughter arrives. They will have shared similar adjustment problems and similar fears. They will have had occasional mixed feelings in the beginning and will usually be able to reinforce the new parents' feelings that the adoption is worth the hard times, that things can be worked out. Sometimes meeting the adopted child that friends have worried over, and seeing that child well, happy, and contributing positive things to his family, puts new parents' minds to rest more than anything else. Having this kind of support group helps fight the sense that total responsibility rests on their shoulders; and finding other adoptive families, particularly couples who have adopted an older child, is a good step for any couple during the in-between period.

The period following agency approval is a little different for the DeSandos and the Allens. Already parents, they find the waiting not so hard. But they are concerned about the impact of the adoption on their other children. These parents are focusing their energies on helping to prepare their children for the arrival of an instant brother or sister.

They have discussed how feelings for new people take time to grow. Everyone will probably feel strange in the beginning, they have said to their children; people may be mad at each other and there will be problems to work out. The new child may feel homesick and grieve for his former home. Both the new and the old children may even wish the adoption had never taken place; but that kind of feeling is all right, and it will pass. In time, love will grow, and everything will get back to feeling normal. It just takes working at solving problems, and becoming used to being a family with one more person.

The period of waiting for a referral is almost always a difficult one. Faced with an impending permanent life change, geared up to meet it, and uncertain of what it will bring, parents are often charged with a great deal of energy. They want to get to it, to begin. They alternate between excited anticipation and frustrated impatience. They suffer from what Bruno Bettelheim describes as "in-between" anxiety. They don't know what they will be asked to face up to, what problems they will be called upon to solve, or what disappointments there will be. One of the most constructive ways of reducing this anxiety, Bettelheim says, is to take action calculated to put an end to the tension of the waiting period (1950, p. 134); but such action is denied parents who must wait helplessly for the wheels of placement to turn.

It is a tense period for workers also. Charged with the responsibility for making a lifetime decision for a child and his new family, aware of the magnitude of their task, they often feel a sense of not being up to what needs to be done. They delay and procrastinate, hesitant to make a decision.

And yet there are constructive things that can be done by workers and by families in this period, not to bring about the placement more quickly but to make themselves more ready for it. In this preliminary period, each of the adults involved has a task: the worker to prepare the waiting children as best she can for a new family and to prepare herself to help child and parent adjust; the parents to prepare themselves for their new child. All the adults need to recognize where the child is emotionally and developmentally, in order to be able to listen to him with understanding, talk to him so that he hears, and plan for him realistically.

Child Development

One of the basic tools to help in these tasks is a working knowledge of child development, for although each child develops on his own schedule, the stages in the process unfold with a good degree of predictability. A sense of how children think at certain stages, their common fears at varying ages, the developmental tasks facing them as they grow up, helps workers and parents immeasurably in preparing and planning for children.

Agencies that truly wish to prepare staff and parents to help children should give short courses, calling in outside personnel if necessary, acquainting the adults who deal with the child with the developmental stages in children. Some agencies make this kind of learning not only available but mandatory, using the waiting period before adoption for the information to be shared. For those workers and parents who do not have such a service available, excellent descriptions are to be found in *Child Development* and *The Child from Five to Ten*, both by the Gesell Institute.

Learning to Talk to Children

Another useful skill to learn or to enlarge is the ability to talk with children in a way that draws them out, encourages them to face up to and solve their problems, and recognizes and allows expression of their own thoughts and feelings. Although some adults have a knack for talking with children, others do not. Loving the child and anxious that he learn about the world, develop good moral values, and be valued by people outside the family, such parents constantly send messages that what the child does is not up to standard. This kind of communication with children conveys non-acceptance, disapproval, or impatience, and keeps the child from perceiving how much he is valued as an individual.

Working with troubled families, Dr. Thomas Gordon began in 1962 to devise a course of study that would help parents deal with their children more effectively. If professionals could be trained to communicate with children therapeutically, he theorized, parents with even greater desire to help their children could use these same tools and methods at home, to the benefit of their children and the parent-child relationship. Since that time his methods have spread across the nation. Titled Parent Effectiveness Training (P.E.T.), many of his ideas and techniques are of interest to parents and workers who deal with children.

Essentially, P.E.T. encourages adults to send clear messages to children, rather than messages that confuse or cause conflict in the listener. P.E.T. encourages the use of "I messages" — which reflect the response of the adult to the situation ("I do not like it when the house is a mess") — as opposed to "You messages" — which cast blame ("You are such a slob; you always leave things in a mess"). P.E.T. helps adults define to whom a given problem belongs — the child, the adult, or the relationship — and gives the adult a means of helping the child find his own solutions if the problem belongs to him; ways of communicating non-acceptance of the situation if it is the adult's problem; and conflict-resolving tools when there is a conflict of interest and both child and adult share the problem.

By using what Carl Rogers calls a "reflection of feeling tones" and what Gordon calls "active listening," proper communication with children can do the following things:

1. Help the child know that the adult identifies with him and understands his feelings — thereby establishing an immediate bond between the child and the adult.
2. Clarify the child's feelings, to the adult and to the child.
3. Perhaps open up a way to satisfying the child's need to get his feelings out so that he may find reassurance for his fears and vent his anger and frustration.
4. Help the child understand himself better.
5. Be a good tool for adults talking to children at times when they don't know what to say. P.E.T. doesn't assume that it is necessary for adults to have the ability to understand and solve all the child's problems in order to be helpful to children when they are troubled.

Some agencies, recognizing the usefulness of this kind of training, provide their own Parent Effectiveness Training series for parents in the pre-placement period, and make the course a requirement for parents awaiting the arrival of an older child. Others recommend that parents and staff take advantage of courses available in most communities, or read the book outlining the philosophy and methods. It is not necessary to accept the entire philosophy behind the P.E.T. program to profit from the course and to communicate more effectively with children. Most adults find the philosophy to be thought-provoking, and the techniques useful.

Taking time to acquire a better understanding of the principles of child development and how best to listen to and talk with children is one way for workers to feel more confident of their ability to prepare children for an adoptive placement, and for waiting parents to use the in-between period to prepare themselves to become better parents to their expected child. It is time well spent.

5
Preparing Children for Placement

Early one clear fall morning, Leah Gardner, having finished her coffee, gathers her paperwork into her briefcase and heads towards her car. A social worker with the state Adoption Placement Unit, she is on her way to meet Tommy and Gena. Over a period of months she will spend as much time as possible with them, for it is her job to introduce them to the idea of adoption and to help them deal with their feelings about their past families and their move into a new one. It is her intent that the children grow to trust her, becoming able to share their hopes and fears about an adoptive home and their future in their conversations with her. Like most placement workers, Mrs. Gardner has a deep sense of personal responsibility for the children assigned to her. She is committed to doing the best job she can to prepare them for an adoptive family. In time, she will use her observations and conversations to make recommendations about the type of family best suited to these children. Mrs. Gardner knows that a great deal depends on how well she and the children can work together.

As Leah Gardner pulls onto the highway she mentally goes over what she already knows about the two children. How can she best help them? What will they need from her to be able to profit from an adoptive placement?

One of the most important things in the preparation of children for adoption is that the worker herself be properly trained and able to operate effectively. There must be enough time allowed for the child to establish a supportive relationship with the worker, and for the child to do the necessary emotional work to be ready to move. Mrs. Gardner is unusually fortunate to work in an agency where there are enough workers so that she has the time she needs for the children in her caseload. Anyone who has placed older children knows without doubt that the time not properly spent in the preparatory phase is almost always needed after the child is placed. But the unprepared child, who must deal with his feelings about his adoption after he is already placed, frequently has a longer and rockier adjustment period. Sometimes the lack of preparation jeopardizes the placement itself. The time then needed to help salvage the placement would have been far better spent helping the child become ready for adoption.

Over her several years of preparing children to move, Leah Gardner has refined her skills until she is an exceptionally good worker. But other social workers who choose to use her methods will quite likely find that her techniques, though thorough, do not require more staff time than other means of preparation. Instead, she uses time to its fullest.

Involving the Foster Parents

Mrs. Gardner has timed her arrival at the foster home so that she can spend some time with Gena's and Tommy's foster mother before the children come home from school, to talk to her about the children she has been caring for. Leah Gardner wants to get an understanding of the foster mother's feelings and concerns about the proposed adoption. If she is willing, this foster mother can be an important part of the children's preparation and move into adoption.

Although the commonly held notion is that people often become foster parents chiefly for the money, there are a great many other reasons. Gena's and Tommy's foster mother decided to take in foster children when her own children had all entered school. In this way, she felt, she could do something positive without taking herself away from her own family. One of the questions that Mrs. Gardner will ask her is whether she and her husband have considered adopting these two children. This accomplishes two things: it tells the worker if the foster mother sees the children as adoptable; and it establishes whether a foster home adoption has been considered, and if it has, why the consideration has been rejected. Perhaps the foster parents are aged, or perhaps the agency feels that their home is too crowded to allow the proper individual attention to the children living there. Perhaps there has been a personality clash between the child and the foster parents. Or perhaps the foster parents do not have strong enough ties to the children to lead to adoption. Maybe the child has been in this home for only a short time. Maybe the child was placed on an emergency basis without consideration of the foster parents' preference in a child. Maybe the foster parents have held back on their attachment in order to be better able to help the child move on, feeling that their best contribution to their foster children is a good start towards adoption.

Mrs. Gardner and the foster mother sit with their coffee in the sunny, tidy kitchen and talk. The foster mother explains that she and her husband have no thought of adopting any of the children in their care, but that she finds Gena and Tommy as appealing as any of the children they have taken on. She and her husband are committed to helping these children make their move as smoothly and as easily as possible. She talks about her mixed feelings — sad to lose the children, and happy to have them settled permanently. Mrs. Gardner and the foster mother spend some time talking together about the type of family the foster parents would pick for these children. The foster mother's obvious acceptance of the children gives Leah Gardner a beginning point: the children have fit into this family; they would probably do well if the adoptive family were in some ways similar.

There are specific questions that can be asked to give a framework for understanding the children—information that will help match children to adoptive parents, and that cooperative foster parents are in the best position to provide. Leah Gardner will ask about many things:

1. Eating routines. Are there any feeding difficulties, table problems? Are the children gorgers or picky eaters? Have their eating habits changed since they entered this home? How?

2. Sleeping routines. Leah knows from his records that Tommy wets his bed and has nightmares. But do the children wake at night and wander, or sleepwalk? Do they have night terrors? How hard are they to get to sleep? What time do they get to bed? Do they fuss about bedtime? Do they share a bedroom? Do they sleep with a special object? How hard are they to get up?

3. Self-help. Do they dress themselves, pick out their own clothing? Do they take care of their own bathing and toothbrushing, or do they need to be reminded?

4. Play. What do they like to do with their spare time? Do they prefer small- or large-muscle play? Do they play alone or with others? What kinds of play do they avoid? Do they have special interests? Favorite toys? How much television do they watch?

5. Speech. How well do they communicate? Do they make themselves understood? Are there special body postures or habits of speech they use to communicate certain feelings or ideas? Can they talk about their feelings?

6. Relationships with other children. How well do they get along with the other children in this family? In the neighborhood? Do they prefer to play with children who are older, younger, or their same age?

7. Experience at school. Are they strong, average, or weak in their academic skills? How well do they get along with people in authority? With other children in their classes? Is it likely that they will be able to graduate from a regular high school? Would they be good candidates for a vocational/technical school?

8. Functioning in the family. How have they adjusted to this home? How do they respond to reasonable requests; does every issue escalate into a battle? How do they handle routine chores and expectations? How have they been disciplined? How are they about expressions of affection, about touching? Do they like parents to initiate exchanges of affection, or do they initiate them? Do they prefer men to women, women to men? Do they need a lot of approval? In what form?
9. Self-control and antisocial areas. Do they bedwet? Soil? Lie? Steal? Set fires? Act out sexually? How is their control of impulses? How do they take care of possessions?
10. Sex. What has this child been told?
11. Fears. Are there specific things they are afraid of? What? How do they handle these fears? What is their experience with and relationship to animals?
12. Personal makeup. What kinds of feeling does the child have about himself? How does the child handle failure, stress, happiness, anger, physical and psychological pain, anxiety?

It will also be a good idea to make an appointment with the child's school, interviewing teachers and other involved adults for their impressions.

Meeting the Children: The First Visit

Soon there is the sound of a school bus stopping at the driveway. Leah Gardner watches as the bus doors open and a blond figure jumps out, dashes up the walk, and hurls herself into the kitchen; Gena is home. Along with Gena, a younger boy stands at the open door of the school bus. Carefully he reaches his small foot down the steps. Deliberately he comes up the walk and in the door. Gena, having tossed her red sweater in the direction of a hook, says, "Hello. You must be Mrs. Gardner. Miss Jones said you were coming today. Do you like cats? Have you seen our kittens? The teacher said I did real well in school today. Hurry up, Tommy, come meet the new social worker."

Tommy comes just inside the kitchen door, from where he watches Gena and the adults in the kitchen carefully.

Although it takes more staff time, many agencies are now encouraging the familiar foster care worker not only to prepare the child for reassignment to an adoptive worker, but to bring the new worker to the foster home and introduce her to the child with whom she will now be working. The more gentle and non-rejecting are the changes of personnel in the foster child's life, the less chance for these children to feel hurt or abandoned. Even after the children have met their new adoption worker, it would be ideal for their old worker to call them up or to drop by once or twice, so that they know she has not dropped them precipitously but that she is still interested in them and concerned about their well-being.

After a snack and conversation, Mrs. Gardner asks if she might take the children for a walk. She spends time on her walk beginning to know Gena and Tommy. In the course of the afternoon, she asks them if they know why they will be seeing her instead of Miss Jones. She explains that she has a different kind of work to do. Her job is to help children who need a family of their own find just the right place to live. When it comes time for Tommy and Gena to leave their foster home, she will be looking for a place where they can stay, a place where children don't have to move.

The pace taken by the worker in preparing children for adoption varies with each worker and each child. Although some authorities feel that talk about the impending separation may cause such anxiety that it impedes the child's ability to establish a good relationship with the worker, Mrs. Gardner believes it is important to implant at the beginning the idea that she will be moving the children at some time in the future, that a permanent home is the goal. There are several things that must happen before the children are ready for adoption. They must face their feelings about their first family and their separation from it. They must deal with their feelings about moves from other foster families, if this is not their first placement. They must realize that they are foster children in this home and that they will be moving. They must be allowed to express their feelings of sadness, anger, rejection, or anxiety about this move. They must understand that they are entitled to a permanent family. Misunderstandings about adoption must be cleared up. And they should be included in the planning for an adoptive home, with a chance to consider what type of family they would like to live with.

Mrs. Gardner would be well advised to follow the "ten commandments" from a booklet called *Opening New Doors* by Kay Donley, past director of Spaulding for Children.

1. Avoid cliches in talking to children. Children recognize cliches and your use of them will readily and clearly inform the child that you are indeed an adult who does not know how to talk to them. Some of the typical cliches that adults use in working with children are questions, probing questions, such as, "How do you like school? Which class are you in?" Never begin a conversation with a child in that way. Eventually, when you really know that child, such questions may be appropriate, but never as an opening gambit. The best way to begin a conversation with a child is simply to exchange some pleasantries about who you are and how pleased you are to know him and let it go for a while. Children are more responsive to the idea of approaching you gradually, than [to] being physically and psychically overwhelmed by this large thing that flies at them and begins to probe their inmost thoughts. Take your time. You never know at first if you have a very shy withdrawn child or a very agressive one.

2. Assume that any child you are going to work with has some deep concern that has never been adequately understood or answered. I am referring specifically to children in public care, all of whom typically share the experience of having been separated from their parents. In many cases they have also lost a succession of caretakers — house parents and foster parents. In working with the child you may, in fact, discover that someone very skilled and very sensitive has helped him to understand what has happened. But it is safer to assume that no one has adequately assessed the deep and often confused concerns of the child.

3. Understand from the beginning that children in care have been hurt: some part of them has been damaged. Never make the assumption that, because everyone presents this child as

untouched and undamaged, he must be that way. More often than not, the child will have been handled by a lot of unperceptive people. Perhaps this particular child has made an exceptionally good adjustment in the face of difficult and painful circumstances. But as a rule, there are always some damaged pieces of unfinished business tucked away. If you understand that, you will not be dismayed or thrown off balance six months later when someone says: "You know, there's something peculiar about this kid. He's not quite what I would call 'normal.' "

4. Remember that in working with a child your essential task is to learn how he explains himself to himself, and what he understands his situation to be. Unless you really know what is going on inside him, you will not be able to represent him justly or truthfully to residential staff or to potential foster or adoptive parents. It is not simply that you must know where this child is for your own satisfaction. You must be prepared to communicate your understanding to other people. This is not easy.

5. Develop specific concrete tools which will help you communicate with children. Children are not normally interested solely in verbalization as a way of communicating with anyone. They have other available tools and you must find out what they are so that you can use them too.

6. Be prepared to become a dependable, predictable, and regular fixture in the child's experience. You simply cannot pop in on a Monday and say, "I'll see you again sometime soon." The social worker's indefinite promise of returning to his life usually means avoiding him for several weeks and then popping in again. This simply does not work and is, in fact, destructive. You are adding to the child's already increasing fund of knowledge that, as far as he is concerned, adults are undependable, unpredictable, and unknowable. You must regularize your contact.

   Most social workers say, "I really would like to, but I haven't the time." This begs the question, because it is possible to regularize contacts, even if there are long intervals between visits. It is the idea of predictability that is important to the child. If you make a commitment then you keep it. (And I mean you keep it, even if it breaks your back!) If, for some reason, you are unable to keep the appointment you have made, it is important that you communicate directly with the child the reasons why you cannot. I have known workers [to] go to the extent of sending a telegram to a child whom they could not reach by telephone, so strong was their sense of commitment.

7. Remember that each child's experience is unique and that it is absolutely crucial that each child is helped to begin to come to grips with his life. You cannot begin on the assumption that, because you have worked successfully with one or two children who have been neglected by their parents, you know what this experience means to any child. Certainly, you can learn from one situation and apply your knowledge to another. But keep in mind that you are dealing with individuals: deceptively similar experiences have very different meanings for different children.

8. As you work with a child over a period of time, you must help him develop what I call a "cover story." "Cover story" is not a very good phrase because a lot of people think that I mean concealing things and I do not. I believe that a child must have a clear, understandable, acceptable explanation of his circumstances, which he must be able to use at will and comfortably. For example, when he goes to a new school, he will be meeting a lot of new children, making friends and meeting people living in the neighborhood. He will be asked questions about himself and it is essential that he should have a socially acceptable and logical explanation for who he is and where he is and why he is in this situation. Only too frequently, unskilled workers do not appreciate how essential this is and do not help the child develop a cover story for public consumption. Without it the child is left to his own devices and frequently falls into fabrication. A child fabricates when he is not quite sure how people will receive the true facts of his situation. Fabrication, once found out, will very quickly give the child a reputation in the neighborhood for being a spinner of tall tales or, at worst, a liar.

9. Commit yourself always to what I call a multi-faceted or composite view of the child. Remember there is no one true way of seeing and experiencing a youngster. Every person who has contact with the child will have a slightly different point of view and a unique experience. Some people will be enthusiastic about him, while others cannot abide him. What you are

really searching for is a combination of all those perceptions, because buried amongst all of them there is the truth. Somewhere, amongst all those varying views of the child, will be a perception that his potential adoptive parents may make of him. So it is important that you begin to develop that kind of sensitivity and awareness.

10. Keep in mind from the beginning of your work that you are obliged to convey to any caretakers — be they residential staff or adoptive families — a true sense of the child's history. You may think that this is self-evident and that I am being needlessly repetitious in stressing this point. But I think it bears repeating, because many social workers feel they are doing a child a grave injustice by telling the full and sorry tale, and that the only way to spare the child is to conceal certain things. These are usually things the social worker finds distressing or unpalatable, so they are concealed because she feels that this will give the child a better chance in life, a better opportunity for placement, an easier adjustment. Invariably those very things come flashing up anew out of the child's history and past to create problems and difficulties for him and his caretakers. This is a painful area for most social workers but it is one which you must grapple with and come to terms with.

The Life Book: A Preparation Process

The following week, Leah Gardner visits Tommy and Gena again. After they share a snack, she tells them that one of the ways she likes to get to know children is to have them make up their very own books, which tell the stories of their lives. She wonders if Gena and Tommy would each like to begin a book. The children are enchanted. They can hardly wait to begin.

Mrs. Gardner is finding the foster home a good place to work. If it were not, she would try to make arrangements to use a local church or school. Taking out a pack of brightly colored construction paper, a new box of crayons, and some magic markers, Mrs. Gardner sets the children to work. She encourages them to draw pictures of themselves and of their favorite things to do. As the children draw, she talks with them about themselves and their drawings, asking information-sharing questions: What is your favorite color? Your favorite animal? What do you like to do best? Gena dashes off several drawings, with a running stream of conversation to keep attention focused on her. But as Tommy draws, he keeps asking for reassurance that he is doing things right, that his drawings are okay. Mrs. Gardner tells him that there is no particular right way to do his book. He can decide to draw however he wants to. No one can look into his mind but him, she says, to see the picture that he sees. It is his picture that is the best one for his very own book. Later, as they talk, it will be very important for Gena and Tommy to know that what they think and feel can be independent of anyone's approval.

When Gena and Tommy finish their drawings, Mrs. Gardner has them dictate stories about what they have colored. She writes these comments down to go into their books. Now she invites them to draw a picture of something that they hate to do, or something that makes them angry. She wants to establish that she knows all children have things that bother them, and that Gena and Tommy can share some of their uncomfortable feelings with her and still be accepted.

When they have finished these drawings and dictated a little about them, Mrs. Gardner brings out two large manila envelopes. She asks the children to print their names on their own envelopes. Collecting their drawings and the paragraphs about these pictures, she tells them that they have worked hard, and promises them that she will keep their work safe in their envelopes until it is time to put it into a book. In this way she is conveying the importance of their activity to the two children.

As demands on her time allow, Mrs. Gardner will be seeing Gena and Tommy regularly, so that she becomes a part of the children's expected schedule. Some workers take their children out for walks, ice cream, or meals; or occasionally bring small gifts like balloons or a coloring book; or remember them on their birthdays or on special occasions with a card or a note in the mail. They want the children to know that their worker cares, and to look forward to their visits together.

On the following visit, Mrs. Gardner shows the children their manila envelopes of drawings from the previous week, and asks them if they would like to do some more work on their "life books." When they seem interested, she takes out two photograph albums and helps the children begin. (Often these albums are available at discount stores very inexpensively. If not, bound spiral notebooks may be used or the pages may be stapled or tied together.)

The first pages in their books will include the drawing each child made of himself last week, with his dictated comments. An early page will show the child's birth information: date and time of birth, place, weight, length, or any of the facts available from the child's birth certificate or hospital records. Because Mrs. Gardner knows that often foster children are very unclear or uninformed about their prenatal growth, she will spend a visit talking with them about how they grew in a first mother's body. The children may want to draw or to cut out from magazines illustrations of pregnancy, prenatal life, and newborn babies. (Free magazines filled with these pictures are available in obstetricians' offices.) They may wish to draw a picture of what they looked like as brand new babies, aided by the birth information shared with their worker plus her concrete interpretations ("You were this long, and you weighed just a little less than this package of potatoes"). The beginning of the book should include a physical description of the child's biological parents, giving their ages at the time of the child's birth, their coloring, height, and weight. Frequently the child is interested to know his birth parents' first names.

The life book works well to help children explain who they are and where they came from. Without the personal history of a lovingly kept baby book, without well known references to the personal past ("When you were little you had blond hair and you used to turn your dinner dish upside-down on it when you had finished eating"), the child needs someone who confirms whether his fragmented memories are fact or fiction, who can embellish a glimpse of times gone by before it fades completely away.

> The youngster who has spent the major part of his life in care is often uncertain about why he came into care, why changes in placement were made, why other children moved on and why

staff left; he may not know the names of the various people who have looked after him, let alone their current whereabouts; the same is true regarding the children who shared his life for certain periods; nor does he know what the future is likely to hold since long-term plans are rarely made (Pringle 1975, p. 134).

To help them begin to reconstruct the happenings in their lives, Mrs. Gardner in another visit gently leads the conversation towards how Gena and Tommy came to be living here. Their first mother had grownup problems; she did not live with their first father. She found it hard to take care of two little children by herself. The agency helped find Gena and Tommy this place to live, where they could be looked after. Leah Gardner talks with them about how they must have felt when they first came to live in the foster home. She knows that when their mother abandoned them four years ago, Gena and Tommy were seven and three. Much of their growing up has taken place in this foster home. Moving into a new family can be good for children, she lets them understand, but it may be frightening at first. Because Gena and Tommy are no longer frightened here but feel comfortable and safe, Leah Gardner hopes to use their change in feeling as encouragement when the time comes for the children to move into a permanent family. She ends the visit by asking them to draw pictures of the foster home and of the family they are now living with, and adds them to their life books.

Many times children bring up their own memories about the things that led them to be placed in a foster home. Gena and Tommy have not done this. Pacing herself, in part by the children's questions and in part by her own sense of how quickly to proceed, Leah Gardner begins to talk in subsequent visits about the details surrounding Gena's and Tommy's separation from their first mother. She encourages Gena to tell Tommy what she remembers about the loss of their mother and to serve as a family historian to him, though she stands ready to correct any distortion or fantasy that Gena may have. Gena begins to fidget, tapping her crayon against the table, swinging her foot. First their daddy went away, Gena tells Tommy. Then their mommy was very sad and she cried a lot. She also yelled. One

day when they got up in the morning, there was no one in the
house. They were afraid because their mother was gone and
they were hungry. They cried. Finally a man came and took
them to an office. Then they came here. They never went back;
they never saw their mother again. Mrs. Gardner encourages
Gena to talk about how she felt. Gena says in a very quiet little
voice, "I was scared. I wanted Mommy. I didn't know where
she was or when I was going home. Why did my mother leave us
alone? Why didn't she come back and take care of us?"

Leah Gardner is now entering a very important psychological stage with Gena and Tommy. She knows that children who
have lost their parents almost always assume the loss to be their
own fault — they feel that they were bad children and drove their
parents away.

> No matter what the realistic reason for the separation, the child
> seems to experience first — either consciously or unconsciously —
> a feeling of abandonment, which contains elements of loss,
> rejection, humiliation, complete insignificance, and worthless-
> ness. In addition, he is flooded with a feeling of complete help-
> lessness, of lack of control over what is happening to him. The
> child reacts to his sense of abandonment and of helplessness
> with a feeling of anger at the parent he feels has deserted him.
> The feelings of helplessness and insignificance further stimulate a
> need to deny them. Instead of facing the unacceptable feeling
> that he has no control over the harsh blows of fate, he tries to
> deny this with the exact opposite feeling — that really he is totally
> responsible for the abandonment. As an attempted self-
> reassurance against his inner feelings of helplessness and insignif-
> icance, the child blames himself for all the incidents leading up
> to the separation. It is as though he is declaring that it is not true
> that he is a helpless, unimportant pawn — actually he is the
> important one, completely responsible for everything that has
> happened. This self-blame also helps him deny his anger at his
> parents. He is the one who is bad, not they.
>
> He seeks for a specific badness within himself on which to
> blame the events of the separation. He usually singles out the
> current problem that he is attempting to master at the particular
> stage of his physical and emotional development that is
> coincident in time with the separation. It may be a feeling of
> failure and shame, that he has disappointed his parents by not

learning fast enough how to walk, or how to control his sphincters according to their expectations. Or it may be a feeling of badness associated with some unacceptable impulse, such as anger at his mother for various reasons, or rivalry with a younger sibling, or competition with father or an older sibling, or sexual interest in his mother. Any of these shameful or guilt-laden feelings may be given full credit by the child as being responsible for the actual separation and placement.

Thus, as an example, Johnnie—whose mother had died in childbirth—felt completely responsible. He unconsciously felt that his anger at both her and the new baby was the cause of her death, of his father's subsequent inability to care for him, and his final placement in a foster home (Littner 1956).

This tendency can also be seen in some children with serious illnesses; they have diabetes "because I ate too much sugar," or rheumatic fever "because I ran around too much" (Wolff 1969, p. 73).

Mrs. Gardner will explore with Gena and Tommy their ideas as to how they came into care, trying to ferret out where they blame themselves. Whatever the facts that caused Gena's and Tommy's first parents to be unable to take care of them, the events can be reconstructed and presented in a nonjudgmental and understanding manner to the children, helping to counterbalance any feelings of self-blame or badness they may have. Leah Gardner will encourage the children to talk freely about their biological parents and the hurt and anger they may have stored up against them. At the same time she will not downgrade or blame their parents for their inability to care for the children. As the children sway between defense (the parents were fine) and criticism (the parents were no good) she will help them to see their parents as people with virtues as well as shortcomings, whose troubles came in part from their own unhappy childhoods. Gena and Tommy, too, have experienced difficulty from their own unsettled lives, so they may be able to understand and accept this explanation.

She will not expect the children to accept that their mother gave them up "because she loved them." She knows it makes more sense to them to talk about their mother giving them up because she couldn't take care of them, or be as good a parent as she wanted to be. She will help them see that their mother continued to feel concern for them after she left them, by calling to notify a caretaking agency that her children were alone. She talked with a social worker about her problems, and finally she released them for adoption so that a permanent plan could be made. Leah Gardner will let Tommy and Gena find their own way to include this aspect of their past in their life books, integrating the sad with the happy times. Part of her importance to these children is as a stand-in for the missing people from their first family, who could have given them an idea of who their people were and how they came to be separated, providing information but not necessarily resolving all the issues. Part of her importance is to help the children better understand their past so that they can move on to another family, and part is as someone who knows about these children and their past and still likes and respects them. This may give them more of a sense that they are not bad children, and that a new mother and father may find them lovable.

Mrs. Gardner is now ready to talk with Gena and Tommy about their status in the foster family and what that means for their future. There are a number of ways that she may help the children understand foster care. If there are other foster children in this home who have moved in or out during the past four years, that can be a good starting point. Looking at last names is another way to begin. Although some foster children use the foster surname, most do not. Their entry into school where they learn how to write their own last names is often the first time they clearly recognize that they are somehow different from their foster families. Because Gena seems to have a clear idea that she is a foster child, Mrs. Gardner chooses to focus with Tommy on the difference that he has noticed between the last name he uses in school and his foster parents' last name. She tells Tommy, with Gena listening, that he has been cared for in this home during the time that it took for the agency and their mother to make a good plan for them; for everyone to be sure that they would never be able to return to their first home. Now it is time for Tommy and Gena to have a new family, a family to belong to and to share a last name with, a "keeping" family.

Tommy's eyes puddle up and his lip quivers. Gena is wiggling frantically. She is bursting with questions: "Do we have to move? We like it here! Will I have to go to a new school? Don't our foster parents love us? Why don't they want us to stay?" The hard questions pour out. Tommy is crying now, his head down, the tears dripping off his nose. Mrs. Gardner hands him a tissue.

Like all of us, Leah Gardner has had frustrations, separations, and losses of her own. It is hard not to identify with the pain of a foster parent losing a child and with the child about to be placed. Sometimes workers become quite uneasy about the pain of replacement; they feel guilty for being involved, for carrying the news of the impending separation, for setting the process in motion. It is these feelings, coupled with an unrealistic workload, which accounts for the number of children who are presumed to be prepared for their move into an adoptive home, but who have never really been helped to understand their separation from their original family or the reasons they are being moved again. If the worker has found her own feelings too threatening or unpleasant, if the worker has avoided helping the child deal with loss and rejection, the child goes into his new family still raw and hurting from the past. It takes him additional time to heal over, to trust again.

Responding to the children with warmth and understanding, Mrs. Gardner assures them that the foster parents do care about them, but that they are not adopting parents. She tells Tommy and Gena that everyone knows it seems hard to move, but that the foster parents and the agency all feel that the children need a place where they can belong for good, a family that is a keeping family, so that they won't have to move again.

In those instances where the foster parent is able, it often helps to have the initial discussion about moving include the foster parents as well as the children and the social worker. This gives the foster parents a chance to express their concern and affection firsthand to the children. It also helps prevent a child's fantasy that he or she has been snatched away from the unwilling foster mother and father by the agency or the new parents. Foster parents can add their verbal approval of the plan for the children to find a permanent home. If the worker has been able to help them understand how important they can be in assisting children to make a good start in an adoptive home, the foster parents may be happy to be involved in the preparation and moving procedures. In order to be able to have a three-way conversation, both caseworker and foster parents have to face the reality of their own feelings and their reluctance to face pain with the child. The foster parents must be sure of their commitment to the plan for an adoptive placement, and be able to withstand grief, anxiety, and accusations of rejection from their foster child. Experienced caseworkers have found that if the parents can be involved in a positive way to help the child accept separation this can reduce further fantasy and free the child to go on (Chema et al. 1970, p. 451).

For some time after their conversation about moving, Gena and Tommy continue to bring up their feelings about the change. Sometimes they are angry. Sometimes they are worried. Gena tackles the problem by deciding that Mrs. Gardner should adopt them, and this common reaction is dealt with firmly. The children swing sometimes to being excited and unrealistically convinced that a new family will make life perfect, and then back to being upset because the foster family is not keeping them. Mrs. Gardner does not rush the children to resolve their feelings. She knows that it is important for them to be able to have full expression of their reaction to the planned move. A child who is not allowed feelings of grief over a significant loss may fall back on more primitive measures of defense — to deny the pain of loss, for example, and to feel nothing. If a child were consistently reared on this basis, deprived of the possibility of experiencing grief, he might become an impoverished person, without quality or depth in his emotional life. We need to respect a child's right to experience a loss fully and deeply (Fraiberg 1959, p. 274).

Tommy's foster mother reports that he has started to suck his thumb again. Mrs. Gardner tells her that many children over five years old show regressive behavior either during preparation for placement in an adoptive home or during the early months following placement. This behavior shows that the child's early dependency needs may not have been fully satisfied; he is attempting to fill a void (Lawder 1958, p. 3). She encourages the foster mother to continue to be supportive to Tommy and to allow him the thumbsucking as he seems to need it.

As time goes on, Mrs. Gardner begins to talk with Gena and Tommy about their role in finding a new family. She wants them to feel involved and to be a part of the decisionmaking process, so that they will be less likely to have feelings of helplessness. At the same time she wants them to have the sense that finding the right family for them is her responsibility.

Mrs. Gardner continues to use the life book as a means to help with the transition to an adoptive home. She explains that she will be looking for the right family, but says she needs Tommy and Gena to help her understand what kind of a family they would like to live in. She encourages them both to draw a house that looks like a happy place to live and to tell her their ideas on what makes a house happy, so that she can write it down for their books. Mrs. Gardner tries to get a realistic view of what type of family and setting the children see themselves as fitting into. She has them draw or cut out magazine pictures of the kind of parents and family they would like to live with, and she writes down their verbal instructions on what they want in a new mother, a new father, a new family. She also provides ways for them to bring out their fears and worries. She has them draw the things that they are afraid might be bad for them in a new family, and she adds their descriptions about potential unhappy or unpleasant happenings to the life books. Mrs. Gardner's skills will be used fully as she tries to decipher the real meanings of what Gena and Tommy tell her, allowing them to express their concerns and not trying to dismiss them with a lot of intellectual and verbal explanations.

Sometimes children hold real surprises for their workers at this stage of preparation. They may have totally unreal fantasies, both good and bad, as to what their new families will do with and for them. Any effective attempt by the worker to reassure them will have to include an understanding of their private terrors. When asked to talk about what they want in new parents, some children reveal a very poor concept of what being a parent means, because they have received so little loving and nurturing care. Some children have little or no understanding of how families function. Some children reveal fears about having to compete with other children in a family, insisting that they want to be an only child. Perhaps this is the best plan for such children. Or perhaps they need the reassurance that any prospective parents have been studied to ascertain that they will have enough love for another child. They may need reassurance that any couple selected would not find adoption a second-rate method of having a child, nor find the child their second choice. Often these feelings can best be dealt with by having the child cut out pictures as puppets to represent parents, children, and themselves. As the child speaks for the characters he has created, his real concerns tend to surface, and his worker can better reassure him. She may want to use these same puppet characters to redo the scene that the child has just played, correcting distortions and allaying misconceptions and fears.

In addition, workers sometimes need to reassure children that though they cannot adopt them personally, they find the children to be appealing and lovable; the worker's own appreciation and positive feelings about the child should be expressed.

Leah Gardner also has the children include in their books current information about themselves. They can draw or describe their activities, hobbies, interests, or experiences at school. If available, snapshots can be included of themselves at various ages, of their foster home, or of things that are special to them. Information about injuries and hospitalizations should also be included. Some foster care workers are sensitive enough to have thought to take pictures of previous foster homes; these pictures can serve as mementos to include in the life book. The time required to take these pictures or to file an annual snapshot of a child in foster care is minimal, and the significance to the child is immeasurable. He has an ongoing history; he has not lost his past each time he moved or was assigned to another worker.

This is a good time for Mrs. Gardner to get the foster parents involved in the life book. Although she will leave the decision to the children as to how, when, and with whom they will share their books, Mrs. Gardner will encourage the children to share the contents of their books with their foster parents. It will provide a chance for these parents to show their positive feelings for Gena and Tommy and their acceptance and approval of their past, their present, and their future. They may also be able to provide developmental information to include in the books. Ner Littner suggests that one of the caseworker's primary tasks is helping the foster parents do as much as they can to help the child move. This includes helping them with their own feelings about the placement and about separation. It also includes having them take as much responsibility as they are able to, both for preparing the child for the separation and for physically moving him.

The more capable the parents are of doing this, Littner explains, the more opportunity the child will have to vent rather than repress his separation feelings. In addition, the child is more apt to feel that he has the parents' permission to leave them and to live with and love his new parents (Littner 1956, p. 17).

Sharing the life book with the foster parents also gives them a chance to see concretely their own contributions to the child, and to feel that they are a valuable and permanent part of their foster child's history.

Leah Gardner will encourage the children to use their life books as a way to explain who they are to their new parents. She may have them include pictures and comments about foods that they love and hate; people that they love and hate; things that make them feel good and bad; some of the things that they are afraid of. She wants the book to express feelings, so that the child is less concerned about what his new parents will think of the things he considers unacceptable about himself, less fearful that his new parents wouldn't want him if they knew what he was like inside.

Indications of Readiness for Adoption

Although some children do not show such early indications that they are ready to be adopted, Gena and Tommy are beginning to talk positively about their adoption by the time that their life books are finished. They have met all the usual requirements to be able to move into an adoptive family. These requirements include:

1. The child's ability to adjust to the loss of old parental ties and to accept new parental relationships. This implies some sense of trust in the adoptive parents' willingness to accept the child.
2. The child's emotional acceptance that he cannot return to his own parents and that this relationship cannot be revived.
3. The child's expression of explicit desire for adoption.
4. Behavior that indicates the child's motivation to adjust to the adoptive situation (Kadushin 1971, p. 34).

One of the constructive things about the move into an adoptive home is that it can be a planned move. Very often there is little or no time to prepare a child for the separation from his biological family or from subsequent foster homes. If enough time is allowed, the pacing and the preparation in the adoptive move can frequently help undo damage from previous separations. It can demonstrate that not all moves are bad, that change sometimes works for the better. It can also give agency personnel an opportunity to dispel resentment in the child — who sees social workers as appearing only when things are bad — by demonstrating that they can care in a planned, satisfying way. Thus the child may be able to have more positive feelings about the role of the agency in his life.

Mrs. Gardner is also the placement worker for Maggie and for Danny. She will use some of these same techniques in preparing them to be adopted. Let's look in on some of her early visits with Maggie.

Preparing the Quiet, Less Verbal Child

Maggie, at nine, has been moved successively since her parents divorced. Living with one relative after another, she has turned into a quiet, nonverbal, suspicious child; she often seems cold and uninvolved. When Mrs. Gardner first approaches her with the idea of making her own life book, Maggie is not enthusiastic. She will do it if she has to, she says, shrugging her shoulders. Maggie's diffidence may come from her tendency not to demonstrate anticipation; or from a reluctance to share her life with Mrs. Gardner; or from her desire to avoid remembering the things that have happened to her. Mrs. Gardner handles Maggie's lukewarm reaction by telling her that she may be more interested in doing her book in the future, and letting the subject drop.

She concentrates instead on getting to know Maggie better in their hour together. Like many workers, Leah Gardner often carries a few inexpensive props: a frisbie and a jumprope for very active children like Gena; crayons and paper; a deck of cards; and a ball and some jacks. Today she spends a short while teaching Maggie to play jacks. Maggie learns surprisingly quickly, although she is very quick to criticize herself. She does seem to drop some of her tight control, though, and plays the game with increasing skill and enjoyment.

Mrs. Gardner knows that children like Maggie often find it hard to let themselves care about or hope for things. She now makes the first in a series of promises to Maggie; the next time she comes, she says, she will bring Maggie her own set of jacks. She intends to try to establish at least a tentative feeling of trust with Maggie while they are working together, helping Maggie to see her as a person who raises hopes and who follows through, who doesn't disappoint her. Leah Gardner suspects that Maggie may have gone to the various homes she has lived in with an increasingly strong need to have the placement work out, but with diminishing hopes that her need would be met. Every time Maggie has become settled, there has been one more disappointing rejection. Even if Maggie can just come to suspect that it is safe to trust again with Mrs. Gardner, she will be better able to make a move into an adoptive home.

Because these children are so sensitive to being let down, if she should have to miss a scheduled visit Mrs. Gardner will explain to Maggie directly instead of going through a third person. If this is not possible, she will talk to Maggie as soon as she can, before Maggie has retrenched into her feelings of rejection or disappointment.

At another meeting, Mrs. Gardner reopens the possibility of making a life book by taking Maggie out to shop for her album. Overcome by the seduction of being allowed to pick out her own book from all the brightly colored covers, Maggie is hooked. She too starts willingly to work on her story.

There are other snags in the process of preparing Maggie. Whenever she becomes anxious about information being shared or about the impending move, Maggie does not ask questions to relieve her anxiety, nor does she seem to hear reassurances from her worker. She seems to want to deny that anything is bothering her, to "forget" that the subject exists by changing the drift of conversation. She is quick to say "I don't know" when asked about her feelings. Leah Gardner tries to encourage Maggie to say "I don't want to talk about it," as a more accurate expression of her hesitation. She has learned that the things that a child doesn't want to share can reveal areas where there are deep concerns or inarticulate feelings, and that even if these areas are never discussed freely, the inability to discuss them can be used as an emotional barometer to provide additional understanding of a quiet child.

Mrs. Gardner tries to help Maggie with her feelings. She asks Maggie how she felt when she left her parents' home at the time of their divorce and went to live with an aunt; Maggie replies with a very defensive "I don't know." Mrs. Gardner volunteers that she knows how other children have felt when similar things have happened to them: they felt sad, angry, frightened, lonely, and as if they must have done something bad. Sometimes they felt that they were even the cause of their parents' divorce, or of having been sent away. By sharing with Maggie that she knows that children have these feelings at the time of separation, Leah Gardner tries to give Maggie permission to let herself acknowledge her own feelings.

In some ways, Mrs. Gardner explains, Maggie's first parents were not grown up inside, although they looked as if they were. The part of them that was not grown up won out and made them act unwisely over disagreements. In fact, they quarreled so much that they decided to separate, just as any people do when they cannot get along together. Moreover, neither parent was grown up enough to be able to manage the care of Maggie without a partner to share the responsibility; so now the agency is there to help find parents who can take care of her (Glickman 1957, p. 274).

Leah Gardner could also use a knowledge of psychodrama to help Maggie get to her feelings, showing her how other children might express emotions with their faces and with their bodies. She could ask Maggie to demonstrate these same feelings with her body and with her face. "How do you look when you are angry, Maggie, can you show me?" "How do you look when you are frightened?" In time, Mrs. Gardner could return to the question about Maggie's feelings at the time of separation from her original parents, and Maggie might be more able to show or to tell her how she felt.

The use of drawing materials can also be a good tool with a child reluctant to put her ideas and feelings into words. Many times it is easier for a child like Maggie to respond to "show me" rather than "tell me." After making a drawing, perhaps the child can respond to a direct request to tell what the picture shows.

In talking to Maggie, there are times that Mrs. Gardner might be misled to construe silence as understanding. She would be wise to double-check to be sure she is being heard. She might say things like, "Can you tell me what you heard me say?" to ascertain where she has been tuned out, or where her words have not connected. If she tries to maintain eye contact, it makes it more difficult for Maggie to drift away from the conversation into her own private thoughts in order to deny what is being said.

When a child is hesitant to verbalize because the subject is hard for him to talk about, the worker may try asking the child if he would like the worker to guess. Given his permission, it is often easy to tell the child what he seems to want to say, helping him to put it into words by saying, "I think you are feeling or thinking . . . . Is that right?" Even very nonverbal children will frequently correct a misinterpretation if it is stated out loud.

As Mrs. Gardner talks with Maggie, she begins to understand various misconceptions Maggie has about why she had to leave each of the families with whom she has lived. Among Maggie's problems, she discovers, is an inability to express anger, especially against her first parents. It is not unusual for children to have destructive wishes towards their parents. A child who is separated from his own parents finds his hostile wishes towards them more dangerous than does the child who still has the physical presence of his parents as a reassurance that the loved persons have not been harmed or destroyed by the child's own bad wishes. In the absence of their parents, some children cannot tolerate their own dangerous fantasies; there is no reassurance against the omnipotence of their thinking, and they worry that these thoughts may cause their parents to die. This kind of thinking also encourages some children to believe that their first parents *are* dead. And society encourages this fantasy, because an orphan is often perceived with romanticized importance; he is an object of pity, while the foster child is felt to be of little value.

Maggie's stored-up resentment towards the various adults in her past who have disappointed and rejected her slips out in bits at a time. To help her focus these feelings and to get them out into the open where they can be dealt with, Mrs. Gardner might use the "empty chair" technique with Maggie. Placing an empty chair in front of them, she would encourage Maggie to try to see someone in the chair with whom Maggie has unfinished business, someone she would like to try to talk to. After giving Maggie some time to focus both on the chair and inward, she would ask Maggie who the person in the chair is and encourage her to talk to this person about what is left unfinished between them. She could ask Maggie to tell the person in the chair how she feels about him or her and what he or she has done or is doing to her.

Then Mrs. Gardner could have Maggie reverse roles to become the person in the chair — helping the child play the role by giving her word cues, asking her to sit as the person sits, to show with her face how the person looks, to move as the person moves. These and other techniques from psychodrama training can be useful tools for working with quiet children.

With whatever technique, Mrs. Gardner should encourage Maggie to deal directly with her feelings about the people in her past and what has happened to her. She should be receptive to Maggie's "feeling tones" and accepting of what the child has to say and the way that she says it, not allowing her own guilt or fears about the move to cause her to send subconscious messages that anger and hostility are not welcome.

Eventually, Mrs. Gardner comes to feel that Maggie, too, is ready for an adoptive family. It is time to begin the search for a permanent home.

6
Matching Families and Children

Today Leah Gardner plans to stay in the office and concentrate on paperwork. Glancing out the window at the grey, oppressive winter sky with its threat of more snow, she is glad that she is not scheduled to be driving any distances. She settles herself at her desk, pushing things to the back and piling stacks higher to clear a workable area. Here she spreads out several manila file folders, each containing the summary of an adoptive home study for an approved family that is looking for a child between seven and twelve. Mrs. Gardner wants to get a feel for each family, to see what type of child they have requested and what their worker feels they are best able to accept. In these home studies she hopes to find the right families for Gena and Tommy and for Maggie. Setting to work, she moves her glasses down from the top of her head and begins to read.

Each time a worker reaches this point in the adoption process there are four questions that need to be considered if the "match" is to be a good one:

1. What kind of a child is this couple most eager to have?

2. What are the worker's needs and biases?
3. How does this child structure his reality?
4. What kind of family does this child seem to want? To need?

With these questions in mind, Leah Gardner will try to find appropriate parents for the children in her caseload.

What kind of child is this couple most eager to have? Mrs. Gardner will be looking for the types of physical appearance and personality that each couple finds attractive or unattractive. She will study the assessment of what makes them feel like good parents, what kinds of behavior make them feel intimidated, what kinds of behavior they feel unable to accept. She needs to know how much they will want to change a child: how much improvement do they hope to see, and how long do they expect this amount of change to take? Are they aware that there is no way to predict how the child may change? Can they accept the child as he is if he does not improve? Can they stay committed to a child who does not seem to be benefiting from their care? Can they get and use outside help if they need it?

What are the worker's needs and biases? At the same time that she is looking at parents, Leah Gardner would be wise to screen her own personal biases. Just as there are commonly held opinions about older child adoption in general, there are biases held by many workers that prevent their being able to place children as individuals. Among the most common of these are:

1. Never place a child out of the biological order; that is, only place children as the youngest in the family. This premise overlooks the ease with which many families are able to add a child older than their oldest youngster. It shortchanges the many older adoptable children who can benefit from being given permission to regress to the level of the family's younger children, to act younger than their actual age as a way to fill their own unmet maturational needs. Depending upon the personalities of the children involved, adding a child at the top end of the family can be very satisfying and workable.

2. Never "twin" children; that is, never place a child in a family where there is another child of the same age and sex, or in the same grade. This opinion is so widely held that many workers never have had any personal experience at all with such placements, refusing to try it despite evidence that families who do "twin" children, either by birth or by adoption, often successfully help the children minimize competition and focus on each child's individuality.

3. Never place children with single parents. In spite of the large numbers of children growing up well-adjusted in a biological home with only one parent, this opinion often denies children their chance for any permanent parent at all. Single-parent placements can be useful for many types of emotionally disturbed children; for children who are unable to form attachments to more than one person at a time; and for teen-agers, who frequently do quite well in a single-parent family.

4. Only place children with experienced families; that is, put them only into homes where there already are children. There are some kinds of children who do need a home with other children, just as there are some children who need to be placed where they have no competition. To assume that experienced parents are always a safer placement overlooks the additional task involved in making a family blend together when more personalities are present. Sometimes it is safer, sometimes not.

Mrs. Gardner needs to give some thought to her own biases, acting on what she knows from her own personal observation rather than relying upon opinions she has heard. She needs to give herself permission to be innovative and flexible, not always to follow predetermined guidelines.

She should also take a look at her own needs as a child placement worker. What is her attitude toward the children she is trying to place, toward the families she is reviewing? Esther Glickman (1957) explains that each of us has unconscious needs that have grown out of our own lives. A worker may be searching for his own perfect family; problems in his own childhood may result in his needing excessive dependency gratification from parents, or needing to be the father's favorite, or needing a symbiotic closeness to a mother. These personal needs must be understood, the unrealistic search abandoned and replaced by other satisfactions, in order for the worker best to serve the children whom he places.

Occasionally workers overidentify with a child, wishing to possess the child for themselves and finding it hard to share. No family seems adequate, or doubt exists about any family's ability to give to the child as well as the worker can.

An additional source of difficulty to workers is the great responsibility and significance of the placement decision. The worker wishes to match child and family wisely enough that the placement is permanent, that it works to the benefit of child and family; but instead he gets bogged down in a sense of personal inadequacy and fallibility (Glickman 1957, pp. 94–97). When this happens the worker needs to proceed, using if necessary the training and experience of the supervisor; the child loses most if no permanent plan is made. The worker needs to accept that he or she is not responsible for the child's pain at the loss of his original family; to acquire the skills to help the child and the new family adjust to one another; to be willing to take the responsibility for the matching process, but not willing to assume full responsibility for the ultimate success or failure of the placement.

How does this child try to structure his reality? Mrs. Gardner should spend some time in looking for patterns in each child's behavior. Children form expectations of life in early childhood and then work hard, though unconsciously, to make life conform to this understanding and to meet these expectations. The child tries, without conscious intent, to get each new personality in his life to match his picture of how things are and where he fits in. As he is able to reproduce responses and events again and again, the familiarity of these happenings reinforces his sense that his expectations are valid and his environment predictable. He feels a sense of personal equilibrium.

This need to play out the past in the present is called recapitulation. One example of how it works can be seen in children who have been abused, or controlled by strong physical coercion, or who are afraid of their own aggressive tendencies. These children expect to be physically mistreated. They tend to precipitate the feared happening by behaving in ways tailored to frustrate an adult; thus pushed to the edge of his own personal control, the adult strikes or spanks the child, thereby allowing the child to say to himself, "I knew it. That's how they all are. This always happens to me."

Because of this tendency to recapitulate, Mrs. Gardner should look for similarities between her own emotional response to each child and the responses he has elicited from foster parents, knowing that the child will most likely evoke a similar response from adoptive parents.

In addition to patterning reactions, there is often an unconscious attempt to pattern events. This can be seen in Maggie, whose original home was broken by divorce. At the time her parents separated, Maggie was at the point in her development where little girls usually compete with their mothers for the father's attention. Since she left her first home, Maggie has lived a number of places. Each time the foster mother has complained that Maggie plays up to the foster father, somehow coming between the couple. Sometimes she openly prefers the father, ignoring the mother and thereby setting up rivalry; sometimes she behaves so differently with each parent that tension springs up between them as they try to decide on the best method to deal with her. But each time, Maggie has tried to reconstruct her perception of her past experience, where she believed she was the cause of her parents' disharmony. Although this pattern of behavior has resulted in her being evicted from home after home, Maggie continues with it; she is most comfortable when her present reality duplicates her perception of her known past.

Gena too shows signs of a recapitulation pattern. Gena's original parents were unable to meet her needs for care and finally deserted her. Now Gena seems bound to drive other parents away. She feels that her parents left her because she wanted to be taken care of and loved, and so Gena does two things: First, she acts in an overly competent manner, denying she needs caretaking. This independence rebuffs adults and prevents them from being able to nurture her. In response, they draw back, recapitulating the original desertion. At the same time, Gena's need for affection cannot be denied, and her need for attention and physical contact is so incessant that adults pull back in order to gain some space and time for themselves. This additionally reinforces Gena's conception that her need for love drives parents away.

Gena and Maggie will continue to try to establish their patterns in any home where they are placed. Therefore, adoptive homes should be found where the parents will be able to resist being drawn into these destructive patterns. Maggie will need parents so strong in their own relationship that she is unable to come between them. She should have a mother who can allow her to have a special relationship with her father and who can wait for Maggie to come to the realization that mothers can be a source of pleasure and support too. Gena should join a family that encourages self-reliance, but is also warm and physically demonstrative. By understanding the patterns that prospective parents are likely to experience with each child, Mrs. Gardner will be more able to predict what strengths these parents will need in order to live with and help their new children. She can help them plan how to deal with the behavior patterns, eliminating some of the frustration in the placement.

What kind of family does this child seem to want? To need? Mrs. Gardner has worked with each of the children on their life books. Through listening to them talk, she has some understanding of the kinds of families they dream about, the kinds of ideal parents they hope she will find. Gena, for example, has said repeatedly that she would like to live in the country where she could have a pet. She says that what makes her feel good is having someone to listen to her and to talk to her. She hates being alone, her mother going away, and her teacher picking on her.

Mrs. Gardner has her own special criteria for a family for

Gena. She is looking for a family where the parents put a positive value on articulateness and sparkle, because Gena is a verbal child. If Gena can receive positive responses to her need to talk, her verbal winningness, it will help her value herself more quickly in the new situation. Likewise, parents who like to talk to their children will find Gena interesting and enjoy her verbal spontaneity. They should get genuine feelings that they are doing a good job as parents early in the placement.

It is important for Leah Gardner to look for ways to match the children's patterns and personalities with the responsive behavior and actions that will make the new parents feel early validation. If there are some areas that cause the new parents to feel pleasure and delight in their child in the beginning, the parents and the child as well will all feel that they belong to each other more quickly and be better able to tolerate more difficult areas of adjustment.

The meshing of the needs of the child and of the parents can do much to achieve smoother integration, especially at the beginning. Although it can be argued that children need to be exposed to different forms of living to encourage them to expand and cope, it is more important for the child to be accepted from the first for himself as he is. This is more likely to happen naturally when the needs of the child and of the adopting family are compatible. If along with this contentment there is capacity for healthy giving and growth, both child and parents will derive greater benefit from the placement. Such blending helps the child to fit in more readily, to begin to feel secure sooner, and thus to make new ties and to take root earlier after placement. And if the adoptive parents can allow room for change in the child, along with appreciating him for how he came to them, a good match has been made (Glickman 1973, pp. 192-195).

The preliminaries are over; the preparation of the children is under way; matching criteria have been considered. The process of family building is about to begin.

7
Maggie

The Placement Process

Leah Gardner rests her head on the palms of her hands, rubbing her eyes gently. Taking a deep breath, she shakes herself slightly and starts to work again, reviewing one family after another. She is concentrating particularly on her search for an adoptive family for Maggie, whose disapproving foster mother is compounding the difficulties that already exist.

Nine-year-old Maggie's own comments about her future family have not been very helpful. Unlike some children, who trouble their workers with unrealistic fantasies of a new family headed by a current TV star who lives at Disneyland, Maggie's comments show no expectation that an adoptive family will be any better than the other families she has known. She has asked only for parents who don't fight loudly at night and for a mother who doesn't slap. She would like to have a room of her own, she says, because she likes to be alone. Maggie has been steadfast in her insistence that she does not want to go into a family with other children. Understanding that the presence of other children makes Maggie retreat even further into her quiet shell, Leah Gardner agrees that a childless couple would be better.

In trying to plan for ways in which Maggie could give pleasure to her parents and share something with them that is not dependent on chatter, Mrs. Gardner is focusing on Maggie's enjoyment of learning. Because Maggie picks up new skills well and seems to get pleasure from learning in a one-to-one situation, Mrs. Gardner hopes to find parents who enjoy teaching. She feels that Maggie needs parents who are openly loving, to give her a chance to receive some of the affection that she has missed; parents who are comfortable with their feelings and who can encourage Maggie to acknowledge her own; parents who do not feel rejected by quiet people, who are not threatened by silence.

As she reads through the Reillys' home study, Leah Gardner is struck by the numbers of places that the couple seems to fit the profile she has in her head for parents for Maggie. They are childless. They want a daughter in Maggie's age range. Their worker sees them as having a calm, well-working relationship.

Jack is described as a quiet man who speaks up readily when he has something to say. Maureen is used to his silences. Though comfortable with him and sensitive to his nonverbal messages, she is also good at drawing him out when she needs to in a way that gives him time to muster his thoughts without feeling rushed or pressured. Both Maureen and Jack have said that they would feel more comfortable with a withdrawn child than with a child who acted out his insecurities physically. Their home is described as quiet, serene, and orderly; it would probably be a comfortable setting for Maggie, who Mrs. Gardner feels would not do well in a boisterous, active family.

Maureen has expressed the hope that her new daughter will some day develop as good a relationship with Jack as she has had with her own father. It sounds as if Maureen might be less bothered than some wives if Maggie played up to her new father to the exclusion of her new mother.

Both Jack and Maureen like to cook. Their worker advises

that they might not do well with a child who was a fussy, picky eater, but Mrs. Gardner knows that Maggie has never been a feeding problem.

The report says that Maureen is especially looking forward to having a little girl to cook and sew with. Maybe this sharing of domestic skills could give Maggie's mother a chance to work with her to counteract some of Maggie's lack of responsiveness toward and suspicion of mothers.

Jack, the home study states, loves going to museums on the weekend; Maggie loves outings. It would seem that they would be able to enjoy one another on day trips. Certainly living in the city with so many sources of enrichment and parents who make use of them could help Maggie close some of the gaps in her deprived background.

Mrs. Gardner feels a growing sense that the Reillys may be the right family for Maggie. She talks with their worker, who agrees that Maggie looks like a good possibility. The wheels begin to turn for Maureen and Jack and Maggie.

Following staff agreement, the Reillys' worker calls Maureen at work to talk to her about Maggie. Although Maureen has waited for this call impatiently and thought about it daily, she is still caught off guard when it comes. Her worker calls as Maureen is doing some typing at her desk in the secretarial pool. Answering the phone casually, Maureen tenses up as she recognizes her worker's voice. Her heart begins to pound and her hands tingle; fighting back nervousness, she asks if the worker has any news for them. Yes, the worker says, he is calling about a nine-year-old girl that the Reillys might be interested in. Her name is Margaret, but everyone calls her Maggie. Maureen feels a dizzying surge of excitement. A little girl, just the right age, how wonderful! Maggie, the worker goes on, is well-behaved and quiet. Not a talkative child, she can be suspicious and distrustful. Although of average intelligence, she is a grade behind in school. The worker wonders if Maureen has any questions she wants to ask before she and Jack decide if they are interested in coming in for more information about Maggie.

Controlling her voice with difficulty, Maureen makes an

appointment to meet with Maggie's worker. Overwhelmed by her feelings she hangs up the telephone and rushes to the ladies' room to indulge in a good, happy cry. Her eyes spilling tears, she feels both wonderful and a little scared.

Two days later, Jack and Maureen sit in their worker's office looking at a picture of a solemn, delicate little girl with large eyes and curly hair. In spite of their worker's reassurance that if Maggie is not the appropriate child for them another will be found, they have a sense that with this picture their life is being changed forever. Mrs. Gardner, who has come to the meeting, explains why Maggie is available for adoption. She tries to make Maggie as real to the Reillys as she can. She tells about Maggie's difficulty in relating to adults, especially to mothers. She shares Maggie's past experiences, her fears, her difficulty in school. She presents as accurate a picture of Maggie as she is able. Anything she says that causes the Reillys concern now will surely cause more difficulty later if Maggie should be placed with them. If Mrs. Gardner is not completely honest now, she would most certainly deserve the distrust and justifiable anger she might get from the Reillys later on — distrust and anger that would prevent them from being able to profit from her help if the placement is difficult.

Because as time passes Maggie will return again and again for information about her birth parents, it is important that the social worker present them as sympathetically as possible to the adoptive parents.

> We can help adopters to do this by presenting natural parents to them as living people, shaped by life forces often beyond their control, and having strengths and weaknesses as all of us do. It is unfortunate that background material is so often collected with a view to uncovering pathology, with emphasis on the problems rather than the good healthy factors which are also present. It is most important that adoptive parents and their children be able to see in natural parents some similarities in personality, skills or interests. Whether it be music, knitting, carpentry, mathematics or physical likeness, these points of identification help tie the two families together. Understanding an unmarried mother's loneliness which led her into unwise physical intimacy, or the warm-

hearted but impetuous young pair who anticipated marriage and then found they were not really in love, or the married woman who allowed herself to have an affair in her husband's absence even though basically loyal to him; sympathizing with this can help adopters feel, "There, but for the grace of God, might I have gone too" (Rowe 1966, pp. 222-23).

This information should be not only discussed with the prospective parents but also given them in written form, so that they will have information to refer to as their child comes to them with questions in the future. The written report should be composed in such a way that if read by the child in later years he will continue to be able to view his birth parents sympathetically and with understanding.

Occasionally sensitive information is withheld on the assumption that the adopting family might react negatively. Workers make value judgments of what is good and what is bad. This technique is morally insupportable. If the life and future of a child are to be entrusted to his new parents, they can be trusted with all the information pertinent to his individuality (Baas 1975, p. 509).

This information can also be vitally important to the adopting family. One of our daughters, for example, came to us from a foster home that was being suddenly closed because it had been determined that the children there had been exposed to sexual abuse. Hesitant to share this information, our daughter's worker deliberately omitted mentioning the abuse to our agency or to us. This information would have made no difference in our willingness to adopt our child, but it would have saved us valuable time and lessened our concern at her seemingly unreasonable terror of men and of bedtime. By the time the information was obtained, our daughter had begun the road back to health, losing some of her fears. How much better we could have helped her if we had been trusted with the source of her difficulty.

Each family will have its own questions when presented with a child. It is always helpful to know:

1. When is this child's birthday?

2. Why is this child not living with his biological parents? What are their backgrounds (job history, interests, talents)? What is the biological family's medical history?
3. What has the child been told about his first family? What was his last contact with them?
4. How old was the child when he came into care? Where has he lived? If he has lived in more than one other family, what were the reasons he moved?
5. How is the child's physical and emotional health? What is his history—shots, allergies, dental care?
6. How well does the child's worker know him? How long has she been assigned to him?
7. How does this child feel about himself? How does he respond to other people?
8. How does this child handle failure, anger, anxiety, fears, happiness, success, pain, disappointment, sadness, affection, discipline, daily routines?
9. Does he understand about adoption? About foster care?
10. Why did they pick this child for you?

Parents can get a good idea of the worker's sincerity by the kinds of detailed information that is volunteered.

At the same time that Jack and Maureen are getting a better feel for Maggie, Leah Gardner is sizing them up. They seem sincerely interested in Maggie, to want to be good parents to her. She is watching for their response to information that she shares, so she might notice areas of initial concern or discomfort. These are important signals to both the worker and the couple, alerting them to possible sources of tension or difficulty later on in the placement. It is important that neither parent nor worker covers over these gut feelings with intellectual reasoning. Workers may need to give more information in the area of concern, and parents may need more time to decide whether they want to open themselves up to living with the problems that are anticipated. Parents should ask themselves:

1. Why am I concerned with this information? What am I afraid might happen?

2. If this were my child doing this, how would I feel, what would I do?
3. Where might this child disappoint or trouble me?
4. Where might I fail this child?

The more they hear about Maggie, the more excited Jack and Maureen become. When can they meet her? How soon can they take her home? Mrs. Gardner slows them down. Maggie is going to need a good deal of time to get ready for the move. Although the Reillys are understandably eager to get on with things, that will not be Maggie's tempo. She has no reason to believe that this move holds anything more for her than past moves. She will need time to become comfortable with Jack and Maureen, to deal with having to make the change to a new environment one more time.

Maggie, Mrs. Gardner points out, has not responded to her experiences in life by being openly hostile and angry, but by pulling into herself to become guarded, secretive, aloof. She seems to have made a barrier between herself and adults that will keep Jack and Maureen at a distance.

> Children who adapt by withdrawing pull into themselves. They feel unable to cope with their external world in a direct way. They often isolate themselves from others by frequent illnesses or with activities, such as hobbies, which they can pursue alone. They may hide out in fields, alleys, treehouses, bedrooms, or in their inner world of fantasy. Children who adapt by withdrawing may do so emotionally rather than physically. In a sense, such children "tune out" and often act as if they don't hear. Thus they avoid external demands. When "tuned out," they often create their own world of fantasy which protects them from conflict and the possible hurt and involvement that go with it (James and Jongeward 1975, p. 138).

Distrustful of everyone, Maggie will need a chance to know Jack and Maureen before she can see anything positive about moving in with them. It will probably take several weeks of visiting before Maggie even begins to relax. It will be important that the Reillys follow Maggie's pace, that they don't crowd or rush her. Mrs. Gardner cautions them that it is likely to be a long, long time before Maggie is able to trust them, to love them, to become responsive. She talks with them about the impatience and exasperation they will feel as they wait for Maggie to react favorably to them.

Somewhat subdued, Jack asks, "What is the plan? How do we begin?" Mrs. Gardner asks the Reillys to help her prepare Maggie to meet them by making a picture album. Include several snapshots of each of you, she suggests, doing things you normally do and showing Maggie's new environment—the apartment, the neighborhood, the school, anything to help make the proposed move more real and less threatening to Maggie. Leah Gardner will use this family album as a way of introducing the Reillys to Maggie, then the Reillys will have a short visit with Maggie in the foster home so that she can meet them on her own territory.

The foster home is often a favorite place for the first meeting between child and prospective parents. It lets the child meet the intended family where he feels comfortable, and it discourages the child's fantasies that he has been snatched away. It also gives the family the chance to get a better understanding of how the child lives. Occasionally there are reasons for choosing some other location for the first meeting—perhaps the child in question has foster parents who are angry that they are not being allowed to keep the child; perhaps the foster parents have had close contact with the biological parents and it is felt that confidentiality would be breached by their meeting the adoptive parents; perhaps there is a sibling in the home who is not being included in the placement, and whose strong feelings about the proposed move could cause problems during this first meeting. When these or other circumstances make it inadvisable to use the foster home, a more neutral location such as a park, zoo, or shopping center is usually chosen.

During the Reillys' first visit they may want to take Maggie out for a walk or for an ice cream so that they can spend some time together. Later there will be one or two all-day visits; if things go well, Maggie will then come to spend some nights with them as a transition to making the permanent move. Not only will this gradual pace give Maggie the time she needs, Mrs.

Gardner explains, it will also give Jack and Maureen a chance to shift into being parents a little at a time — to figure out rules and routines, to get over their feelings of strangeness with their new daughter.

Jack and Maureen leave their appointment and head for home, stopping to buy a roll of film on the way. Suddenly they wish they had a camera that made instant prints. Where is the quickest place they can take their film to be developed? Finally, the pictures are taken and printed. The album is put together for Maggie, with appropriate descriptions. Maureen takes the finished book to the agency on her lunch hour and drops it off for Mrs. Gardner. She only wishes she could find a way to package some of the love that is waiting for Maggie along with the pictures.

More and more agencies are encouraging parents to make family albums for their new children. It is such a good tool to help introduce parents to children that parents may want to make such an album even if their agency does not suggest it. Pictures can be taken while the family is waiting for a referral and the album assembled after a particular child is found so that the captions can refer appropriately to that child.

Mrs. Gardner makes an appointment to meet with Maggie's foster mother alone on her next scheduled visit with Maggie, to try again to involve her in the plans being made. She knows that often such support and inclusion in the placement process can make a difference in how well the foster parents prepare the child to leave their family and fit into a new one. Workers can often help the foster family minimize their tendency to make the child feel guilty about coming to like his new parents, and can help neutralize negative feelings they might project as a result of their own sense of loss and rejection. She will continue to express understanding for the foster parents' feelings, appreciation of their services to this child, and the hope that they will be part of the placement team as a parting gift to the child for whom they have been responsible. Although she always tells the foster parents about a proposed adoption the same day she first tells the child, she talks to them separately to avoid any prejudicial comments they might make out of guilt feelings for not keeping the child or rivalry with the new parents.

When Maggie comes home from school, Mrs. Gardner takes her aside to talk to her about the Reillys. She explains to Maggie how she has gone about looking for a family, how families are selected for adoption. She tells Maggie that she is thinking about a particular family for her and asks if she would like to know something about them. Maggie sits, her arms crossed tightly, her face closed down. She doesn't respond. Leah Gardner brings out the album. Here are some pictures of the family, she continues; let's look at them and see what we think. Drawing her chair closer to Maggie, she begins slowly to comment upon the pictures Maureen and Jack have selected. Turning the pages, she tries to gauge Maggie's response. Here is the new daddy in this family, she tells Maggie; how does he look to you? Do you think he looks happy or sad? Which picture do you like the best? Maggie doesn't say much; she mumbles short answers.

Leah Gardner is uncertain what is going on behind the shutters of the very quiet child beside her. In order to get in touch with Maggie, she sits in the same position herself, with the same expression. "If I looked like that what would I be feeling?" she says to herself; and what she feels is, "Show me. Prove that we need to be doing this. I don't want to have this conversation."

Ner Littner (1956) has outlined several stages in the child's reaction to a proposed placement. When the child is actually told about the planned separation it seems to give him permission to become consciously aware of some of his feelings and fears. But the full impact of the separation may not show itself until there is some concrete evidence—such as pictures, or the first meeting with the new parents. It is then that the most severe anxiety reaction shows itself. No matter what the child has been told or how much verbal preparation he has been given, some children still remain hopeful that the adoption will not really occur. There seems to be a fantasy, conscious or unconscious, that something will happen to prevent the actual final separation.

With realization that the placement is imminent, anxiety symptoms are frequently observed. Restlessness and hyperactivity, tenseness, vomiting, sleep disturbances, crying, eating and bowel upsets, thumbsucking, bed-rocking, head-banging, and masturbation are all common at this stage. These symptoms may occur with varying degrees of resentment, withdrawal, depression, or despair; or even with physical reactions such as colds, sore throats, tonsillitis, toothaches, asthma, or intestinal difficulties.

A move has a maximum and a minimum time limit, Littner notes. At the same time that the worker is preparing the child to move, she tries to avoid starting the actual placement process until there is a suitable family waiting, in order to prevent a psychological sword of Damocles from hanging over the child's head. She tries to adapt the placement process so that it accommodates the amount of new experiences and anxiety that the child can tolerate at the time without becoming overwhelmed (Littner 1956, p. 4).

The following week Leah Gardner arrives at the foster home in time to talk with Maggie before the Reillys arrive. She and Maggie wait outside, sitting on the stone wall beside the driveway, talking. As the Reillys drive up, their first introduction to their new daughter is a glimpse of her scurrying into the back seat of her worker's Volkswagen. There she sits, hunched down, arms crossed, scowling. Maureen takes the initiative. Getting out of her car, she taps on the window of the VW. "Hello," she says. "I'm Maureen Reilly. Can I come in?" Maggie nods slightly and Maureen climbs in beside her. Jack, following Maureen's lead, gets into the front seat on the passenger side. Mrs. Gardner ditches her plan for the best way to introduce this child to her new parents and climbs into the driver's seat. "Who wants an ice cream?" she asks.

On the ride back to the foster home, following a trip for ice cream and some time spent at the neighboring playground, Maggie is still very quiet. Watching her, the Reillys notice that it is very difficult to catch her eye—she tends always to be examining her feet or looking just past them or sitting sideways when they talk to her. Maureen is very aware that Maggie is looking them over, but she hasn't the slightest notion of what is going on under that mop of curls.

At the foster home, the Reillys meet Maggie's foster mother briefly and some of the other members of her foster family. They go over the pictures in their family album with Maggie and tell her a little more about themselves and how they live. With some children, Mrs. Gardner would encourage the child to share her own life book at this time. Maggie, however, needs to become more comfortable with these new people in her life before she can include them that intimately; so Leah Gardner waits for another time. Before they leave the foster home, Jack and Maureen make arrangements to meet Maggie at the agency at the end of the week for a visit to the Children's Museum.

Comparing impressions later, Jack and Maureen are surprised that they have had somewhat different responses to Maggie. Jack feels quite comfortable with her. But Maureen feels a little challenged by Maggie, although she can't quite put her finger on the reason why. Maybe Jack just understands better how it is to be such a quiet person. He certainly feels calm and good about how the afternoon has gone.

Both Reillys agree that Maggie looks a good deal like the picture they were given at the agency, except that the slight scowl on her face, which they had thought might be the sun in her eyes, seems to be her normal expression. There is a deep crease between her eyebrows and her mouth is held very tightly over her teeth. Both Jack and Maureen have a much clearer understanding of some of the information Mrs. Gardner gave them before they met Maggie.

The first several meetings with a new child often contain kernels of behavior and reactions that will be common to the new relationship for some time to come. At this point, when the child is the most anxious and the least able to admit it, his behavior often reveals how he distrusts and fights the situation. Children tend to show clearly what they are afraid of, what they misunderstand, and how they try to defend themselves when under stress. Chances are these typical patterns will continue for a while after placement and it is wise for workers and parents not to assume that the overly active child, the bragger, the controller, the afraid or shut-in child, is merely showing a first-time reaction. Instead of covering over the behavior with rationalizations that the child behaves thus because he is nervous, it is wiser to assume he is presenting pieces of himself that will be around for some time.

Occasionally after meeting a potential son or daughter, adopting parents find their own anxieties mobilized. Confronted with the reality of what they are about, they may decide that not only are they not interested in adopting this particular child, they are not interested in adopting an older child at all. Other times they find it difficult to warm up to the child they have met — there is something about him that turns them off. If this is true they may just need to spend more time with the youngster, letting him grow on them and becoming more confident of their ability to be parents to him. They will need to gauge their own feelings as objectively as they can. If there are hesitations, it is important not to rush the decision. It is much better for couples to face the fact that this is not the child they have been waiting for than to feel that they are obligated to take the child out of concern that they may do further damage by "rejecting" him. They need not fear that there is no way to stop the wheels that have been set in motion, that they must do what is expected of them. At this point in the placement process the child is not nearly so vulnerable to those feelings as he will be later when he has invested more of himself in the relationship. Adopting parents cause the most damage when they damp down their concern about their ability to accept a particular child and take him regardless of their inner reactions. It is important that they recognize that the child has been waiting a long time for just the right niche — a family that is able to accept him for who he is, and that takes joy in who he is becoming. Workers must curb their own disappointment and feelings of being rejected or their fear of being criticized professionally. They must allow — and even help — prospective parents to say no to a child if it appears that the match is not a good one.

The planned visit to the Children's Museum goes well for

Jack, Maureen, and Maggie. The Reillys feel a sense of pride in Maggie's attractiveness. Although she is not particularly talk-ative, she examines each exhibit and seems to listen to explana-tions of them. Neither Jack nor Maureen is sure that Maggie is enjoying herself — or them — but she does seem interested in the things they are seeing. When the trio returns to Mrs. Gardner's office, the Reillys are beginning to talk as if they have made the decision to adopt Maggie. They have started to say "your mom" and "your dad" in reference to themselves and to talk about "our apartment" and "your room" in a way that definitively includes Maggie as one of the family. Following their lead, Mrs. Gardner encourages Maggie to share her life book with her new parents as a way of beginning to bridge the gaps between the past and the unfolding promise of the future.

The life book is not only an important tool in preparing children for adoption, it is also useful in the placement process itself.

> As [the child] is able to share his book with his new family, he identifies himself with them and asks them to accept all of him. A real sharing of self begins with this tangible evidence that [the] new parents do know and accept all about the child; it becomes the child's way of adopting his parents. It helps adoptive parents bridge that period of the child's life that they can never share in fact, gives them basic concepts of their child as a total person, and also combats their need to deny the past, and helps them accept less fearfully the recollections the child will bring out. The child's experiences can be told to child and parents, but words alone never make the facts so real as the book, and words are more easily pushed aside because they are hard to hear (Chema et al. 1970, p. 456).

As Jack and Maureen show with their actions their interest in Maggie's life book, their caring about and acceptance of who she is and how she feels, it becomes harder for her to deny their intention to be good parents to her. Their actions are much more convincing than verbal reassurances can ever be.

After they have looked at Maggie's life book, Mrs. Gardner adds to the back of it the pictures from the album Jack and Maureen have made, thereby ritualizing the joining of child and family. She demonstrates to Maggie that she expects these two people to be part of her life for some time to come. She extends the invitation to Maggie to spend the next Friday night and Saturday with the Reillys.

During this preliminary period, Leah Gardner should be accessible to the Reillys and to Maggie. The new parents may need help as they crystallize their impressions of their new daughter and come to understand better who she is, how she functions, and what plans need to be made to help her become one of them. The worker, whom Maggie knows, must convey confidence to her that these are safe people for Maggie. The child's chance to share her own impressions and fears and to express ambivalence is part of the work of her making the move into her new family.

At the same time that she is supportive and involved, Leah Gardner lets Maggie and the Reillys begin to find their own ways of dealing with each other.

> When the preparation has been soundly done, the caseworker can often remain rather quietly in the background during the introductions. She must be ready to make suggestions, help over an awkward moment or step into the center of the stage if this should prove necessary. [But] the more the child and family can find their own way of relating the better. The agency can provide the framework and opportunities, but it cannot actually create a family (Rowe 1966, p. 241).

Maggie's overnight visit with the Reillys starts when they pick her up at her foster home. As they settle themselves in the car, Jack notices that Maggie neglects to put on her seat belt, although he thought that Maureen had explained clearly to Maggie on their last trip that they always wore seat belts and why. Maybe he is just overreacting because he feels a little nervous, but he senses that Maggie deliberately didn't wear her seat belt. He can't quite put his finger on it, but there was something defiant about the way she looked at him when he reminded her.

At the apartment, Maggie is shown to her new room. Jack and Maureen have been of two minds about how to get it ready for her. Maureen thinks that Maggie will feel more welcome if everything is prepared and waiting for her; Jack thinks that she will feel more that the room belongs to her if she is involved in the preparation. They have compromised by getting her furniture ready and in place but waiting to paint and decorate until this visit. Maureen is a little apologetic, explaining that the room will look better the next time Maggie comes. Jack gets out some paint samples, which he spreads on Maggie's bed. It is difficult to get the girl to commit herself to one color or another — she doesn't seem to care. Finally, though, she settles on a surprisingly bright pink. Maureen would have guessed Maggie to be a more neutral, pastel type of child; but it is her room, and she does seem to like the brighter color. Jack promises that first thing in the morning he and Maggie will go buy the paint, brushes, and rollers. Maggie has never seen anyone paint before and she asks a few questions about how they will do it.

When the questions peter out and a tour of the rest of the apartment is finished, the sitting begins. Jack and Maureen are feeling awkward; they don't know whether they should entertain Maggie or leave her to her own devices. They haven't wanted to shower her with presents on this first visit, but maybe they should have planned to have some toys for her to play with. Before her next weekend Jack is determined to get some games or something that they can do together. For now, he gets out a deck of cards and begins to teach Maggie how to play gin rummy. Maureen goes to the kitchen to begin dinner. As she peels potatoes and makes the salad she listens to Jack and Maggie talking in the living room. She can't believe it. There is a little girl here in their home. She understands Mrs. Gardner's pleas for caution, for deliberate recognition of Maggie's tendency to side with the man in the household and make the woman feel rejected; but she isn't feeling that way at all. It just seems wonderful that Maggie should be playing cards on the living room floor with her daddy.

After dinner, the three play some more games of cards and watch a little television, and then it is time for Maggie to go to bed. After she is in her pajamas, Jack and Maureen go into her room to tuck her in. Maureen is determined to try to stop acting like a hostess and begin acting like a mother. She leans over and gives Maggie a hug and a good-night kiss. Maggie lies woodenly, but she doesn't draw away. Turning out the light, the Reillys start to close Maggie's door. "Oh, please leave my door open," Maggie cries. "I don't like to sleep in the dark." It is the most genuine statement of feeling they have yet heard. "I used to hate going to bed in a dark room when I was your age," Maureen tells Maggie. "We'll just leave your door open and turn on this light in the hall. Okay?"

Much later, as she stops in before going to bed to check on Maggie, Maureen is surprised to find her lying silently, still awake. Maggie insists that everything is fine with her—she just isn't feeling sleepy. But in their bedroom, Jack and Maureen try to figure out what is going on with their new daughter. Is she homesick? Afraid? How can they help her if she won't tell them what is wrong? What should they do? It is going to be hard always to have to guess what is happening inside her.

Jack decides to stay up a while longer and read. He sits in the quiet living room, reading and thinking. We'll just have to give her time, he guesses. She will eventually come around. When he finishes his book and checks on Maggie, she is asleep, the covers over her head.

Maggie visits with her new family the next two weekends. Each time her parents feel more comfortable with her and less comfortable with the visiting. It is hard to know whether they should correct or discipline Maggie, when she is not actually living with them full time. Maggie tends simply to sit around unless one of them makes a suggestion or gives her something to do. Maureen feels a little bit like a cruise director, arranging activities and entertaining. The Reillys also feel that it would be a relief to end the contrivance of the visit. They think that they are as far along in their relationship with Maggie as they can be before she moves in. They feel angry at the social worker. Why doesn't Mrs. Gardner just let them have Maggie so they can get on with the business of being a family? What has to happen before Maggie can move in?

The period between the time parents decide they want to adopt a particular child and the day the child actually comes to stay for good is often frustrating. Weekend visits, although a good way to get to know one another better, are still no substitute for living together as a family. Parents may feel stiff and ill at ease. They frequently resent the worker if it seems that she is needlessly prolonging this rather artificial period of separation. Sometimes what is going on in the foster home carries over and puts additional pressures on the new parents, who feel they can nurture their new child so much better than his present caretakers.

Parents may feel that there are plenty of indications that the child is ready to make the move before the worker agrees that the proper time has come. It can be a difficult time for everyone—child, foster parents, adoptive parents, and caseworker. Agencies are more often requiring this extended visiting, because they have seen how much more smoothly the child adapts to his new parents if he has had the chance to let go of his old life before he loses it permanently. When he has been able to close his relationships with old friends, old neighbors, old family, he seems more ready to turn openly to his new friends, neighbors, and family. And the time it takes for him to say those good-byes—though hard on his new family, who just want to get him home for good—may later spare several months of more difficult waiting for the child to be able to accept his new life.

Mrs. Gardner is also anxious to end the visiting period, knowing that Maggie is acting up increasingly in her foster home and that her foster mother is becoming more and more resentful at having to provide a home for this child. But it is important for Maggie to have the chance to say her good-byes, not just to run away, but to face up to the impending separation.

D. C. Krugman, a social worker himself, writes of how sometimes workers move children too fast because they want the process to end for themselves. Dealing with the pain of everyone involved in the process, they are called upon not only to help the children and adults tolerate such pain but to deal as well with their own feelings stirred up by the impending separation. Transfer of children from one setting to another, he says, has overtones of guilt, jealousy, anger, and anxiety, as well as positive anticipation for the future. The social worker, in the middle, sometimes hopes to evade some of the expression of such deep feelings. It is not easy for workers to face the sorrow of a foster mother who is being separated from a child, nor is it easy to face the anger of a child who is not yet sure the move is necessary. It is sometimes even harder to hold back an eager new family from too rapid movement into the psychological living space of youngster to whom they are still strangers. Under these conditions, everyone's need to get the move over with may prompt workers, Krugman says, to grasp at all indications that things are going well and to end the process before everyone becomes too upset (Krugman 1971, p. 536).

Mrs. Gardner is watching for several of Krugman's signs of readiness in Maggie:

1. Awareness that a change is going to occur.
2. Anticipation of some positive features of the change.
3. A chance to experience and to talk about anxiety or ambivalence in relation to the change.
4. An opportunity to test reality in the new situation.
5. Some outward evidence of the child's moving toward the new setting with some amount of acceptance.

Bridging Procedures: From the Past to the Future

Continuing her support of those involved, Leah Gardner begins the bridging ritual she has found helpful to displaced children and their adopting families. When she next sees Maggie, she brings along some candles, candle holders, and a box of matches. Setting the candles up in a row, she counts—one candle for the biological family, one for each of the other families with whom Maggie has lived, one candle for the Reillys. She explains to the girl what she is doing. Taking another candle, she lights it, saying that the candle she holds represents Maggie, who was given the blessing of being able to love when she was born. Maggie lived with her first family and "grew" a love for them; that love came from her inborn ability to love.

Now Mrs. Gardner lights the first candle. When Maggie moved from her first parents' home to live with her aunt and uncle, she says, Maggie grew a love for them; and she lights the second candle. Mrs. Gardner points out that the love that Maggie grew for her second family in no way diminished her ability to love her first family. And even though she went into that home still loving her own parents, she reminds her, she was capable of growing to love the new adults with whom she was living. Knowing Maggie's history and having talked about it with her, Mrs. Gardner goes on through the homes where Maggie has loved, lighting the appropriate candles. She omits those experiences where Maggie has not felt love towards her caretakers.

Finally she comes to the Reillys. She talks again about Maggie's ability to grow a love for her new parents and their desire to come to love Maggie. She reiterates that it is safe for Maggie to grow a love for Jack and Maureen. And she points out that it is not necessary for Maggie to relinquish any loving feelings for the special adults in her past — to "blow out" any candles — before she comes to love her new parents and light their candle.

Later, Leah Gardner will explain this same ritual to Jack and Maureen to help them better understand that Maggie's love for past parents does not interfere with her ability to love them — just as their love for others does not interfere with their ability to love her. Love is not a diminishing commodity. This same candle ritual can be used profitably to make the same point to children about to receive a new brother or sister, who worry that there will be competition, or that someone will be loved "best" or "more."

Mrs. Gardner will encourage Jack and Maureen to allow Maggie to keep the candles in her past lit; the more love Maggie has, she points out, the brighter her life can be. In the beginning, before Maggie has come to love them, she explains, they will probably want to "blow out" candles from Maggie's past; and she urges them to find ways to work on lighting their own candle without feeling that their child's memories are a threat. If this ritual seems meaningful to Maggie and to Jack and Maureen, Leah Gardner might repeat it with the three of them at the time Maggie moves in for good.

With a younger child than Maggie the placement process

would have gone quite differently. The life book might be prepared for a toddler by the worker to serve as a personal history, something like a baby book. Unable to work well with words, a toddler would need more chances to have experiences with his new parents in his foster home, if at all possible. One of the best ways to place preschoolers or young children in general is for the adopting parents to visit the foster home on several consecutive days so that the child — less able to remember over a time span — remembers them from day to day and builds up a sense of familiarity. Meeting new parents under the blessing of the foster parents also seems to give young children psychological permission to form the new relationship. Many times there is an actual "laying on of hands," with the adoptive parents coming at different times of the day and sharing in the physical caretaking of the child. For example, they might take over the feeding begun by the foster mother at mealtime, or finish the child's bath. When it comes time for the child to leave the foster parents for his new home, he should be included in the packing process. And the foster parents should actually pick the child up and hand him over to the new parents, in order that the child might experience permission to become close to his new mother and father.

Another bridging technique that Mrs. Gardner can use is a three-way conversation among the Reillys, Maggie, and herself before the final transfer is made. There are a number of things that need to be said: why Maggie is moving to the Reillys'; how long they expect her to stay; what they will do when they run into problems. Somewhere near the beginning of the placement, or even during visiting, the adults involved should communicate to the youngster that:

1. It is permissible to talk about feelings, worries, and the past with the new family.
2. The adults expect that everyone will feel strange for a little while. People will make mistakes, and sometimes misunderstand one another.
3. The adults expect that sometimes Maggie and her new

parents will disagree and get angry at one another, but that will be all right.

4. Everyone intends to work hard at building the family; love will grow.

Even if the child involved has no trust that the new parents mean these things, the statements are often useful later on when trouble arises. Then the parents can remind the child of the conversation, reassuring him that this difficulty is one of the kinds of things that was expected from the beginning.

Finally the day arrives when Maggie is to move in for good. Mrs. Gardner makes sure that Maggie understands before she goes that this is not a visit but the final trip to the Reillys'. She sets things up so that the Reillys will pick Maggie up at her foster home, and she asks that all the members of the foster family be present to say their final good-byes. And Maggie Reilly goes home.

Beginnings

Once Maggie moves in, there are some rather significant changes for Maureen. After talking about it and thinking it over for some time, Jack and Maureen decided that Maggie needed a stay-at-home mother, so Maureen quit her secretarial job to become a full-time housewife and mother. During the first few days after Maggie arrives, Maureen finds herself caught up in the excitement of a dream come true. The Reillys are keeping Maggie home from school the first week to give her a chance to really settle in, and Maureen just can't get enough of looking at her new daughter and doing things with her. By the weekend, however, the pace is beginning to slow down. All that concentrating on just Maggie is starting to take its toll on Maureen.

In addition, Maureen is feeling fatigued from her work change. Her daily routine has lacked its usual structure; there has been no one to tell her what to do, no particular time for coffee or lunch. Although Maureen has looked forward to the pleasure of more free time at home, her hours have turned out to be crowded. For example, on weekday mornings Maureen and Jack have always just grabbed coffee and something quick for breakfast. Now there is Maggie, and Maureen must fix a breakfast more suited to a growing child's needs. Lunch is no longer an eat-out affair; it has to be prepared every day. The extra cooking for breakfast and lunch means dishes to wash, groceries to keep on hand.

Then there is the laundry. When Maureen was working she sent out most of the clothing to be cleaned or laundered. Now that she is at home, she feels that to save money she should take on this task herself. Although this makes sense economically, it takes a good deal of time. To further complicate things, Maggie, who was dry at night during her weekend visits, has begun to wet the bed just as her foster mother had warned she might. Knowing that Maggie had been a bedwetter in her foster home, Maureen had talked to her about it before she moved in. Lots of children wet their beds, she had told her, particularly when they were moving into a new family; and if Maggie wet the bed at night it was perfectly all right. No one would get upset; no one would embarrass Maggie. It was nothing to worry about. Maureen and Maggie worked it out that Maggie would put any wet sheets into the laundry hamper and remake her bed with dry ones. But now Maggie's bed linen has to be washed daily, Maureen discovers, or the odor becomes a problem. And just those sheets and the pajamas make nearly a full load.

It seems to Maureen that she spends half the day in the far reaches of the apartment house laundry and the other half running up and down the stairs to put the wet clothes in the dryer or to put clean clothes away. Maureen is grateful that at least Maggie's bedwetting does not interfere with anyone's sleep. It would be much worse if Maggie woke up at night crying and needing to be helped with a wet bed. Maureen remembers assuring her social worker that a bedwetter would be no problem. Although it does not make her like Maggie less, to have said it would be no problem had been too simple. Now she knows that you can't be sure how you are going to feel about any behavior until you have lived with it for a while.

Next week Maggie will be in school; that should solve a different problem. Surely their daughter will begin to make friends with some of the other children in the apartment building or on the block, once she has met them at school. Then perhaps Maureen will have to do less entertaining and directing. With some time alone, Maureen should be able to figure out a more normal schedule for herself.

During the weekend Maureen gets some badly needed time off. She goes shopping and spends some deliciously unhurried time looking at wallpaper samples and curtain material. With growing excitement she decides that with all the time she'll have after Maggie starts school, she might be able to do some of the things she had to postpone while she was working. Maybe she can get her bedroom and the kitchen repapered and new curtains made and hung.

By four o'clock Maureen is spent but happy. Loaded down with yards of material and two very awkward, heavy wallpaper books, she maneuvers up the narrow stairs to the apartment. Wait until Jack sees what she has in mind, she thinks; he'll love it. At the door, she can barely rearrange her bundles enough to reach the bell. She lets it ring, but there is no response. Where is everybody? She rings longer—still nothing. Grumbling to herself, she unloads her packages one at a time and digs in her purse for the key.

The apartment is very quiet, but the living room is a disaster. The couch cushions are in piles on the floor; the dining room chairs are tipped over. What on earth has been going on here? Where is Jack? As she hangs up her jacket she sees a note taped to the closet door. "Hi," it says. "I've taken Maggie to the playground. Back for supper. Love, Jack."

Maureen tidies up the apartment, and then starts dinner. Hearing Jack's key in the lock, she calls out that she is in the kitchen. As she puts the broiled chicken on plates, she and Jack catch one another up on the day's activities. Jack is sorry about the mess. He and Maggie were playing and it got a little out of hand, so they went to the park. Maggie hangs around during the conversation, saying little but listening to what is going on.

After dinner Maureen gets out the wallpaper samples and the material she has brought home. Jack likes her selections but is concerned about spending the extra money. After all, they have just taken a sizable cut in pay. Does Maureen think they can swing the expense right now? Maureen feels deflated. She can't remember when Jack has ever questioned how she was spending their money. Maybe they are a little short on cash, but she'll be careful about expenses. After all, she reminds Jack, before Maggie came they would go out to eat once or twice a week. Now they are eating all their meals at home and saving that money. She points out to Jack that things have not changed much for him, but that she needs something to do with her time and energy besides cooking and doing laundry. Maggie sits quietly during this conversation playing with her silverware. But as things grow more tense between Jack and Maureen, Maggie drops her fork to the floor with a clatter. Jack and Maureen look at each other, chagrined. For a moment they had forgotten their daughter.

"I'll tell you what," Jack says. "You get your bath and I'll help Mommy with the dishes. Then we'll read a story. Okay?" By the time Maggie's parents have her tucked up in bed, with her door open and the hall light shining in, things are back to normal. Maureen explains that she can't return the fabric because it has been cut from the bolt, but she offers to postpone ordering the wallpaper. Jack tells Maureen to go ahead and order everything. He guesses that he is worrying about their financial situation more than he needs to.

The next morning, Maureen wakes up to an empty bed and a silent bedroom. She listens for Jack. Much whispering is going on out in the kitchen. Things must be under control. There is a knock on the door and Maggie comes in carrying a large tray with toast and orange juice and eggs. Jack follows closely behind with the coffeepot and two cups. Maureen is being served breakfast in bed. Off to such a storybook beginning, the day gets better and better. At church, the Reillys introduce their new daughter to their priest, who shakes Maggie's hand, smiling warmly and welcoming her into his parish. Maggie looks adorable in her new dress and patent leather shoes, her soft curls framing her face. Sensing Maggie's shyness, Maureen holds her daughter's hand protectively as Jack hovers over his family. Obviously proud of his new daughter, he receives the heartfelt congratulations of his friends with a big smile. At

home, after lunch, the three Reillys decide to spend the afternoon seeing an exhibit of antique toys. Then it is home and bath
and getting ready for tomorrow's first day of school. Maggie will
be attending the same school that Jack and Maureen went to
when they were growing up. They reminisce with her about the
teachers and the routine they remember. Maggie seems surprisingly relaxed about starting a new school. After all, she tells
them, schools are pretty much all the same.

As expected, Maureen finds that things do go somewhat
more smoothly when Maggie is in school. A pattern emerges in
her work at home, but Maureen still feels disorganized and a
little pressured. It is hard for her to get much done on her
redecorating project. She can't decide whether to make the
curtains or strip wallpaper first.

Convinced that her first job is getting closer to her new
daughter, Maureen stops her other projects as soon as Maggie
gets home. She greets the child with a snack each day, sitting
down with her at the kitchen table. But Maggie doesn't seem to
have much to report. Getting information from her about what
went on at school is almost impossible, which somehow makes
Maureen feel left out. Unless her mother suggests that they do
something particular together, Maggie tends to eat her snack
and then go to her room. Maureen is trying to decide how to
handle that. She guesses she will just let things work themselves
out.

Sensitized by the workers' warnings of Maggie's difficulties
in relating to mothers, Maureen is uncertain about how to
approach her daughter. And Maggie is little help. Maybe
Maureen should just tell Maggie that she'll be working on the
wallpaper and that she is available if Maggie wants her for
anything. Maureen has the feeling that Maggie is constantly
watching and evaluating her to see if she measures up as a
mother, but there is never any clue as to what Maggie wants or
expects a mother to do.

Maggie is similar to those newlyweds who expect that their
new mate will automatically know what it is that they want
without being told, and will prove their love by doing it without

being asked. People who act this way are sometimes called "love-testers."

> The tragedy in the love-tester's life is that other people are likely to constantly fail the tests because of the stringent (unexpressed) conditions for passing. The love-tester says, in effect: "You pass if you do exactly what I want you to do (or say exactly what I want you to say), but you fail if you do (or say) anything else." This, of course, means that the likelihood for failing is infinitely greater than the likelihood for passing, especially since the love-tester usually feels that the partner should know what he has to do or to say to pass without being told (Wahlroos 1974, p. 282).

Although Maggie spends many afternoons in her room very quietly, she is always around as soon as Jack comes home. She is not a lot more talkative with her daddy, but somehow things seem to be more comfortable between them. Unlike Maureen, Jack never seems to get tired of taking the initiative with Maggie, which is surprising because he has always been such a quiet person himself. Jack and Maggie spend so much time together that sometimes Maureen misses the long evenings she used to spend alone with Jack. Then she feels guilty. It certainly isn't Maggie's fault if she needs some time with Jack.

By the time Maggie is put to bed at the end of the day, Jack and Maureen are tired. They face the rest of the evening with different needs. Maureen needs a chance to talk alone with her husband. Jack needs the time to tune out, to watch television quietly, to have some privacy. Maureen doesn't know exactly how to balance their needs and Maggie's. There ought to be a way to make time for just the two of them, to stop the unpleasant changes that are affecting them. Somehow even talking in the small apartment is hard; it always seems that Maggie may be listening. Maybe if they could go out alone they could get back into their usual tempo with one another. But dinners out are expensive, and now they would also have to find and pay a babysitter for Maggie.

The Family Mobile

The trouble at the Reillys' is typical of new child placements. It would help Maureen if she understood that families work very much like mobiles. This concept, put forth by Virginia Satir (1972), points out that each family is "strung together" like a mobile. Every member has his balanced place, and a relationship to every other member and to the whole. Each member is affected by the behavior of the others. Any time there is a change in the family mobile—a child getting married, a grandparent coming to live, a new child joining the family—the mobile is set to swinging violently off balance. It can't work smoothly again until each member has found his new place and settled down. Until this new balance is found, the members of the family mobile feel strained with each other; things are constantly shifting; pulls and collisions keep occurring. In the Reillys' case, things are more complicated: not only has Maggie's coming caused Jack and Maureen to redefine their own roles to include that of "Mom" and "Dad," but Maureen is also feeling the rearrangement that comes from a job change.

Because the family is being redefined, there is extra strain on the parents, particularly on a mother who feels it is her job to settle everyone else down. Sometimes parents become deeply frightened by the disorganization, the colliding needs of various members, or the different member who seems impossible to absorb into the group. Because they are locked into their places by fear that the whole mobile will never work as a unit once more, it becomes harder for them to shift things around and to deal with the change. The trick of regaining balance is for each member of the family to have a secure, truly individual place and to feel comfortable, to have fun, in that place. The more the parents can do to maintain their own positions of balance with each other and with the various other parts of their family system, the more quickly changes can be made and the whole can resume its balance. Jack and Maureen would be wise to tackle their personal difficulty head on—to make time to be together and regain the sense of closeness they have shared in the past. They may decide to do this by scheduling their time differently. Perhaps they could get up earlier and spend some time together before facing the day with Maggie. Perhaps they could balance off their different needs after Maggie is in bed, with some quiet television time and some talking time. Maybe they should look at their budget and decide that money spent on time for the two of them alone is as essential as money spent on any of their other needs. However they resolve it, their need for time alone together is a very important part of their regaining a comfortable balance.

Maureen's concerns come and go. Often when she is feeling most put upon by Maggie, the situation is defused by the sound of the little girl's voice saying "Mommy." Maureen finds that she can't stay irritated very long. There is something about having a daughter that both builds up and eases the pressures in her life. Maureen is increasingly aware that although she is sometimes exasperated, she is coming to love Maggie.

The Odd-Man-Out Triangle

But there are still some problems. Although Jack is making a real attempt to spend as much time with Maureen as he does with Maggie, the family is not running smoothly yet. Finally things come to a peak. Maureen spends, at long last, an entire day stripping wallpaper, letting everything else go. By nightfall she is overtired. She knows that she has pushed herself too hard, but it is worth it. The job is finally done. Everything is in a mess when Jack comes home. The bedroom has piles of stripped paper on the floor and the furniture is all pushed together in the middle of the room. Dinner is not started. Jack gives Maureen a quick kiss on the top of her head and then settles down in the living room for his daily time with Maggie.

Maureen steps through the mess and makes her way into the kitchen. She decides just to ignore the dishes in the sink left over from breakfast and to get through dinner so that she can soak herself in a hot tub. There is little conversation during the grilled cheese sandwiches and soup—not one of Jack's favorite dinners, but easy to prepare. Jack talks a little about his day at work. Maureen expresses her relief at having the wallpaper down. As Maureen clears off the table and starts filling the dishpan, Maggie and Jack disappear as usual into the living room. What happened to those evenings when they were both working and Jack used to help make supper and clean up? Being a full-time housewife is not what it is cracked up to be, Maureen silently complains.

Maggie comes into the kitchen for a glass of water and Maureen's anger escalates as she sees one more dirty glass to wash before the kitchen is clean. "Damn it!" she shouts. "You'd think I could get a little help around here!" She leans her head against the kitchen cabinet and begins to cry. Jack is there immediately. Putting his arms around his wife, he asks her over and over what the matter is. All the pent-up frustration comes out as Maureen begins to tell him about the lack of response from Maggie, her feeling of being put upon, her sense of being left out. Maggie stands in the kitchen doorway, wide-eyed. Jack feels terrible; he had no idea Maureen was so upset. Why didn't she try to make him understand before this?

Maureen ought to look at that question when she feels calmer. For in some ways she has been playing at Maggie's game of love-testing. She has expected her husband and her daughter to recognize what it was she wanted and needed without her telling them. When they didn't, she felt unloved and used. If she is to work things out she will have to begin to send clear "I messages": "I need . . . ," "I feel . . . ," "I want . . . ." Not only will this help her with her own feelings but it will establish that in this family such communication is expected. Maureen has been working at cross-purposes to her own needs and also reinforcing the trouble her daughter has, because she has not told people how they could help her feel better. The best way to help Maggie over her difficulty in expressing herself is for her parents to set an example of how to use direct communication.

Although Jack was warned by the social worker of Maggie's tendency to draw fathers and mothers apart, he has thought that Maureen's own strength, her trust in the depth of their marital relationship, would head off any problems. He should give some thought to the old saying "two's company, three's a crowd," and be more sensitive to the dynamics of "odd man out" in his family.

Any couple that adds a child, whether by birth or by adoption, immediately forms a family triangle. As soon as this triangle is set up, there is the potential for an odd-man-out situation. Mother and child can form a bond that makes the father feel left out. Similarly, the mother or the child can be the one who feels left out. Particularly in the early stages of adoption, when tensions and fatigue are running high and new roles are being defined, it is likely that someone will feel excluded at various times and in various situations.

Sometimes these positions harden into inflexibility; two parts of the triangle lock together and the third member is permanently excluded. But in most families an effort is made to prevent the odd-man-out situation from becoming the family pattern. If the third member is a newborn baby who is demanding the mother's immediate attention, the father usually understands and modifies his own demands. At the same time, the new mother does not let herself become totally preoccupied to the exclusion of her husband. In time, the new father and mother develop a closer relationship to the baby, making it easier for them to view him as one of them rather than as a competitor. When it does happen that either of the parents feels uncomfortably left out, he lets the partner know so that the problem can be remedied. Eventually each member of the triangle comes to feel that he has his own place in the affections of the other two. Feeling good about himself, he is able to be both dependent and independent; and he can observe closeness between the other pieces of the triangle without feeling excluded. He knows that he will get his turn, that time will be found for him.

The odd-man-out triangle that comes about when an older child is adopted is usually more vexing than that formed by the addition of a new baby. The adopted child usually has had a long history of being the odd man out. It may be the only way he knows how to relate, to get attention, to feel at home. Past experience may have taught this child to respond only to a mother or only to a father. He may feel uncomfortable with any closeness that his parents express towards each other, and try constantly to come between them. It is important that the new parents understand what is happening when they see one another feeling left out or their child excluding himself, and that they act to minimize this fragmentation of the family. They must teach the new child that in their family there is no need to set up this destructive competition, reassuring him that no one will be left out. They may need to help him learn how to relate to both parents.

The way the odd-man-out triangle works depends largely upon how the parents handle it. If they are confident in the strength of their own relationship, if they can tell each other when they feel left out but can also allow each other the chance to form independent relationships with their new child, the situation will resolve itself. As the child has time to see that his family does not work on an odd-man-out basis, the family can form a unit in which no one feels he is on the outside.

If the new child joins a family where there are other children in addition to the parents, the situation becomes more complicated. Imagine the number of triangles, and the potential for someone being odd man out, that can exist in a family with one child when a new member is added:

- mother, father, old child;
- mother, father, new child;
- mother, old child, new child;
- father, old child, new child.

Now picture a family where still more children are involved, and see how increasingly easy it becomes for someone to be the odd man out. What prevents this kind of problem from becoming impossible is that as each child has entered the family the parents have had time to work out ways to avoid the odd-man-out situation. When the new child enters such a family the old children tend to be temporarily pulled into a scramble with him. The addition of a needful sibling who is also an experienced odd-man-out manipulator is unsettling. But the old children have also had the experience of working in a family where this is not the usual state of things. In time they regain their old sense of trust, their ability to share and feel comfortable, and they help the new child settle in with a diminishing number of recurrences of odd man out.

After a good clearing of the air, things take a turn for the better at the Reillys'. Maureen is reassured of Jack's commitment to her. Jack is more sensitive to the pressures on Maureen. Both of them try to send clear early messages to each other to prevent tensions from building up again. Though Maggie is still not able to express her needs, the Reillys feel that as they set a clear example it will become easier for her to tell them what she wants. The family routine is changed so that Maggie and Jack give Maureen a hand with the dishes after supper, and that is becoming a good family time for the three of them. Maureen has begun to ask Maggie for help — giving her things to do like helping fold laundry and put it away, and involving her in the preparation of meals and the setting and clearing of the table. Interestingly enough, Maggie seems to enjoy being included in the work. She is developing a sense of competence about her cooking skills as she fixes breakfast with her daddy on the weekends and helps her mommy make supper at night. Both parents are enjoying teaching Maggie, contributing to her increasing ability in the kitchen. Her having jobs to do makes everyone see Maggie as able to contribute, to be a working part of the family unit — and that feels good to all three of them. Jack is amused to see how many things Maggie does just like Maureen. Sometimes as she ties on her apron and washes her hands at the sink she looks like a miniature version of her mom. She also seems to be relaxing, coming out of her shell a little. Now when she smiles her eyes light up and the smile looks real, not mechanical.

Although chores can be annoying, many older adopted children seem to enjoy being allowed to participate in adult work. Working alongside their new parents often gives them a sense of pulling their own weight in the family, and develops rapport between children and their new parents. Cooking in particular seems to give children a sense of competence, of being able to take care of their needs for nourishment.

Just as things are getting better and everyone is feeling more comfortable, Jack's parents come for a visit and there is an upset. The senior Reillys now live several states away. Jack's father has found it hard to get away from work long enough for a trip to meet his new grandchild. Pictures have been sent and Maureen has kept her parents-in-law as up to date as she could by letter, but both Jack and Maureen have been eager for Jack's parents to come. On the first three-day weekend the older Reillys drive up. Jack wants Maggie to make a good impression on his parents. He knows they have been apprehensive about the adoption of a child as old as Maggie, and he wants them to see firsthand how well things are going and to come to love Maggie, who is their first grandchild. But Maggie is obviously uneasy about the visitors. She wants to know where they live and who they are.

The evening before the planned visit Maggie asks her daddy what she is supposed to call his parents while they are visiting. Jack tries to figure out what is behind the question, because it is asked in a way that suggests that Maggie needs more than a simple answer; but he has little luck getting an idea from Maggie.

The question about what to call members of the family sometimes comes up as soon as a new child enters the household. Some children start addressing their new parents in parental terms right from the beginning. But others find it hard to say "Mom" and "Dad." They tend to avoid the issue by not calling their parents anything at all. Many times children will ask what they are to call their new parents or a new relative. There are a number of common reasons for these questions:

1. The child may be voicing a reluctance to use parental terms, or may have his own ideas as to what he wants to call his parents to differentiate them from parents in his past (Mom and Dad instead of Mommy and Daddy, for example).

2. The child may be asking his new parents to define how they feel about him and the new relationship, to be sure that it is permissible to call them Mom and Dad.

3. The child may be trying to figure out whether he is

accepted as a member of the extended family by the new grandparents or the new aunts and uncles.

The best way to have this discussion about names is to find out what the child's preference is and also to clearly express how you feel about what you would like to be called and to have other people be called.

Jack talks to Maggie about the impending visit of her grandparents and explains that she may call them Grammy and Gramp if she would like to. He talks about his parents and tells her some of things they will all do together, trying to make the upcoming visit seem as pleasant as possible. Maggie does not have much to say.

When Jack's parents arrive, Maggie seems like a different child. She has to be coaxed out of her room to meet them, and then she hangs on the fringe of the group as far from the conversation as she can position herself. Her face has a closed-down look; she seems dull, dumb, not quite normal. In the kitchen, Jack asks Maureen, "What on earth has gotten into Maggie? She acts as if she had an I.Q. of about ten."

"Don't be impatient with her, Jack. Remember how she was when she first met us? She's just shy."

But Maggie's behavior, designed to put others off, may be more than just shyness. It is sometimes seen in children whose experiences have not led them to value themselves; and it is most often apparent in their interactions with new adults, especially grandparents, teachers, and other important people. It may come from the feelings that the child has about himself as the source of his own displacement; but it also is frequently an outgrowth of his interactions with troubled parents who have used caustic or cruel humor in dealing with the child, causing him to doubt his own value and damaging his ability to love and respect himself. "A child usually accepts as reality the things that he continually feels and perceives, especially if no one expresses contrary opinions. Hence, a despised child tends to accept as reality that he is despicable, and a loved one that he is lovable" (Chapman 1971, p. 19). It is not the occasional unkind statement by a parent that causes this problem, but rather the daily hammering without the background of love—

especially if both parents are involved or if one parent stands by silently while the other degrades the child—that engenders a low self image in the youngster.

> Only a child who has at least one person whom he can love, and who also feels loved, valued, and wanted by that person, will develop a healthy self-esteem. He can then become confident of his own chances of achievement in life and convinced of his own human value. Where this positive environmental attitude toward an infant is missing from the start, the consequences become obvious in later childhood and adult life (Goldstein, Freud, and Solnit 1973, p. 20).

If a child likes himself, and feels confident of his ability to cope with life, his expectations of success most often bring him success, which makes him more confident. This growing self-assurance makes him seem attractive to others. Because he likes and respects himself, he regards others in the same way.

But those children like Maggie, who lack self-confidence, who do not particularly like themselves, may expect to fail. As a result, they don't try very hard to master skills or make friends; and their lack of effort causes them to fail. The more they fail, the more they expect to fail, and a vicious circle takes shape.

It is understandable that Jack wants Maggie to perform in certain ways—to prove herself as a new grandchild and himself as a new parent—but he should not put subtle pressures on her just to relieve his own tensions about the impression she is making. On this visit he would probably do well to take the spotlight off his daughter as much as possible, allowing her to watch her new grandparents from the sidelines until she feels more comfortable with them. In time, he may want to help her modify her behavior when meeting new people—so that she doesn't come out looking dumb or acting in a way that turns people off, and so that adults and children outside her family will respond to her favorably, boosting her image of herself.

Sometimes it helps to give children like Maggie something to do—food to pass, water to pour. Sometimes it helps to teach these children socially acceptable ritual phrases that can be used to enter into the social niceties without a great deal of personal exposure: "How do you do; hi; nice weather; fine; okay;

thank you; you're welcome; please; nice to meet you; see you around; good-bye." Sometimes it helps to include them by talking about something that they are involved in, allowing them a chance to add to the conversation if they feel comfortable in doing so or to sit quietly if they do not.

The "Nothing to Do" Problem

Jack begins to watch Maggie more closely after his parents return to their home. He had grown accustomed to how very quiet and shut in she seems much of the time. When he talks to Maureen about it, she says that she is even more concerned about Maggie's inability to structure her time. Maggie has not made any friends at school; she comes home every day to hang around the apartment. She doesn't seem to be able to find anything to do, so she just sits around, lies on her bed, or stares out the window. Lately, Maureen has deliberately refrained from making suggestions for things they might do together, hoping that Maggie would become bored enough to find some way to amuse herself. But so far this has not worked. Maureen suggests that this weekend the three of them stay home rather than plan an outing, so that Jack can get a better idea of how Maggie is when there is nothing arranged for her to do.

By the end of the weekend Jack knows just what it is that bothers Maureen about Maggie. She does nothing — absolutely nothing. Occasionally she may wander about, looking out the window. But most of the time she just hangs around. She doesn't even seem to get tired of sitting when Jack is almost out of his skin from the boredom of inactivity. How does she stand it? What is the matter with her? Certainly it can't be normal for a nine-year-old to spend an entire weekend just sitting passively, eating, and sleeping.

What Jack and Maureen are seeing in their daughter is not an uncommon phenomenon in older children from unsettled backgrounds. In a normal family parents respond to their children as individuals. Bowlby points out

> In a family a young child is within limits encouraged to express himself both socially and in play. A child of eighteen months or

two years has already become a character in the family. It is known that he enjoys certain things and dislikes others, and the family has learned to respect his wishes. Furthermore, he is getting to know how to induce his parents or his brothers and sisters to do what he wants. In this way he is learning to change his social environment to a shape more congenial to him. The same occurs in his play, where in a symbolic way he is creating and re-creating new worlds for himself. Here are the exercise grounds for personality. In any institutional setting [or in very disorganized families] much of this is lost; in the less good it may be all lost. The child is not encouraged to individual activity because it is a nuisance; it is easier if he stays put and does what he is told. Even if he strives to change his environment he fails. Toys are lacking: sometimes the children sit inert or rock themselves for hours together. Above all, the brief intimate games which mother and baby invent to amuse themselves as an accompaniment to getting up and washing, dressing, feeding, bathing and returning to sleep—they are all missing. In these conditions, a child has no opportunity of learning and practicing functions which are as basic to living as walking and talking (Bowlby 1965, p. 64).

This kind of beginning, which robs children of the reinforcement of their play activities, is often combined with multiple moves that keep the child from developing a play environment where he feels comfortable. Because his total environment is often new and strange, he lacks the support of knowing what is expected. He does not understand how to function in one familiar family or community. He is at a loss as to how to get along, to join in. Although there may be opportunities for play in his new home, the new game or situation threatens him because it may define one more time his strangeness, his lack of belonging. Therefore the child tends to give up on the potential for fun before he explores it. "As a result these children lack concrete and marketable peer skills which prevent them from making contacts with other children, furthering their lack of pleasure resources. They also have trouble appraising fun potentials in things they have not been exposed to frequently before" (Redl and Wineman 1952, p. 93). "Many of

these children simply do not know how to have fun" (Trieschman, Whittaker, and Brendtro 1969, p. 102).

There are some concrete things that Jack and Maureen can
do to help Maggie learn to play. They can begin to establish a
sense of play with her — incorporating games into the routines of
the day, much as parents do with very young children. They can
actively involve themselves in games, letting her see their enjoyment. They can take the time to teach her to play the games
that other children her age know, instead of assuming that all
nine-year-olds have played hide-and-seek, dress-up, dodgeball,
hopscotch, kickball, checkers, house, rummy, jumprope.

Redl and Wineman, who worked with children who had
little idea of how to play, describe the steps they took to help
these children. They point out that, whereas most children have
a "resource pool of satisfaction images" to fall back upon, these
deprived children have not developed such a resource. There
seem to be three ways to help such children build up their own
sets of resources:

1. *Name giving.* Teach the activity with frequent use of its
   name so that the name can be used first by the adult as a
   point of recall for the child and later by the child himself as he thinks of things to do.
2. *Props.* If there is special equipment for an enjoyed game
   or experience — such as a checkerboard, a puppet stage,
   craft materials — the sight of this same equipment serves
   much like the calling of its name to bring to mind the
   memory of the pleasure attached to the particular prop.
   Adults can deliberately store these props where they
   will be noticed by a child looking for something to do,
   or they can bring the prop out at strategic times when
   the child drifts aimlessly.
3. *Promotional buildup in between.* Here the adult brings
   up in conversation with the child the fun that was
   shared playing a game, thus helping him keep his
   memory of the pleasure fresh (Redl and Wineman
   1952, p. 131).

Finally, because children like Maggie frequently do not recognize their own feelings of having a good time, Jack and Maureen may need to point out to her the times that she is enjoying herself, so that she may come to recognize those feelings and have the words to define them.

Passive Aggression

As time goes by, Jack and Maureen begin to notice another trait in Maggie — carelessness. She seems to have no idea of what things cost. Last week she lost her brand-new spring jacket. When questioned about how she might have lost it, she just shrugged her shoulders and mumbled "I dunno." This week she has misplaced her sneakers and brought home a note from the teacher saying that she must have another pair for gym. Jack and Maureen have explained to Maggie that all of them have to be careful about the money they are spending; they have gotten angry; they have punished her; but still Maggie seems totally unconcerned about the problem.

There is also a problem with the dishes. Maggie doesn't seem to be able to pay attention to what she is doing and she drops plates or bangs glasses almost every time she helps. Lately Maureen has begun to wonder if it is worth the breakage to insist that Maggie continue to dry the dishes. What is the matter with the child?

Her room, so carefully furnished and decorated, is a disaster area; toys and clothing are everywhere. Things will be ruined if Maggie doesn't begin to take better care of them, but it is a major job to get her to pick things up. She "forgets" until it is time for bed, or if Maureen sends her in to start on the task at a reasonable hour, Maggie stalls and fiddles and procrastinates, accomplishing little. Even Jack is annoyed with Maggie. It seems to take her forever to do anything she is asked.

Carelessness, stalling, disorder — all common traits in children but often carried to an extreme in a child like Maggie. The anger inside her, unable to be expressed, builds up. The depth of her rage makes her feel guilty, so she acts unconsciously in ways that frustrate the adults around her — both to vent her anger and to get them to punish her and relieve her feelings of being bad. Children who do these kinds of things are sometimes referred to as "passive-aggressive" children. Afraid to let their anger out directly, they do it indirectly—by dawdling, forgetting, daydreaming, bedwetting, losing things, breaking things, hurting themselves or others "accidentally." Often they respond to adults with a shrug of the shoulders, a blank look, or infantile behavior.

Bettelheim says that this behavior is frequently seen in children who feel totally overpowered by adults. Certainly children who have been moved around for the convenience of others often feel that their lives are under someone else's control. Bettelheim points out that in children often

> the first freedom to retaliate reveals itself in hostile procrastination. They do not dare to be openly aggressive, but they hostilely inhibit the actions and movements of the adults around them by not getting dressed, by losing things for which the adult must then search for hours, by slowness of speech or movements, by endless and meaningless stories to which we must listen, by blocking exits, or by walking so slowly or so immediately ahead of us that they reduce us to standing still. Thus they block our freedom of action, or movement, as theirs was once blocked (Bettelheim 1950, p. 210).

There is another aspect to passive-aggressive children. Frequently they say "I can't" to excuse themselves from unwanted or unpleasant tasks. They fail at assigned tasks, or do them so badly, or take so long to do them, that the exasperated adult takes over and ends up doing the work himself. If you can't do anything, after all, no one expects you to do anything. If no one expects you to do anything, there is little chance of punishment or failure. If you take long enough to do things you don't have to worry about whether you measure up to the standard of the person in command. You don't have to worry that that person will give you more things to do. And you don't have to worry about doing things so well that you stand out or make others resentful of you.

Probably the best way for Maureen and Jack to deal with Maggie is to begin to make her responsible, to stop making excuses for her, to stop bailing her out. Maggie needs to begin to see that her actions do not relieve her of responsibility, and that she can do a competent job when she chooses to. The consequences of her actions should be logical and not punitive, underscoring the effects of her choices. If she dawdles in the morning, then she is late for school. If she does not put her laundry into the hamper, it does not get washed. If she loses things then she does without, or the item is replaced with something she may not like as well, or she is given jobs to do to earn half the price of the replacement. When she uses the phrase "I can't," Maureen and Jack can point out to her that she is actually saying "I don't choose to," or "I don't choose to try." When she does an unsatisfactory job, she should have to do it over until it passes.

At the same time, a real effort must be made to help Maggie express her anger more directly and appropriately. When she is obviously angry, her parents should point that out to her, helping her express it by giving their permission for her to feel angry. "I can see that that is making you angry, Maggie," they can say. They can talk about acceptable ways to let anger out—foot stomping, crying, clay pounding, hammering—so that Maggie comes to feel less awed by her own anger and can learn to release it. Some families use the phrase "You don't have to like it, you just have to do it" to help their children recognize and accept their anger at an imposed task. When the anger is expressed in a passive-aggressive fashion Maggie's parents can say to her things like:

1. I think you are mad because you have to dry the dishes.
2. I think you are losing things to make me angry.
3. I think you are stalling about cleaning your room so I will change my mind and say you don't have to.
4. I think you are taking a long time to pick your puzzle up because you want me to do it.
5. Tell me in words, not with your body.

When children like Maggie become more able to let their anger out in words and stop their passive-aggressive behavior, several things frequently happen. They begin to feel better about themselves because they are gaining competence. They see themselves as able to make choices in their lives that bring them good feelings, both from within and from without. Their senses of self-worth and self-esteem improve. As they are allowed to vent their anger they get over their fear that something terrible will happen to their parents because of the anger the child directs at them. They also see that there is no need to fear retaliation from parents.

If they are bedwetters, they often begin to be dry much more of the time, giving credence to the view that bedwetting can be a way of letting out feelings of anger, tension, or fear while asleep, a way of asserting oneself, manipulating, or getting even. With help from attentive parents, children who wet their beds only sporadically can often figure out when they wet if something has happened during the day that has made them angry. Everyone feels better when the child can let his feelings out verbally instead of wetting the bed.

Problems of Giving and Receiving; Greed

Maureen and Jack are coming to realize that much of what they need to do for Maggie involves giving: giving her resources to fall back upon for having fun; giving her positive experiences to modify her negative feelings about herself; giving her things to do so that she feels one of them and sees herself as a competent contributor; giving her encouragement and permission to have her feelings and to express them. But giving to Maggie is difficult, because she does not seem to be able to take what is offered. Maureen likes to pick up a new piece of clothing or a small toy for her daughter when she is out shopping, but Maggie never seems comfortable accepting these gifts. Her response is often a suspicious "What did you get that for?" Many times she will put aside her presents, not wearing the new socks or not playing with the new toy. Then Maureen feels rejected; it is as if she has offered something of herself to Maggie only to have it turned down. At first Maureen thinks that this is an outgrowth of Maggie's need to reject mothers, but it seems that Maggie responds the same way to gifts from Jack.

Many older adopted children have difficulty with gift-giving. Some of them respond by demanding more and more. Especially in the beginning, they want to have *all* the attention, *all* the love, *all* the food, *all* the toys. They are frequently impossible to satisfy. No matter how much they get, it is not enough. Bowlby (1965) writes that deprived children often select a giving person whom they settle on to make up for the privations of their early lives, and then make excessive demands on that person for unlimited food, money, privileges. Having been frustrated and denied in the past, they have built up what Redl and Wineman call "neglect edema"—a situation where their past deprivations swell and fester until any frustration, no matter how small, is lumped together with the frustrations in the past. When confronted with a new situation with a giving adult, the child builds up an intolerable greed tension, with exaggerated ideas of the loving adult's ability and willingness to accept all the aspects of the child's behavior and to satisfy all desires. "If the hostile adult of the past was one who thwarted pleasurable experience, then the loving adult is just the reverse, i.e., categorically permissive. The underlying emotional slogan becomes, 'If they love me, they will give me anything I want, let me do anything I wish' " (Redl and Wineman 1951, pp. 258-59). This expectation is doomed, for it would be impossible and unwise for the new parent to be totally giving and permissive.

Other children, who respond more like Maggie, have trouble with gifts for other reasons. Some of them, aware of their own hidden anger and guilt, can't accept tangible expressions of love because they feel they are bad and don't deserve anything. Some children focus themselves not on the offering itself but on their suspicion that the reason for the gift is to make them beholden, so that their parents can make demands in return. They respond to gifts with expressions like "So what," "I don't like it," or "I don't want it." Sometimes this goes even so far as to include difficulty with taking and passing food at the table, reflecting perhaps the interchangeability of food and love in our culture. The child seems to be asking, "Why are you giving me all of this—what are you going to expect in return?" Many newly arrived children eat very little or refuse to eat at all for the first day or two (Trieschman, Whittaker, and Brendtro 1969, p. 140). Not only are these patterns observable with gift-giving and the receiving of food, but they also extend to other kinds of giving, most noticeably the exchange of affection and the receptivity to praise. The response of the child is often to act up, to express how "bad" he is inside. "Acting up is a child's way of communicating his private reservations about his public image," says Ginott (1965, p. 39).

Parents of any of these kinds of children frequently experience difficulty with them. Those parents who face impossible demands from their new children are put in the uncomfortable position from the beginning of not measuring up to the child's expectations and needs. Bothered by their own inability to meet either the excessive demands or the obvious responsibility to set some limits, they come to see themselves as depriving parents and/or the child as greedy and selfish.

Those children who are suspicious of what the parents are going to want in return often distress their new parents. The parents *do* want something from the child. They want him to love back, to be glad to be in their family, to change behavior, to become sensitive and giving in return. And because of his own needs, the new child is not able to reward them in this manner. When their new child rejects the things they offer, these parents feel as if it is themselves and their love that the child is refusing.

"Buckets"

One of the tools for dealing with the stresses of these problems is the concept of "buckets." Imagine for a moment that each of us enters this world with a tiny arm through the handle of a tiny bucket. As we grow larger, our buckets grow larger. Much of what we become, how we respond, and how we see ourselves is determined by what goes into this bucket. The newborn baby cries because his empty stomach gives him a sense of distress. Someone big and caring responds with comforting food and the baby feels noticed, nurtured, safe. Along with his full tummy goes a sense of "full bucket" — that is, he feels that he has worth and is noticed (which is the beginning of his self-esteem), and that the world is a good place.

As the child grows, if his parents continue to put good feelings into his bucket by the way they interact with him, the level of good feeling that he has about himself is high: he feels confident, good, competent. Sometimes the child's parents slosh his bucket and spill a little by being angry, critical, or inaccessible. Perhaps an accident, an illness, or a disappointment slops out some of the good feelings. But if the child is lucky enough to have nurturing, giving parents, the level of good feelings in his bucket remains high. Before long the child learns that life is basically good. He likes himself and other people. Soon he begins to dip into his own bucket and ladle good feelings into the buckets of those around him, tentatively at first and then more freely as he discovers that the response to his sharing brings him additional good feelings. As long as things go well and he is surrounded by people who are happy and generous, the outpouring and receiving become his life pattern and all is well.

If, however, the child is born into a family that does not meet his needs or convey to him a sense of personal worth, the level in his bucket remains low. The closer the bucket is to empty, the more tightly the child clutches it, for fear that someone will slosh out some of the precious, life-sustaining contents. If this child lives in a family where everyone is "low bucket," the terrible scarcity prevents any ladling of good feelings from one person to another. It becomes impossible for the child to share anything of himself with others. Unless something happens to help this child learn how to give and to receive, it is likely that his state of scarcity will make it impossible for him to share with a marriage partner or children of his own when he grows up.

Feeling threatened, such children often try to raise their own levels of good feelings by constantly and indiscriminately demanding that others give to them. This tends to make those around them even more guarded. Some children go so far as to construct a "cover" for the top of the bucket to prevent any loss. Unfortunately, this cover also prevents any good feelings from getting in; they just hit the surface, roll off, and are lost.

When an older adopted child first enters a family, his level of good feeling about himself is dangerously low—either because his previous placements offered him little or because the pain of the move has upset his emotional balance. As a result, the child will demand more and accept less from others in his new family; some, who feel angry, will also watch carefully for the chance to strike out at other family members, causing everyone else to feel "low bucket."

However the new child reacts, he enters a family with a set of new parents who are usually feeling strong and giving. These parents are eager to dish out their good feelings expansively. What do they run into but an older child whose bucket is impossibly low, who is unable to cooperate in the family giving, who demands excessively, or who is not even able to accept the good feelings ladled his way.

If the parents can keep their own spirits high, they can usually give themselves time—time to reassure the demanding child that his needs will be met, time to help the closed-up child relax, time to go back to the early infant-like days and start to make up for the lack of earlier affection. When this happens, things usually go well and the placement most often works out.

But it is vital that the parents find other ways to replenish their own buckets while they are filling the child's, until he is able to begin to give back to them. The amount of love, energy, and wisdom ladled out by the new parents must not be allowed to so deplete them that they run dry—for then the placement becomes so costly that it has little chance to succeed. Parents may have to choose when and how they will give to their new child, to avoid becoming so drained that they start to dislike the youngster and see him as a threat. And it is also important for the parents to find ways to help the child give to himself—to fill his own bucket and to enhance his own sense of self-esteem.

Low Self-Esteem

Low self-esteem is one of the most common characteristics in newly adopted older children. In order to help these children come to value themselves, it is important for parents to understand how self-esteem develops. It is never too late for people to learn to feel better about themselves. In a study to determine what leads to high self-esteem, Stanley Coopersmith found that there were four major factors: *significance, competence, power,* and *virtue.*

Significance is the degree to which a child feels approval, love, and acceptance from the important people in his life. It is marked by warmth, responsiveness, interest in and liking for the individual as he is. It comes, in part, from the type of care that the child receives, which serves as evidence that he is of worth to those who are doing the caring. Accepting parents enhance the child's self-esteem by support and encouragement in times of need and crisis, marked interest in the child's activities and ideas, and rational discipline which includes more indulgent attitudes towards training and assertiveness (Coopersmith 1967, p. 38). Significance seems to be communicated to children primarily through the way their parents *act* towards them, not by what their parents *say.* People perceive that they are loved when they see that others are doing things for them out of active concern (Coopersmith 1967, p. 29). Many times the thoughtful things that caring parents do for their children without being asked are the first evidence a child has that he is noticed, that his parents want him to have pleasure, that they value him enough to want to give to him—that he has significance in his new family.

Fair and consistent punishment, surprisingly enough, is another way that the child seems able to recognize that he belongs, and that his parents assume responsibility for him. The child seems to accept the punishment as an expression of his parents' active concern for his life and growth—which is evidence of being loved.

Praise is another means by which parents can demonstrate that they are aware of their child and value what he does. One of the areas of frustration early in placement is that "low-bucket" children do not seem able to accept praise or believe in its validity. Perhaps this stems from past feelings of "badness," which make the child quick both to discount compliments and to accept derogatory comments. Perhaps these children are reluctant to accept praise because they fear that they will be expected always to continue to do as well. Part of the child's difficulty with praise may be learned from adults around him.

> Adults and many teachers have fallen into the habit of always pointing out mistakes and incorrect behavior and generally ignoring good behavior. If children are playing gently at home, parents tend to leave them alone. But if the kids start climbing or walking on the sofa, one of the parents soon pays attention to them. . . . Before the child has formulated completely his system of praise, ignoring him when he is doing well and paying attention to him when he is doing poorly is teaching him that it is appropriate to self-ignore good behavior and to self-rebuke poor performance (Felker 1974, p. 89).

Felker goes on to point out that children learn "bad" as one of the first self-evaluating terms; this indicates that much of the social environment is designed to teach children self-derogation rather than self-esteem.

Whatever the reason, parents of newly adopted children often find that when they give praise it helps matters to focus on the job well done rather than on the child's inherent goodness. "You did a good job," and "That was hard work," seem to be less quickly discounted than "You are a good girl [or boy]." This kind of praise is less likely to produce the misconception that the new parents expect their child to live up to a "wonderful" label all the time. It is also useful in helping the child learn how to praise himself. Self-praise is an underdeveloped skill in many of these children—partly because society looks down on "bragging," and partly because the children have lived with adults who did not teach them how to praise themselves. Some of these children remain dependent on outside praise for much of their lives because they have never learned how to reward themselves in this manner. It is important that this tendency be reversed, because the healthy art of self-praise is always available, independent of outside interactions.

Felker explains that rewarding the self, particularly with words, is related to self-concept. It is useful to regard the verbal labels and descriptions that the individual develops in forming the self-concept as a pool of statements that he uses to refer to himself. If the child learns only negative words, he will say predominantly negative things to and about himself (Felker 1974, p. 17).

Teaching the child to engage in self-praise not only reinforces his positive behavior, it also teaches him a new set of self-referent ideas. To say, "I did well on that" not only reinforces what was done, but attaches to "I" the label "well-doer." This skill of praising oneself can be nurtured by asking the question, "Don't you think you did well on that?" The child's response can then be linked with a statement of praise, such as, "I think you did a tremendous job, too," or "You must feel good about that." When the child becomes more accustomed to giving self-referent verbal reinforcement, the adult can ask, "What do you think you should say to yourself?" If the child replies that he doesn't know, the adult can ask, "What do I say to you?" or a similar question, to help involve the child in the evaluative, praising process and to give him permission and encouragement to feel pride in himself (Felker 1974, pp. 86–87).

In addition to giving such praise, it is important for parents to be available and to communicate their acceptance of the child when he is experiencing difficulties, so that the child does not believe that parental acceptance depends on complete success and tranquility.

It also helps the child build feelings of significance if he lives with adults who accept his ideas and values, even if they do not necessarily agree with them. In this way the child can come to respect himself, gain assurance in deriving his own values, and learn to trust himself as a locus of experience (Coopersmith 1967, p. 35). To do this parents must believe that the child has a right to his own opinions, and trust that their child is able to solve many of his own problems. The best way to communicate this kind of respect and trust is for parents to avoid the tendency to jump in immediately and make the child's decisions for him. Rather they should send the child the message that he has the ability to make good choices for himself, and encourage him to find his own solutions. Ginott suggests the use of the following phrases to foster this kind of independence and to communicate to the child that he has significance:

If you want to.
If that is really what you like.
You decide about that.
It is really up to you.
It is entirely your choice.
Whatever you decide is fine with me (Ginott 1965, p. 90).

This approach is also useful in helping the child develop a sense of *competence,* the second major factor in the development of self-esteem. Maureen and Jack are already on the right track in trying to help Maggie feel more competent. They are demanding that she contribute to the work that needs to be done in her family, and they are encouraging her to develop self-care skills through their cooking lessons. The more adult skills they share with Maggie — handling her own money, making plans, learning housekeeping, going places on her own — the more able she will be to see herself as a potentially competent person. When there is something that Maggie does not know, Jack and Maureen should not say something negative — that she is too young, too dumb, or too inexperienced to understand. Rather, they should try to break the task or the information down into simple, sequential parts so that Maggie gets the positive sense that she can grasp new, unknown things. They should provide Maggie with experiences in which she has a high ratio of successes to failures.

These parental actions are particularly important to children like Maggie who are behind in school. The majority of older adopted children come into their new families with some kind of school-related difficulty. Many of them, thrust into the highly competitive classroom environment, where almost everything they say or do is evaluated, see themselves as losers. In a discussion of children under pressure, Sula Wolff points out that failure at school, for whatever reason, is one of the major stresses in childhood and can set the stage for lifelong feelings of inferiority. It is particularly damaging for the developing child, because it often lasts throughout his entire school career. The psychological defenses that the child must use to cope with the chronic anxieties aroused by this situation only add to his difficulties. This is true even when the child who fails appears not to care at all about his shortcomings; even when his teachers find him poorly motivated, uninterested in his work, restless, and easily distracted (Wolff 1969, p. 167).

To complicate the problem, the child who experiences difficulty in learning is not usually allowed to maintain his tenuous self-esteem by avoiding the areas where he does not do well. Rather he is expected to spend *more* time in those areas, further underscoring his feelings of incompetence.

Frequently, older adopted children have grown up in homes where learning, exploratory activities were disapproved of or punished. Maybe such activities disrupted a tidy, smoothly running adult-centered household. Maybe the potential hazards worried an anxious mother. Perhaps a harassed, overburdened mother could not provide either the time or the space because of overcrowded conditions. Whatever the reasons, these children often develop an attitude toward learning marked by passivity, fearfulness, frustration, or irritability; they take little joy or satisfaction in learning new things. In contrast, the child who is actively encouraged to explore new experiences masters one of the basic lessons of early life — learning how to learn. This child finds that mastery brings joy and a sense of achievement. He is rewarded both by his own feelings of competence and by his parents' pleasure in the newly acquired skill, which further reinforces the child's willingness to seek new fields to conquer (Pringle 1975, pp. 42-43).

Children who are confused or behind in school often do not know how to go about unraveling their difficulty. Either they have not been encouraged to formulate and ask questions about what they don't know, or they are embarrassed to ask questions, feeling that they will only demonstrate their own inadequacy or stupidity to the teacher and to the other children in the class. They need help from parents and teachers who are able to say "I don't know" or "Let's find out." They must be taught to ask questions.

There is another difference between children with positive self-concepts and those who view themselves negatively. Children with positive attitudes tend to link statements of personal failure with success statements. They say, "Sometimes I succeed," or "Usually I can do it right." Children like Maggie, on the other hand, tend to say, "I always do it wrong." Children who are quick to assume failure can be helped through encouragement, through parental teaching of basic skills, and by verbalization of the fact that they can improve: "You blew it, but you will do better another time." It is also helpful to point out what they did right, especially in evaluating schoolwork. Here the adult can count and score the number of right answers rather than the number of mistakes. When the child begins to recite a litany of his faults, the parent can break in and help the child make a similar list of things he did well.

Underdeveloped Vocabulary

Another factor interfering with a sense of competence in many older adopted children, particularly at school, is their lack of a working vocabulary. Many of these children come to their new families not knowing the words for ordinary household items, foods, clothing, parts of their bodies. Often their range of experiences has been meager, and this gets in the way of their understanding conversations or scholastic material dependent on knowledge of vacations, zoos, circuses, geography, construction, or time sequences. Here it is important for the new parents to remember that the ability to communicate is a learned skill. By going back to missed preschool and early experiences, by talking to him about what he experiences and by responding to and developing what the child has to say, language development can be enhanced and vocabulary enlarged.

Experts attribute some of this lack of language to the general living conditions from which these children frequently come—overcrowding combined with few play materials or books—where children play outdoors most of the time and parental concerns are rarely focused on their development and abilities as much as on basic matters like health. Often children have more contact with other children than with adults; as a result, their language environment is less rich and possibly also less clear because of competing noise. Perhaps parents and children do less together, and communicate verbally with each other less often and less proficiently. Often the noise level is high in the home because the television or radio is constantly on (Wolff 1969, p. 168; Pringle 1975, pp. 90–91).

Some feel that these differences in verbal ability are more noticeable because children in working-class foster homes often move into middle-class, more verbal families upon adoption. Mia Pringle explains that language in working-class homes tends to be simpler and less individualized. Middle-class families encourage their children to listen to and respond to increasingly mature speech patterns; stories, nursery rhymes, and word games are often included as an important part of the daily routine. In these homes, conversation is freely engaged in, for example, at mealtimes, during shopping, and at bedtime, rather than being regarded as time-wasting chatter. There is also a common difference in the style of childrearing, with working-class homes favoring an "authoritarian" form of discipline and middle-class homes tending towards "democratic" discipline. In democratic homes, the reasons for expected behavior and rules are explained, verbal means of control are preferred to physical ones, and the child's views and wishes are taken into account in making decisions. So in addition to the greater inclination for verbal exchange, there is a greater need for it in democratic homes. This means that there are more frequent, prolonged, and reciprocal interactions between parents and children. These foster two other kinds of behavior: a readiness to approach new problems with an open mind, and a sense of personal independence.

The use of simpler, less individualized language — more common in working-class homes — is likely to mean that small or subtle differences among objects, people, and situations are ignored; also, the nuances of wishes and feelings will be more difficult to convey with more restricted speech. In consequence, children in these homes grow up less sensitive to their own emotions and those of others, and less able to distinquish the finer shades of meanings (Pringle 1975, p. 49).

At every age, children from middle-class homes are ahead of those in working-class homes when it comes to verbal skills.

The whole mode of language differs, from a smaller vocabulary to the use of shorter, simpler, and often incomplete sentences. There are also specific ways in which older adopted children do not communicate well:

1. They rarely observe or specify how they or others are using words.
2. They overgeneralize and operate on assumptions.
3. They send incomplete messages, relying on the receiver to fill in:
     "He isn't very . . . *you* know."
     "As you can see . . . well, it's obvious."
4. They use pronouns vaguely:
     Child: "We went and so they got upset."
     Adult: "Wait a minute. *Who* went *where? Who* got upset?"
5. Often they do not send a message at all but behave in relation to others as if they had. This usually is related to an inside wish that never gets put into words.
     Child: "She never."
     Adult: "Now you mean your mother. Have you told her?"
     Child: "Well, she's supposed to know."
     Adult: "But have you told her?"
     Child: "Well, no."
6. They leave out whole connections in their messages:
     Adult: "I'm sorry I was late today."
     Child: "Oh, that's all right. Mark was running around the block." [Translated: "Oh, that's all right. My dog Mark got out of the house and was running around the block. I had to run after him. It took some time to catch him so I was late, too."]

The trouble with this kind of communication between the child and his new parents is that the parents are constantly groping and guessing, trying to decode what the youngster has inside his head or his heart (Satir 1967, pp. 71-73). Talking with the child is often extremely fatiguing and frustrating.

It is important for the parents to continue to try to help

their child with his verbal skills. Certainly, the ability to communicate with other people can greatly determine what kinds of relationships the child is able to have. Limited verbal ability also affects the child's response to formal education, particularly reading and writing, the key skills to scholastic progress. Pringle states:

> Probably the . . . most crucial factor which promotes intellectual growth is the quality of the child's speech environment: not merely how much he is talked to, but how relevant, distinctive and rich the conversation. The most essential element is the reciprocity of speech between child and adult, the latter imitating or responding to conversation. Hence, the mere presence of adults or just listening to conversation (on TV for example) is insufficient (Pringle 1975, pp. 90-91).

Verbal skills are also important to a sense of *power,* the third aspect in the development of self-esteem. Coopersmith defines power as "the ability of an individual to influence the course of action by controlling his own behavior and that of other individuals." There is little question that having the word names of things gives the child more power over his environment because he can identify and ask for things instead of having to rely on another's guesswork. It also gives the child more control over himself as it allows him to internalize limits, to control thought — and through it, behavior — and it provides a verbal means to release tension, anxiety, and frustration.

Power is also manifested by the recognition and respect the individual receives from others, and by the weight that is given his opinions and rights. Here is another area where allowing the child to solve problems, to make choices, and to develop areas of competence directly enhances his personal feelings of self-esteem.

The fourth element in the development of self-esteem, *virtue,* refers to how well the child assesses his ability to meet ethical and moral standards. This can be a problem area, because two of the very common early behaviors in older adopted children are lying and stealing. Wanting their child to become a trustworthy person, parents find it hard to know how to respond forcefully enough to dishonesty so that the child will understand how strongly they feel without him feeling personally devalued. Jack and Maureen are about to run into this problem with Maggie.

Honesty

For the past several months things have been going well at the Reillys'. Maureen and Jack are through the initial adjustments to being parents. They have settled in to their new life comfortably, and have begun to trust that things will continue to get better for them and for Maggie. Although they have continued to attend the post-placement group meetings that their agency provides for older child adoptions, they have had fewer and fewer things to discuss. Maggie has become much more relaxed. She is more open, easier to talk to, and somewhat more spontaneous. She has made a friend, a little girl who lives in the apartment next door, and they spend their afternoons visiting back and forth, playing with dolls, and dressing up.

The phone call from Maggie's teacher catches Maureen completely by surprise. There is some difficulty with Maggie at school, the teacher says; could Maureen come in to talk about it? Maureen tries to get a clue as to what the problem is but the teacher insists that she would prefer to wait until they can sit down together and talk. Maureen is apprehensive. What can be so bad that the teacher won't tell her over the phone? There have been some problems with Maggie's progress at school, but she is trying hard and seems to be doing better. Could the school be thinking of holding her back again?

Trying to appear nonchalant about it, Maureen attempts to draw Maggie out about how things are going at school. The child insists that everything is fine. Jack is also concerned. Does Maureen want him to try to take time off from work so he can go to the appointment too? Maureen tells Jack that she'll handle it, but inside she really doesn't want to go to the conference at all, with Jack or alone.

The next day the bubble bursts. There is a serious problem with Maggie, in spite of her protestations to the contrary. It seems that Maggie and another child have been observed several times leaving the playground at recess and visiting the drugstore on the corner. This is strictly against school rules, and Maggie has been disciplined for it. Yesterday some of the children went to the drugstore again, Maggie among them. Although Maggie paid for two candy bars, she did not pay for several others that she had stuffed under her shirt. She was caught and the school was called.

Maureen is stunned. What on earth is going to happen? Why would Maggie do such a thing? How could she have insisted with such innocence that she was having no problems at school? It just doesn't make any sense.

There is more, the teacher continues. Maggie's class has been having quite a spell of trouble with things disappearing — pencils, treats, lunch money. Yesterday one of the children lost fifty cents, the same amount of money that Maggie used to pay for her candy. Maggie said that her mother had given her the money and the teacher wants to know if that is true. No, Maureen didn't give Maggie any money. Come to think of it, Maggie has been having a lot of candy lately. Maureen hasn't seen her with it, but there have been candy wrappers in her wastebasket and in the pockets of her play pants. And there have also been several small toys around that neither Jack nor Maureen bought. Maureen has just assumed that these things were gifts from Maggie's after-school friend. Now she is not so sure. Maureen tells the teacher that she would like to discuss the situation with her husband before deciding how to deal with it. She and Jack will get back in touch with the school.

Stay calm, Maureen tells herself as she heads for home. But inside she is furious. Just wait until she gets her hands on Maggie. How dare that child do this to them! And then to lie about it as well! Maureen is also frightened. What are they going to do? What should they do? Why is Maggie stealing?

There are no simple answers to Maureen's questions. First of all, there seems to be no general meaning to anything that children do — from bedwetting, to being anxious, to running away, to stealing. The significance is personal and specific to each child. Each act can carry a host of different meanings. We do know that stealing is a typical trait in older deprived children and it has been postulated that it may be an outgrowth of separation from people in the past who were a source of love and gratification — an attempt to regain the lost love relationship (Bowlby 1965, pp. 37, 45). It is thought that sometimes children steal food to fill the void left from inadequate mothering in the earliest infant days, when so much of the child's sense of well-being was tied to responses to his hunger. Frequently, children who steal also convey the attitude that they take things because life has treated them badly and now it "owes" them something to make up for past injustices. Sometimes older children seem to take things because they do not really believe that stealing is wrong, or because they are overwhelmed by their desire for the stolen item.

Whatever the reason for Maggie's stealing, Jack and Maureen would be wise to avoid labels such as "thief" and "liar" when they talk to Maggie, and rather to concentrate on the result of the action if they are to keep from further eroding Maggie's diminished sense of self-esteem.

In most cases stealing and lying can be eradicated. Here are four parts of the process that seem to work most successfully:

First, Jack and Maureen should confront Maggie with their knowledge of the thefts. How they do this will depend on the Reillys' own style of childrearing — maybe they will yell, maybe they will spank, maybe they will voice disapproval and disappointment, maybe they will punish. The important factor is that the problem be brought out into the open and their disapproval be clear. It is not good to set a child up by asking if he has done something when the parents know that he has. It encourages lying as the child hastens to deny the act, and it involves the parents in not being totally honest with their child.

Second, further temptation should be minimized, by preventing Maggie from being in situations where it would be easy for her to steal. Her teacher should be careful not to give Maggie time alone in the classroom, and Jack and Maureen should curtail Maggie's access to stores on her own. Care should also be taken to avoid leaving tempting items such as sweets or money lying around where Maggie can easily take them.

Third, responsibility should be assumed for observing Maggie closely enough so that she does not have the opportunity to take things and not have it be noticed. If there are unexplained items like toys, money, or candy wrappers around, Jack and Maureen should follow up: "Where did this come from?" or "Where did you get the money to pay for this?" If Maggie is evasive or says that the item was a gift, her parents should check the story out. If Maggie responds to their questioning by shifting the guilt to them — "You don't trust me" — she should be told that the lack of trust is unfortunate, that her parents would like to be able to trust her, and that is why they are helping her to stop stealing.

Fourth, and most important, Maggie must not be allowed to benefit from her stealing. Her parents should make her return things that she "finds," and replace or pay for things that she has taken and cannot return — either by using her own allowance or what she earns through her own effort.

"The Downs"

As time passes, the incidents of things disappearing at school slack off, though on several occasions Maggie brings things home which Maureen makes her return to the school's lost and found. The stealing situation seems to be improving, but things are not so good between Maggie and her mother.

In the past Maureen has been able to work out or learn to live with Maggie's problems. There have been some times when she has needed the help of the parents' support group, and she has been glad that their agency had this kind of post-placement service available. But although Maureen has actually handled Maggie's stealing quite well, the episodes have shaken her deeply. She has the uncomfortable sense that Maggie is not to be trusted. She does not like to have to act like a suspicious policeman towards her daughter. And now she has the underlying sense that additional trouble with Maggie could come at any time. Her serenity and pleasure in mothering are gone. She feels inadequate, resentful, and frightened. Because she blames Maggie for the way things are going she has lately become increasingly critical, impatient, jealous, and angry with her daughter. This makes things even worse; she feels guilty and down on herself. It is hard to do things for Maggie because Maureen finds herself begrudging the effort.

The two major causes of adoption "failures" or disruptions in older child placements are *fear* and a sense of *being out of control*. The fear usually contains elements of:

1. Worry that the child will never improve.
2. Anxiety that the child will become involved in major lawlessness, immoral behavior, or personal failure.
3. Hopelessness, growing from a sense that there is no solution to the child's problem or that the parents will not be able to implement a solution should one exist.
4. Guilt arising from the belief that it may be shortcomings in the parents which are causing the problem.
5. Panic that the adoption was a mistake, that things can't work out with this child.
6. Concern over the effects of the adoption upon the family as a whole or its effects on particular members of the family.

The sense of being out of control usually comes from three sources:

1. The parents think the situation is hopeless and that nothing can be done to avert a permanent disaster — either the child is ejected from the family causing him additional emotional damage for which the parents will feel eternal guilt, or the family is stuck with the crisis brought upon it by this child and things will never again be normal or pleasurable.
2. The parents conclude that the child is not normal. He has no conscience. The parents can't make him do the things they want him to do or stop doing the things that frighten them.
3. The child's behavior or personality evokes such strongly negative responses that the parent feels he or she is being turned into a terrible person against his or her will.

Obviously, when things get to this point something has to be done to alleviate the fear, and to restore the sense that problems can be overcome. Maureen may be able to get enough help from Jack so that she feels better. If he feels as bad as she does, they will still have the support of other parents involved in older child adoptions to draw upon. And if matters stand as they should, they also have a working relationship with their social worker, whom they can call on for help, reassurance, and advice. If their other friends understand that adoption is not a second-best way to become parents and that adopted children are just as "real" to their parents as biological children, then the Reillys may find that talking over their problems and their feelings will help them deal with some of the pressures.

Unfortunately, parents in real difficulty with a placement are sometimes unable to avail themselves of help. When parents decide to adopt, Sula Wolff points out, they are forced to make a deliberate choice involving someone else's child. Because they have personally set the wheels in motion that led to their adoption, they may see themselves as the active manipulators of their child's fate much more than do most biological parents. When their child is not happy or does not behave perfectly, they sometimes blame themselves (Wolff 1969, p. 130). Often they also deny themselves the chance to find help through talking about their problems; they hide their pain, fearing that friends, family, or social workers will respond to their difficulty by pointing out that they brought the situation upon themselves. As the television commercial says, "You asked for it—you got it." Finally, adoptive parents sometimes also harbor the fear that their worker might decide that this is a bad placement and remove the child from their home—something that almost never happens except at the parents' request.

By the time of the next post-placement parents' meeting, Maureen is desperate enough to express her inner feelings. And she is relieved at the response, both from the other couples and from the workers. Most adoptive parents of older children, it seems—especially during the first year—have times when they feel deeply discouraged, when they wonder if they made the right decision for themselves and for their child. They get tired, lose hope. These periods occur at various times and in varying intensities. Frequently, it turns out, there is an initial "down" period that occurs about six to eight weeks after the placement of an older child. Around this time many parents begin both to feel the fatigue of the job they have taken on and to realize the length of time ahead of them in which they will have to continue to put out major effort. They often become impatient, wanting everything to be resolved now because they secretly fear they will be unable to weather the difficult period ahead. This slump is so common that it is sometimes referred to as "post-adoptive depression." Basically, it comes about because the parents — and particularly the mother — are close to exhaustion; they have allowed the levels in their "buckets" to drop too low.

There is no question that adopting an older child is fatiguing. It involves a great deal of physical, emotional, and mental work. There is the physical work of care and responsibility for another person. There is the work of growing to understand and know someone new. There is the work involved in filling the child's bucket, in trying to make up for past deprivations. Because the child comes with problems, there is the work of trying to figure out what to do about them — a complicated job because the child does not come with directions to guide his new parents in their efforts to help him. There is work in trying to decode what the child says and doesn't say. Many times the work load is complicated by the fact that the child seems unable to benefit from what is given him; his ability to take advantage of good care has been damaged by things that happened to him in the past. While his new parents may understand this intellectually, they are still likely to feel inadequate; this makes them anxious or guilty, which increases their fatigue.

Sometimes, as with Maureen, a certain problem comes up that brings things to a head. Part of the problem is often that the adopting parents have expected to find joy, fulfillment, and a sense of purpose through their new child. Instead they find themselves drained and depressed. The higher their hopes have been, the crueler their disappointment when things don't go well. The results are that parents often start to complain and cry, feel resentful and vindictive, get angry, and act helpless and confused. They can become indifferent, resigned, and joyless. Sometimes they become so overwhelmed that they feel temporarily numb and empty.

When this happens, the parents must take steps to reduce their fatigue by cutting out all unnecessary demands. They need to find ways to nurture themselves, to get help with their own feelings and solve their own problems. Sometimes it helps to get away, to recharge and gain a fresh perspective on the situation.

As the parents in the group talk, Maureen finds herself blurting out that she wished they had never adopted Maggie or that they had gotten a different child instead. The reassurance that comes immediately from other parents, that they have gone through the same thing and no longer feel that way, helps. But what helps the most—and what comes as a surprise to Maureen —is that as soon as she hears herself saying the ugly words that had hidden themselves in the back of her mind, her stomach contracts and she knows she really doesn't mean what she said. Relief pours through her. Of course she wants Maggie, problems and all. How could they do without her now? She has become a part of them. Jack and Maureen leave the meeting feeling both more peaceful and more confident. They are now able to focus on the positive again—the progress Maggie is making, her growing confidence in herself, her coming to life.

They have been lucky that their doubts have lasted such a short time. Terrible as it is at the time, facing the possibility of giving up on the adoption sometimes strengthens the adoptive relationship deeply. The adopting parents recognize that there *is* a way out of their problems. They can return their child, but they make a conscious decision not to exercise that option. Instead they choose to continue working things out, to make a permanent, unconditional commitment. This process, which involves choice and rechoice, sometimes happens more than once; but it somehow seems to cement the relationship and is part of making the adoption work out well in a great many families.

By the end of their year together, the Reillys are truly a family. There are still some problems, but Maureen and Jack feel that anyone who is raising a child is bound to run into some difficulty. They can hardly believe that a year ago they didn't even know Maggie; it is hard to remember a time when she was not a part of them. Although they can look back on difficult times, the pain of them is gone. Maureen often thinks that this must be what happens to women who forget the discomfort of labor after their babies are born.

When the day arrives to take Maggie to court to make final the legal aspect of her adoption, there is no hesitation, only joyous celebration. Maggie, outfitted in a long pink dress her mother has made especially for this occasion, makes a bright note in the dimness of the gray building. After everything they have shared, the process itself seems so remarkably simple. Maureen and Jack hold hands while the judge reads through the adoption petition and then signs the paper that marks the recognition of what they already know. Maggie is theirs — permanent, final, real.

8
Gena
and Tommy

The Placement Process

Leah Gardner was lucky to find a family so easily for Maggie among the approved couples in her agency. But finding the right family for Gena and Tommy proves a bit more complicated, and Mrs. Gardner feels discouraged. She began the paperwork involved in "matching" with three specific requirements: a country home; a home where there are other children; a home willing to adopt two children at once. None of the home studies she has yet read combines those characteristics.

Because Tommy shows so many signs of immaturity, Mrs. Gardner decides he needs a father and mother who are not uncomfortable with a little boy who cries easily. He needs parents who can let him find release from tension in thumb-sucking or tears without worrying about what other people think, a family that sets its own standards and is not pressured by outside opinions of how children "should" behave at given ages. Tommy has asked for a new family with room for him to ride his bike. A rural home with ample space for exploring may encourage his personal sense of mastery and ability.

Mrs. Gardner is concerned about the unhealthy dependency that Tommy has on Gena. She does not think that it is good for either of the children; Tommy needs more chance to strengthen his own sense of competence, and Gena needs the time to be a little girl rather than a substitute parent. If Gena and Tommy go to a family where there are other children, Leah Gardner believes, it might be easier for Gena to let her new mother take care of them. A family with other children might also provide a good chance for Gena and Tommy to make more normal brother-sister ties.

Gena has consistently asked for a new family where she could have pets. Certainly a home in the country should have room for animals, as well as providing space for the girl's very active nature. More than that, though, Mrs. Gardner is concerned about Gena's aggressive affection, her physical outpouring of emotion to everyone. Gena needs to have some time with warm, openly loving parents, she feels, to help her recognize her lovability. She hopes that a rural home will ease some of the social pressure on Gena to begin early dating, so she will have the chance to appease some of her hungers for physical love and attention before she enters puberty and becomes sexually mature.

There just doesn't seem to be a suitable match in the agency's file of approved waiting parents. There are parents who would probably be a good match for either Gena or Tommy, but Leah Gardner is looking for a family that can provide for the needs of both children.

At no time does Mrs. Gardner consider separating the children, although it might make the home-finding process easier. The literature on attachment in children points out that in many cases children deprived of parents form a sub-family, with one child assuming the parental responsibility for another. Consequently, the ties between siblings are often even stronger than the ties of the children to their biological parents. These ties are strengthened when the children are placed in a foster family; they tend to cling together to reduce some of the overwhelming strangeness. All of us have experienced how much easier it can be to enter a new group or a new environment with someone else than it is to make a new beginning alone. Even very young siblings may serve to reduce a child's anxiety in stressful situations (Rutter 1972, p. 19).

Children separated from brothers and sisters may never resolve their feelings of loss, even if there are new brothers and sisters whom they grow to love. There may be more drive in adopted adults to track down their remembered biological siblings than there is to locate their original parents, so great a hole does the loss of a sibling leave in one's personal history. For children who have been separated early in life there may be no sense of loss, no need for contact. Others who have faint memories of a brother or sister often find it enough just to know where that sibling is and that he or she is safe and well. But for children like Gena and Tommy, who have had an ongoing relationship, it is extremely important that they do not lose one another. Workers dealing with siblings who are to be separated need to be very sure that the gains from the separation outweigh the losses.

Occasionally there appears to be so much jealousy and competition between siblings that it seems to be better to separate them in placement. But often, if these children are placed together in a secure, permanent home where there is enough love and attention to go around, this jealousy is minimized and true loving ties come through. Sometimes placement personnel are afraid that each sibling has such great needs for nurturing that no family could meet the enormous demand. When this is the case, thought should be given to finding ways to support the adopting family and help them meet the task. Perhaps funds could be provided to hire a mother's helper or temporary household help. Perhaps the children can be placed in stages, with the most needful child first, so that some of the healing process begins to take place in one child before the family is asked to absorb another. This often works well, particularly if the siblings can visit together and if enough support is provided to the child placed second so that he does not feel left out. This kind of placement can give parents a chance to begin to make ties and solve problems in a transitional manner. Interestingly enough, in spite of the common worry that the second child entering the family will cause the first to lose ground, there is often enough relief from the tension of having been separated that the first child stabilizes. Even when progress is temporarily reversed upon the arrival of the sibling, it is most often much more short-lived than when a new nonrelated child joins the family or when another child is born into the family.

Children are sometimes separated, finally, because of a large difference in their ages, or because it is feared that a family cannot be found to accept all the children in a particular group. These separations should probably not occur unless resources such as adoption exchanges have been pursued and given a chance to place the children together. If there are reasons that make separation necessary, the older child or children frequently benefit from being involved in the planning process for the younger ones. This seems to help minimize the resentment at the outside forces that are breaking the family apart. There should be time and help for all involved to deal with the grief of loss of a brother or sister, and help provided for each child to understand that the other has a right to the best life available to him. There definitely must be a chance for the children to say good-bye. If siblings are to be raised in different homes, it is better for the homes to be similar in social, educational, and cultural backgrounds, so that the children can continue to relate to one another easily and have similar upbringings.

If it is decided that children must be separated, they will need protection from the guilt and jealousy that is often stirred up when one child is placed in an adoptive home and another is not. Steps must be taken to prevent either child from intensifying the feeling that one child is "good" and the other "bad." Because sibling rivalry, even in closely attached children, often contains a death wish towards the brother or sister, there should be reassurance after placement that the other child still lives. Pictures should be exchanged, and addresses kept safe, so that the fear of losing the sibling forever to death or disappearance is minimized.

At the same time, workers and parents alike should honor the child's wishes about how and when he wants to keep in touch with other members of his first family. Too often, children who have been separated for a long time are expected to take up their relationship because some adult decides that they "should" have deep feelings for their "blood" siblings and that they "should" maintain contacts in a manner not determined by the child himself.

Mrs. Gardner tells Gena and Tommy that it may take some time to find the right family for them. Sometimes children who expect parents to be found immediately become disillusioned and angry because no parents appear. Sometimes the child waits so long that it becomes too late for placement; the child's openness to a new family passes. His feelings close up, his longings are driven back into the unconscious, and he develops a tough, protective shell. If the youngster understands the reasons for delay, he is less likely to close himself off. He does not feel so unwanted and unlovable if he realizes that there are many people who long for children but that they take a long time to find them (Rowe 1966, pp. 239–40).

Mrs. Gardner should also explain to Gena and Tommy that the first family they meet, or the second or third, may not prove to be just right. The children will have a vote in what happens to them, but she will decide. If the worker assumes the responsibility for the final decision on a family, the child is often more able to handle a situation in which a meeting with possible adoptive parents doesn't work out.

Unwilling to give up on her search for a family that seems right, Leah Gardner registers Gena and Tommy with the state Adoption Resource Exchange; perhaps out of a larger pool of waiting parents a match can be made. The exchange makes several referrals to Mrs. Gardner, but it is the Allen family in whom she is most interested. She writes to their worker to see if they would consider adopting Gena and Tommy.

Before long Bob and Linda Allen receive a call from their social worker. Linda is out, having just left to drive a neighbor's visiting child home. Bob sits at a small table in the den engrossed in seed catalogues, sums, and measurements for next season's planting. Interrupted by the ringing of the telephone, he tilts back his chair, his mind still on the papers in front of him. The sound of the worker's voice brings him rapidly out of the spring planting he has been planning.

"What's up?" he wants to know. Somewhat hesitantly the worker explains that a situation has come up in which she needs guidance from the Allens. She tells Bob that she received a referral from the Adoption Resource Exchange in the mail about a possible placement, but it involves *two* children. Do the Allens want to pursue adopting them? Grabbing a piece of paper, Bob begins to ask questions. He jots down the children's names, ages, and some of the things that the worker tells him about their current situation and their personalities. All the time his mind is spinning around the word "two." Linda is out on an errand, he explains; he will get back to the agency as soon as they have had a chance to talk about it.

"Two." Bob is on his feet walking back and forth as if his trips between the back door and the front window could somehow hasten Linda's return. "Two." They certainly sound good. From a good foster home, with the girl a year younger than Julie and the boy a year younger than Mark — they could slide in just right. "Can we do it?" Bob wonders. "How could we ever swing it financially? Could we really take good care of that many children?" Excitement and impatience mount equally. Where is Linda? What is taking her so long?

Bob busies himself making a pot of tea. At last he hears the car coming up the driveway, and Mark and Julie being directed to the barn to start their evening chores. Then Linda comes into the family room off the back entrance, brushing large feathery snowflakes from her hair. Glancing at Bob's face, she immediately asks, "What are you up to? What's going on?"

Bob stands in the kitchen doorway, a mug of steaming tea in each hand. Giving one to Linda, he says, "Here, you're going to need this. The agency called. They've had a possible referral. How'd you feel about adopting two kids?"

"Two! Wow!" Linda takes a breath, her mind racing.

"What did you find out about them?" Bob goes over the information he has written down, while she listens intently, nodding her head at each pause as if to hurry him along. She struggles to keep her empathy for the children under control, to consider the decision rationally. Can they afford it? Where would the children sleep? Most important, could they handle four children and still find the time to give each one his fair share of attention and nurturing?

Throughout the rest of the day and well into the quiet calm of late evening Bob and Linda find that most of their thinking and conversation is about Gena and Tommy. They alternate between excitement and caution; their hearts tell them to go ahead, but their minds question the likelihood of adjusting to two new older children at once.

When consulted, Mark and Julie get very excited about the possibility of having a new brother *and* a new sister in the family. Their enthusiasm makes it easier for their parents to let their own growing anticipation take hold. All four Allens are in the kitchen the next morning when Linda calls the worker to express interest in finding out more about Gena and Tommy. The worker sets a time for a meeting, reassuring Linda that she and Bob do not have to make a final decision at once. As they get together to exchange information, or after the family meets the children, or even after visiting has begun, the adoption process can be slowed down or stopped. She assures Linda that it is normal for the Allens to feel a little anxious and uncertain. Even if they were not considering adding more children than they had expected, she says, they would most likely have some qualms.

Three weeks later, arrangements completed, Bob and Linda start off early on a Wednesday morning for the two-hour trip into the city to meet Leah Gardner and the children. Packed in the car are thermoses of hot tea and juice, and some fruit and sandwiches for lunch. Linda holds the hand-drawn map showing the directions to the foster home, and the pictures of Gena and Tommy that the Allens were given by their agency. There is only sporadic conversation during the drive, as both adults drift off into their own thoughts.

As they get nearer to the foster home Bob and Linda begin to talk about their nervousness and excitement. There is a last-minute stop at a filling station for clarification of the directions; then they turn down the tree-lined street of comfortable looking houses, watching for the address they have been given. Getting out of the car, they head up the stone walk, holding hands as they climb the front steps. Just as Bob raises his hand to the doorbell, the door opens and Mrs. Gardner steps outside, introducing herself and inviting them in. Bob and Linda go through the motions of shaking hands with the foster mother, but their attention is really focused on the two attractive blond children darting around her. "What appealing youngsters," Linda thinks. "They look enough like Bob to have been born to him." "Why have we been so cautious?" is Bob's first thought. "These are just kids like Julie and Mark, not two-headed monsters."

There is easy conversation among the Allens, the children, and the foster mother. The Allens have brought some more pictures of their farm and of the other children at home to add to the booklet they had sent Mrs. Gardner to use with Gena and Tommy. They settle in the middle of the roomy couch, an excited child on each side. Gena is bursting with questions. She kneels on the seat beside Bob, pointing over his shoulder at the pictures, then dances off to stand in front of Linda, then returns to alight next to Bob. Tommy sits quietly beside Linda who has her arm around him, hugging him into a shared snuggle. Mrs. Gardner encourages Gena to get out their life books, and some time is spent going over the pictures they have drawn and the information they have compiled.

Mrs. Gardner watches Bob and Linda Allen, knowing that the placement decision is really up to them. Gena is so eager to be accepted, to get the move over with, that she will warm up to any parents. Tommy will agree with Gena, as usual. If the Allens want these children, the placement should go well. She is glad that Gena and Tommy are getting a chance to meet their prospective parents first without the other children being present. Sensing the natural pace at which things are going, Mrs. Gardner lets the Allens take the children out alone for the afternoon.

Sometimes it is good for the first meeting to take place with just the parents and the children to be adopted. This may give the new children security and minimize competition, fostering a one-to-one relationship. Other times, meeting the whole family at once is a better plan. The new child may be threatened by adults and need the other children there to dilute the intensity of attention; or the new child may be fearful that the other children will be favored by the parents and need a chance to spend some time with the whole family to see that this is not so. Sometimes the other children have fears about the newcomer and it is unfair to delay their chance to meet him. Often the best plan, if it can be arranged, is for the adopting parents to come to the foster home alone to meet the new child, and then for everyone to make a trip to the new home where all the children can spend some time together.

By the time the Allens return Gena and Tommy to the foster home, the placement is showing signs of being definite. Gena and Tommy have obviously had a good time. The Allens are relaxed and enjoying the children. They want to know what the next step is. Mrs. Gardner asks the children if they would like to visit the farm on the weekend. Gena is impatient. Why do they have to wait? Why can't they just go home with this mother and father now?

Children like Gena often leave their old situations without saying good-bye, to run blindly into the new. Gena will need help in dissipating her anxiety about the move, help that takes into consideration that waiting is difficult for children, who experience a given time period not in clock-counted minutes but according to their own feelings of impatience and frustration (Goldstein, Freud, and Solnit 1973, p. 41). It is important that Gena not deny or repress her feelings of loss, or be protected from those feelings by excessive reassurance, or intellectual adult explanations. The foster parents in this placement will be a help to Gena and Tommy; they understand the purpose of visiting and they want to see the children make a good transition into the new family. They are prepared to let the children go, to handle the change in titles as the Allens become "Mommy" and "Daddy" and they become "the old Mommy" and "the old

Daddy," or are called by their first names, or even "Mr. and Mrs."

Sometimes foster parents find it hard to prepare themselves and the child for the impending separation. They make the child feel guilty about wanting to go home with his new parents after all they have done for him. They may draw away from the child emotionally in order to get themselves ready to lose this child, which makes the youngster feel that he is going to the new home because he was unable to keep the foster parents' love. When this happens, the worker should help the child work out his feelings of anger, resentment, abandonment, betrayal, and guilt.

Just as Mrs. Gardner and the foster parents will encourage Gena and Tommy to recognize their feelings rather than to deny them, Bob and Linda Allen may want to try to set the stage for the children to bring out their mixed emotions as they visit. They can tell Gena and Tommy that they know that it is sometimes hard for children to make family changes, and that it is fine with them if Gena and Tommy have some mixed-up feelings about coming to live with them.

Returning home, Bob and Linda swing by their neighbors' to reclaim their children. Julie and Mark are out the back door to meet them before Bob has turned the engine off. They are clamoring for information: "What were they like? What did you do? What did they say? Are we going to get them?" Reassured that Gena and Tommy will be out for a visit over the weekend, Julie and Mark take off, running in large circles across the yard, shouting, "Hooray! They're coming! They're coming!" The neighbors' dog joins in, barking as he runs after the children. Shaking her head, the neighbor says with a smile, "I hope you two know what you're doing."

During the next two days final arrangements are made for the coming weekend. Bob lets all his other work go in order to build and stain a set of bunk beds for the boys. Gena will be sharing a room with Julie. His children stay close as he works, ready to hand him the level or more nails. Over the carpentry, he talks with Julie and Mark about how they can help Gena and Tommy feel more at home. He points out that the family rules will undoubtedly be somewhat different from what the new children have been used to, and that it may take some time and patience before Gena and Tommy understand how things are done here. All of them will need to use the visiting time to get used to one another. Everyone will be involved in the process of working things out to build a family.

Linda is besieged with phone calls from friends whose children have brought home the news. Some call to offer congratulations, others to voice their opinion that the Allens are crazy. Many offer help, extra clothing, and outgrown bicycles. By Saturday morning there are two new chairs around the family table, the extra beds are ready, and nothing else remains to be done.

This first weekend visit goes remarkably well. There is some indication that Gena is feeling a little frightened—she is constantly on the go and talks nonstop. Tommy seems worried some of the time, wondering out loud what would happen to him if he did something wrong or if he got sick. But actually both children seem to fit right in. There is a quick tour of the house, then they are off to the barn to see the animals. Gena is enthusiastic about everything, announcing over and over, "I love it here, I love it here." All four children get along well together, and there is little disagreement. By suppertime Mark and Tommy have to be called twice before they can be enticed away from the village they are building in the barn, and Julie and Gena have announced firmly their decision that all they ever need to be truly happy is to have each other for sisters. Linda Allen is amazed at how easy it all seems. She wonders why she and Bob hesitated.

Linda panics momentarily as she tries to figure out how to serve dinner to four children instead of just two. For some reason, the fact that there are now two little boys who need to have their meat cut seems temporarily difficult to handle. She decides that she is just tired from the day's excitement. Maybe tomorrow she'll stick to foods that don't need cutting.

Sunday is also good. At dawn, Bob and Linda lie in their bed holding each other and listening to their enlarged brood whispering and giggling together. "You know," Bob says, "this is going to be even more fun than having just two." After a big farm breakfast all the children go along to help Bob with the barn chores. When shown what to do, Gena and Tommy pitch in willingly. They are especially impressed with the milking; each of them takes a turn trying to get the milk to spray into the bucket.

By the time the afternoon brings the visit to an end, Bob and Linda are reluctant to part with Gena and Tommy. It is hard to split the new family up just when it is starting to come together. Even Gena is a little subdued on the ride back to her foster home. The foster parents greet the Allens and the children warmly, listening to the excited chattering of all four youngsters trying to tell everything about the weekend simultaneously. Too quickly, it is time for the Allens to leave. Gena and Tommy walk with them to the car, where there are kisses and hugs all around as good-byes are said and plans are made for "next time." With a chorus of "See you on Friday," the Allens back their car out of the driveway and head for home.

The following weekend goes even more smoothly. Gena and Tommy are becoming familiar with the family routine. There is no doubt in Bob's and Linda's minds that they want these two children. It seems to them that everyone involved feels ready to make the move. After talking to the Allens, to Gena and Tommy, and to their foster parents, Mrs. Gardner agrees. With her blessing, plans are made to eliminate prolonged visiting; the next weekend Gena and Tommy leave their foster parents and go home to the farm to stay.

The Honeymoon

The next several weeks go quickly. Things seem almost too good to be true. It is as if Gena and Tommy had always been part of the Allen family. Gena is such a help. Grown up and remarkably capable for her age, she is up each morning without being called, dresses promptly, makes her bed, and then gives Tommy a hand as he gets ready for school. She can clean a room as well as Linda, and is always asking her mom if there is anything she can do to help. Linda secretly wishes that some of Gena's habits would rub off on Julie. Tommy is a lapful of loving little boy, cute and snuggly, unlike Mark who has come to feel too old for that "baby stuff." Linda doesn't understand why more people don't add a child or two to their families.

But gradually Bob and Linda come to the realization that things are not all perfect with their new children. Gena seems stretched to her limits. Always active and talkative, she now has an almost frantic busyness about her. She seems compelled to outshine the other children. Tommy is at the edge of fatigue much of the time. He cries over nothing and is increasingly dependent on Gena to do everything for him. He is sleeping poorly and waking frequently with bad dreams.

Children come into families in different ways. Some test the limits from the beginning, as if determined to find out what behavior will fulfill their expectation and cause them to be rejected. Others withdraw. Some regress, whining and wheedling others to help them with everything. But many cover their stress by acting cheerful and pleasant, by trying harder and harder, by overreaching themselves to take on adult attitudes and responsibilities not usually seen in children their age. Whether it is because they are numb with grief at the loss of their previous loved ones, fearful of rejection in their new home, frightened at their own built-up anger, or convinced that they have been moved because of their basic "badness," they overcompensate in the beginning as they try to please their new parents and secure a safe place in the new family.

Often this behavior is encouraged by the parents, who are anxious to see proof that they made a good decision in adopting the child, and who want the child to do well as evidence of the "rightness" of their family.

It is impossible for either child or parent to maintain this "honeymoon" beginning indefinitely. Eventually fatigue takes its toll. The child reverts to more normal adjustment behavior, and the new parents are less able to overlook the problems that begin to surface. Sometimes the honeymoon comes to an end gradually; the child maintains his posture of "goodness" at home, but becomes more difficult at school. Frequently children come out of the honeymoon suddenly, pulling out all the stops and beginning to test every limit in the new family at once. The child seems determined to see if he can cause himself to be evicted, to see if his parents are able to accept him as readily when he presents his worst side as they did when he presented his best. It is as if the child feels that being loved doesn't count when he is good, obedient, and loving.

This sudden change in behavior and personality leaves many new parents bewildered and afraid that they have somehow damaged or failed their child. The child in this stage often gets worse no matter what the parents do, and this makes it hard for parents to follow their instincts about how to react. As the testing period continues, some parents find themselves turning against the very child who so delighted them in the beginning. He now seems a stranger who has set them up with high hopes only to let them down tremendously. They feel unfairly used, and need to be reassured that their child has not done this to them deliberately. Other parents take reassurance from that brief initial glimpse of their child's potential to be appealing and pleasant. It makes the testing period less threatening to know that their youngster can behave in more positive ways. Some parents feel relief when the honeymoon ends, realizing that this testing is partially due to the child's emerging trust and the relaxing of some of his effort to win his parents over.

Age Gaps and Regression

The Allens' problems initially surface as they try to help Tommy. After they care for him for a while it is clear that although chronologically he is seven years old, emotionally he is more like Julie and Mark were as three-year-olds—whining, clinging, quick to cry. Bob and Linda know instinctively that Tommy needs help to work through the things he normally would have dealt with much earlier. They spend time rocking, cuddling, and playing with him. But Gena is bothered when Tommy gets this kind of attention. She hangs around, obviously uncomfortable, and becomes giddier and giddier until Tommy, distracted by her excessive, frantic silliness, becomes so tense that it is impossible for him to soak up any of the calm security Bob and Linda are trying to impart. There is never any opportunity for them to spend time with Tommy without Gena there. She seems to be always in the middle. When Bob and Linda make a special attempt to remedy this situation the honeymoon screeches to a halt, and the real work of family building begins.

One day Tommy is moping around the kitchen, left behind because Mark has gone to play with a friend. Linda sets aside her mending and pulls him into her lap in the big kitchen rocker. Stroking his soft, almost white hair against her shoulder, she puts her face close to his neck and ear and sings snatches of nonsense rhymes that soon have him relaxed and chuckling. It is a quiet, happy moment.

Bang — the back door slams open. "Hey, Tommy," Gena calls demandingly, "come on, we need you to be in our play. Tommy, where are you? Whatcha doing?" Coming into the kitchen she says, "Hey, come on. Quit that yucky baby stuff. Let's go." Tommy shakes his head, his face buried in his mother's shoulder. Gena is unwilling to give up so easily. She pulls at his belt. "Come on, come on."

"Gena, leave him alone," Linda insists. "We're busy right now." "Baby, baby, baby," Gena taunts. "Stop that right now," Linda hisses angrily. Gena stomps off down the back hall and out the door, muttering, "I wasn't doing anything. Why is everybody always picking on me? It's not fair." Linda is upset, but she knows from past experience that when Gena gets in this frame of mind it is impossible to reason with her. She settles back to rocking Tommy once more. What happened to the lovable, maternal, responsible youngster that Gena used to be?

Part of Gena's reaction is undoubtedly due to her own relationship with Tommy, which she is unwilling to share. But there is probably more to it than that. Children like Gena, who have been encouraged to prove their worth by premature competence, often are also deprived of earlier nurturing. Both Gena and Tommy need very similar corrective experiences; Jane Rowe explores an analogous situation with two children named Anne and Alice:

They needed to be cuddled, rocked and babied. Anne [like Tommy] required it because she had never had enough consistent mothering to satisfy her craving for love and make her feel sure she was lovable. She could not hope to be independent until she had had her fill of dependency, though of course the time would come when she should be encouraged to move forward. Alice [like Gena], on the other hand, is typical of a group of children who often fool adults into thinking them well adjusted and free from problems. In some ways their behavior is so praiseworthy and desirable that it is easy to miss the basic inadequacies it hides. Children like Alice have been much hurt and build strong defenses against deep feelings of any sort. Love threatens them and makes them feel helpless. They have to regress back to the beginnings of life and relearn how to relate to people. They must actually be helped to be babyish before they can grow up healthy.

Adoptive parents cannot be expected to see this without help. They are more likely to enjoy the youngster's amusingly grown-up ways until they become puzzled and unhappy because of his superficial and manipulative behavior. Their proffered affection is rebuffed by the child who is fighting dependency. . . . [The adoptive parents must let] him know that it is all right, safe and dependable to be a baby (Rowe 1966, pp. 255–56).

When Gena sees Tommy being babied she is crowded by her own frustrated wish to be mothered. If the Allens come to recognize that Gena has many of the same needs as Tommy — though the evidence is to the contrary — and begin to try to fill those needs, Gena will soften up and may suddenly become for a time even more greedy in her infantile consumption of adult affection (Redl and Wineman 1952, p. 63). Sometimes children revert to thumbsucking, using baby talk, wetting and soiling, or demanding bottles. They frequently play with toys and games from much earlier stages and choose for their friends much younger children.

This regression may involve much of the child's day for several months; it may be seen in conjunction with progress — the child improves in one area and regresses in another; or it may present itself in the "age swings" seen in virtually all older adopted children — the child acts in a single day as a two-year-old, a four-year-old, a seven-year-old, and a ten-year-old. It is almost as if the child has to go back to his very beginnings and then progress through all the stages that he has not experienced with his new family. It does not take him a whole year for each age — there may be only two weeks spent "being seven," for example — but it takes sensitive parents to respond to their child according to the age level he displays. New parents find dealing with these sudden switches to be exhausting. It is like pacing yourself to run into a turning jumprope only to find that the rhythm is not constant. Parents who make the effort to keep to their child's age tempo, who use their understanding of child development, who are not afraid that their child will never progress if they encourage his immaturity, find that the child eventually recaptures what he needs to fill the gaps and moves on to behavior more appropriate to his actual age.

Bob and Linda notice that although Gena is bothered when Tommy is babied by someone else, she consistently acts in ways that reinforce Tommy's feelings of inadequacy, discourage his attempts at self-sufficiency, and keep him dependent on her. If Tommy is encouraged to try to do something by himself or for himself, for example, Gena either takes over the task impatiently or is very critical of his effort. Before long Mark and Julie begin to do the same thing. Bob and Linda see this as very bad for Tommy, but it is a hard pattern to undo. They spend time discussing the problem with their children — pointing out that sometimes it is no help to help someone, and that this kind of intervention prevents Tommy from learning to do things. They become alert to situations where the other children encourage Tommy's dependency; they say things like, "Come on, give Tommy a chance. He doesn't need any help. He can do it. He can learn that as well as anyone else." They actively encourage Tommy to try by sending similar messages to him. When something appears to overwhelm Tommy or to make him fearful, they try to break the activity down into its parts so that he can master it a little at a time.

Injuries, Illness, and Doctors

The area in which Gena does let her need for nurturing and her fear of being untended show is in her reactions to illness or injury. She is hypersensitive about her body. Each time she hurts herself she becomes nearly hysterical. Because Gena is so active, she does frequently bang or skin or bruise herself.

Bob and Linda have spent this afternoon balancing the checkbook and paying bills. Now they are relaxing over a hot cup of tea. Suddenly Julie runs in, her eyes large in a white face. "Come quick, Gena fell out of the peach tree. I think she's really hurt."

Rounding the corner of the barn, Bob and Linda can hear her screaming, a shrill cry followed by anguished moans. Gena lies crumpled on the ground, rocking back and forth and clutching her elbow. Neither parent can get any coherent message from her as to what happened or where she is hurt. Julie, Mark, and Tommy are all talking and pointing at once. Apparently, Gena crawled out to the end of a branch to get a particular peach and the whole branch came crashing down. Bob scoops her up, carries her in, and settles her on the couch, hopeful that away from the other children she will calm down so that her parents can get a better idea of how badly she is hurt. Gena's crying subsides to quiet sobs and deep gulps, but she is trembling badly all over and refuses to let anyone touch her arm, elbow, or shoulder.

When there is no change in the next half hour, Linda puts Gena in the front of the van and heads for the hospital emergency room forty minutes away. This is not the first time she has made this trip with Gena, and she dreads it. Not only is a hospital call expensive and a strain on their already stretched budget, but Gena is so terrified of doctors that she is embarrassingly difficult to handle when being examined. Even when not hurt a simple physical checkup can put her in serious distress, panicked all the way to the office for fear that she may need a shot, fighting off the doctor when she has to have her ears checked. Tommy has been no better; on his one trip to the doctor he cried the whole time. Linda wonders if there has been some serious accident or medical trauma to these children in the past.

Not only do most older adopted children share Gena's and Tommy's fear of doctors, but many of them are also very vulnerable to injury or illness. Some theorists attribute this fear to unexpressed guilt over their unacceptable anger at past parents; others feel that it results from the child's sense of having been unprotected against calamity by his original family. Still others think that separation has made the child feel physically vulnerable, more likely to die. Moved children are upset not only when they are hurt or sick, but also when someone else is not well. If another member of the family has a fever, they complain of feeling dizzy and hot. If someone else hurts himself, they search their own bodies to find an old bruise or lump or cut. If they hear about a serious illness or calamity on television or in conversation, they become convinced that they themselves have "kidney failure" or "high blood pressure" or whatever. At first glance this is often read as another way to compete, to resist having to share attention and concern. But for many of these children, their overreaction is a result of real anxiety. The following actions seem to work best to combat health fears:

1. Be careful not to let illness be the primary way in which the child receives care and affection.
2. Take care of physical complaints solicitously.
3. Explain how bodies work—that it is all right to bleed, for example, because blood helps clean out the wound so that it is less likely to become infected.
4. Make it clear that illness is not always contagious—that you don't catch heart attacks or broken arms.

Another technique is to help the child see that his body is equipped to do a good job of healing itself. ("That hurts now, but it will soon feel better." "Goodness, your body got over that quickly.") Parents adopting preadolescent or older boys or girls should explain thoroughly the process of menstruation—that it is not an illness, it is not contagious, it is not the result of injury, it is not fatal — to alleviate any anxiety about this normal part of growing up.

At the hospital, an X-ray of Gena's shoulder and arm proves her difficulty to be a bad sprain. Leaving the hospital she proudly displays the triangular sling, only to discard it the next day, well before the time the doctor advised.

Sharing

Not only are Gena and Tommy overly sensitive to physical ailments, but they are also absolutely intolerant of feeling displaced. They constantly insist: no one better go into *my* room, sit in *my* chair at the table, use *my* glass, *my* bed, *my* toys. Bob and Linda are appalled by their apparent selfishness, their inability to share. But moved children like Gena and Tommy often need a guaranteed place in the family; their own space must not be overlooked or invaded. They need a clear sense of ownership. They are also sensitive to ownership in relationships — no one else better play with *their* friends.

Virginia Satir points out the importance of

> being able to count on managing your own things and partici-pating in the decision about how and when your things will be used by others . . . . This makes it more possible to feel that he can count on others. . . . The use of things often reflects the feeling of self-worth; I care about myself, and I care about my things; I care about you; I care about your things. . . . Sharing . . . is the decision by one person to let another into his belong-ings, to his time, to his thoughts, to his space. Sharing can only be done if there is trust (Satir 1972, p. 276).

Eventually some of this sensitivity to ownership should subside.

Late in the summer, unable to postpone it any longer, Linda spends the better part of a morning rummaging around in the attic for bags and cartons of handed-down children's clothing. Normally the attic is one of her favorite spots, full of pleasant reminders of happy times, sweetly scented by the herbs hung on the rafters to dry. But today the big room seems hot and airless. Everywhere Linda looks there are bags and boxes hastily stored in the rush and confusion of Gena's and Tommy's arrival and settling in. People have been so good to share all these things with them. It looks as if all four children can be pretty nearly readied for school from the garments spilling out of containers onto the floor. But what a job! Linda sits on a discarded footstool, pulls the nearest carton towards her, and begins to sort through it.

After a while Bob calls up the stairs to see if she wants a glass of cold cider. "I can't leave this right now; how about bringing it up?" Linda replies. Soon Bob joins her, carefully stepping over piles of shirts and pants. While they sip from their beaded glasses and listen to the buzz of the summer insects, they become aware of another sound, faint at first, but then growing louder. "You're out." "Am not." "Yes sir." "No way." "You baby."

Shifting position to look out the screened window in the eave, Bob and Linda can barely make out the picture of their two sons, toe to toe, fists clenched at their sides. There is a sudden flash of blue and Gena stands beside Tommy. "You leave him alone, cheater," she shouts. "I'm not cheating, he's out," says Mark. "Is not." "Is, too." "Is not" — the fight escalates as Gena and Mark loudly defend their positions. "I'm telling!" is Gena's parting shot. She runs for the house and can be heard calling for her parents. "Here we go again," Linda says impatiently.

As Tommy has begun to be more capable and secure he has shifted his basic pattern of behavior. The first evidence of his growing self-esteem has taken the form of stubbornness. If Linda or Bob starts a request with "Wouldn't you like to . . . ," Tommy's immediate response is "No." If the other children approach Tommy by saying, "Hey, Tommy, let's . . . ," his response is "No." When given a directive like "It's time to pick up the toys and get ready for bed," Tommy is very likely to say, "I don't wanna," or even "I ain't gonna."

Now that Tommy no longer acts so babyish and his novelty has worn off, Julie and Mark are less tolerant. They have begun to insist that he share things with them, take fair turns, and follow the rules in games. If he whines or cries because he doesn't get his way, they tell him to "knock it off." But whenever how to help with the adjustment period. They may be afraid to hear something that suggests they have made a poor placement. These workers need not assume personal responsibility for problems that arise. Problems are inevitable. Rather they need to support parents by allowing them to blow off steam, to release some of the emotional tension, guilt, or anxiety that has been building up. Workers should watch for their own tendency, because of their personal need to see no problem, to block parental expressions of concern with inappropriate or premature reassurances.

Families often are reluctant to involve their workers in their adjustment troubles. Like the Reillys, they fear they might lose their child if they complain. Sometimes they are afraid that the worker may be insensitive to them, brush them off, or worse yet, blow the problem all out of proportion. It isn't fair to bother the worker, they tell themselves, if the child isn't really doing anything all *that* bad.

Families often feel that they should be able to solve privately any problems arising from the adoption. But when parents run into trouble, professional help can often be useful. To use this resource is not giving up; it is just another way to solve family problems. Maybe someone outside the family will be more quick to see manipulative patterns between the child and the parents. Perhaps the worker can provide additional pertinent information about the child; or can reassure parents that what is happening is normal to placement adjustment. If special counseling is needed, the worker can help get it for the child as he struggles to handle his problems.

Negativism

Bob and Linda should know that Tommy's pattern of docility giving way to stubbornness is not unusual, nor cause for alarm. Discouraging as it is to parents of older adopted children, behavioral changes often seem initially to be for the worse. Negative almost always precedes positive. The child who has previously been unable to express his feelings often begins by expressing anger and resentment. A too docile child is likely to start to assume responsibility for himself by opposing his parents. The new parents might choose to have their child show that he is beginning to trust his family by saying, "I'm glad I'm here. I love you." But the child is more likely to show that he feels at home by daring to skip his chores or by arguing.

Tattling

As a personality shift occurs in one child and problems erupt, the other children in the family are likely to react to disagreements by tattling, or "telling on" their sibling. Tattling can be discouraged by minimizing its gain. It is unfair for frustrated parents simply to say "Work it out" to their children; the tools for compromise and mutual problem solving are not skills that children intuitively have. When one of the children comes to them, the parents can use the incident to show the youngsters how to settle their own conflicts fairly.

The secret is never to discuss a two-person disagreement with only one of the people. As soon as a child runs to tattle, the parent can ask if he or she has tried to settle things first. If so, both children should come and discuss their difficulty with the parent there only as a mediator — making sure that each child listens to the other, understands the point of difference, and tries to work the situation through. Each child should be allowed to state his case without interruption. Because it is human nature to disregard shouted statements, the parent should help the children express their feelings and perceptions reasonably, assuring them that they will each have a turn to talk without interruption, to explain, to rebut. Very heated situations can sometimes be defused by telling the children that they may not shout, and that they may fight only in a whisper; this not only changes the tone but frequently deflates tension because the contenders begin to giggle.

Verbal Handles

Bob and Linda should try to do something about Gena's tendency to side with Tommy. When a fight breaks out and Gena involves herself they can say, "Gena, were you invited in?"

may use their own mistakes as an excuse to give up trying ("I'll never be able to do it, I'm just no good"), it is important for the adults to acknowledge errors and to continue to work with the child. Overlooking or tactfully ignoring the wrongdoing, especially when the child becomes aware of the mistake, backfires more often than not. It comes to be turned into its opposite and interpreted as lack of interest in the child's progress, lack of helpfulness, or stupidity on the adult's part (Redl and Wineman 1951, p. 155).

It is important to help the child grow to believe that everyone makes mistakes. Parents should set an example by openly and willingly owning up to their own errors. This prevents the child from thinking that his parents expect a standard of perfection from themselves or from him. Because most adults have learned to internalize their feelings, children frequently have no idea that their parents experience fear, disappointment, or error. They do not know what adults do when they can't figure out a problem or when they do something wrong, so they lack the skills to deal with similar situations. It is important to point out that sometimes making a mistake is a good way to learn. Questions such as "What did you learn from that?", "How can you improve that another time?", and "What do you want to do about that?" all imply that the child has some choice as to how to profit from his mistake.

When Gena gets into a fight with one of the other children and insists that "it wasn't my fault," her parents should help her focus on what she did that contributed to the difficulty, without focusing on fault or blame.

Setting Goals

Not only are many older adopted children unable to learn from their own mistakes, but they often seem to have difficulty evaluating their own performance and setting realistic goals. The child who is finding school a struggle talks about how next year he will have all "A"s and makes plans about someday going to Harvard. Instead of concentrating on solving current problems, he dreams of the future when he will "play professional ball" or "have a million dollars." When this kind of dreaming is carried too far it prevents the child from learning to set realistic goals for himself so that he can experience success; it ties him to impossible standards, which means that he will almost surely fail.

Some children defend themselves by saying that they could do "A" work (never "B" or "C" work) if they wanted to, and then never making an effort. They fear that if they do try and can't meet their self-imposed standards, they will have killed their dreams. One variety of this behavior can be seen in the child who is so concerned about success in a particular activity that he avoids it altogether.

Many displaced children seem to have trouble setting any goals that are not unrealistically low or high. Either way, they usually come out failing. If the goal is too high and cannot be met, the child sees himself as a loser. If the goal is set too low, its achievement is not an accomplishment. Even when the child succeeds, his sense of self-esteem is frequently so low that he is quick to devalue his success ("Anyone could do that, even me").

Parents can help by encouraging the child to set goals that can be met. They can help the child break complicated tasks into smaller ones that can be mastered, and encourage him to plan out how he might go about reaching his goal. ("That sounds like a good idea; what do you need to do first?") They can emphasize the new things that the child has learned and the possibility of additional learning, rather than focusing on what he can't do. They can respond with encouragement to areas of difficulty. ("You can't do it now, but you will be able to do it.")

They can encourage the child who has academic trouble to set other kinds of goals as well — in sports, personal projects, or saving money.

There are ways to help children feel secure in their competence and their ability to set and meet goals. Several years ago, I clipped from somewhere Edith Neisser's memorable list of standards for "How to Live with Children":

    1. Parental attitudes that say, "You are the kind who can do it."

2. The understanding that it is all right to try—failure is no crime.
3. Provision of plenty of opportunities for the child to succeed, and the setting of reasonable standards so that the child is not constantly falling short.
4. Parental pleasure with a reasonably good attempt, and confidence in the child's ability to become competent.
5. Acceptance of the child as he is, liking him so that he can like himself.
6. Parental guarantees of certain dependable and consistent rights and privileges.

Separation Anxiety

Too soon the children's shorts are put away in favor of the jeans Linda has brought down from the attic. The busy days of harvest and canning, when the Allens store the goodness of the summer against the coming winter days, begin to wind down. Before long, the golden-yellow of the school bus mingles with the other fall colors, accentuating the four blond heads waiting by the rural mailbox each morning.

Tommy, who has spent a lot of his time close to his new mother, is unsettled by his time away at school. He becomes very sensitive to any kind of separation. If his parents leave the house without him he cries and begs to go along, much like a very young toddler, and he becomes unreasonably clinging upon their return. Lately he is bothered even when Linda goes into the bathroom and shuts the door. He stands outside and talks to her as if he were afraid that she might disappear. He is so upset and worried at the thought of being away from home that it is becoming increasingly difficult to get him out the door and onto the school bus. Things are particularly hard on Monday mornings, after Tommy has had two days of not having to leave for school. The last two Mondays, his crying and clinging have been so intense that Bob has ended up dressing Tommy, putting him in the car, and driving him to school. Tommy's teacher says that he seems worried; he tells her that he must go home because his mommy is worried about him or his mommy is sick.

Separation anxiety is a fairly common problem in older adopted children. It is particularly evident at the beginning with children from overseas. The child's fears that he will lose his parents once again are activated when he is apart from them. Even temporary separations make some children feel rejected and deserted, and contribute to their belief that they are being punished because they have been "bad." Some children respond by acting up; others, like Tommy, cling. John Bowlby points out that the stronger the child's inner conviction that he will lose his mother, the more he clings to her (Bowlby 1965, p. 31). Sometimes an unfortunate cycle is set up. The more the child clings, the more the mother needs relief from the clinging. The more the mother tries to discourage the clinging, the tighter the child hangs on. Eventually the mother gets irritated and draws back or pushes the child away. This parental displeasure makes the child even more anxious, which causes him to latch onto his mother more desperately still.

Separation anxiety can also be triggered by a visit from a social worker whom the child associates with a past separation. Workers and parents alike need to be sensitive to this, to talk to the child about why the worker visits and to help him understand that the worker has not come to take the child away.

Although it is wise to avoid overnight separations until the child feels less threatened, the cure for this problem lies in the parents continuing to do the things that temporarily take them away from their child. Linda can help by promising that she will always tell Tommy before she goes out and by keeping that promise. Tommy may also need to know where his mother is going and when she expects to be back. Linda should tell him that she is not angry with him before she leaves, and she should leave matter-of-factly to emphasize that she is not concerned that anything harmful will result from her absence. Gradually, as he learns that his parents will indeed return, Tommy will begin to handle separations better.

More "Downs"

The Allens have managed well throughout the summer, but they are getting tired. They have had five months of coping with newness, of trying to blend two groups of children into a cohesive family unit. The Allens tell themselves that it is normal for children to act up when there is a change. Even when Julie and Mark visit their grandparents for a day or two, they always return home acting as if they need to be assured that the old rules still apply. But this business has been going on for a long time. Bob and Linda had counted on the beginning of school to give everyone a break during the day so that their time together could go more smoothly. But even though they begin each day calmly, determined to be fair and patient referees, it always seems to end with them screaming irrational threats at the children. Lately Linda has caught Bob sitting in front of the evening's fire with a frighteningly grim expression on his face. He dislikes the kind of parent he has become, he tells her. In the past he was slow to spank his children. Now he is spanking more often and with less cause than ever before.

One of the common causes of serious difficulty takes the form of parental self-discovery. The newly adopted child brings out submerged feelings or behavior in his parents that make them dislike themselves. This can be such a severe blow to their self-esteem that they must eradicate the cause of their distress. Sometimes the only way that parents are able to do that is by returning the child.

Part of the "down" comes from the inner fear that the adoption was a mistake. All the things the couple initially feared seem to be coming true. The parent may be having to give up things that were more important than he knew. Often there is panic that the family has taken on more than it can handle.

Sometimes parents succumb to what Karen Horney has described as the "tyranny of the shoulds." They *should* be paragons of honesty, generosity, consideration, justice, dignity, courage, and unselfishness. They *should* be perfect lovers, spouses, teachers, and parents. They *should* be able to endure everything, *should* like everybody, *should* love their children. They *should* always be serene and unruffled and enjoy life. They *should* know, understand, and foresee everything. They *should* be able to solve every problem of their own, and of others. They *should* never be tired or fall ill. They *should* be able to do things in one hour that can only be done in two or three hours. And with older adopted children, they *should* be able not simply to accept and help their child find ways to deal with his problems but also to restore him.

Obviously, meeting all these *shoulds* is impossible, but still the parents struggle to measure up to these impossible goals. Striving to accomplish impossible tasks combined with solving continual problems results in the major cause of the "downs"— accumulated fatigue. There is often no time to digest and dispose of one problem before the next one arises, so the parents never have a chance to feel competent and good about themselves and about how well they are managing. This leads to terrible feelings of inadequacy and incompetence, eroding the parental ego just at the time it needs to be strongest.

There is no question that the entry of an older child into the family stretches the parents greatly, sometimes almost to the breaking point. They are suddenly involved in what may be the hardest job they have ever tackled, and they find that they must dig deep into their own resources of strength just to keep going. The demands are constant, hour after hour, day after day. To face this drain becomes increasingly tiring, and there is no set time for these demands to abate and things to return to normal. The new mother may feel exhausted and find herself hard pressed just to deal with the normal routine of the day. Fathers come home to find everything upset and their whole way of life disrupted. The parents find their sex lives foundering. One partner or both will often be too drained or too put-upon for that sharing of intimacy. There is no time to recoup energies; both parents feel emotionally exhausted. Because they are just barely managing to hang on, any step backwards becomes desolating.

Bob and Linda have to stop trying to solve every problem simultaneously. They should focus their energies on the single problem that bothers them most, and let the others go. That way Gena and Tommy will not be bombarded with too many expectations for change. They will be able to feel some success in modifying their behavior, and Bob and Linda will not overwhelm either themselves or the children by trying to do too much too fast.

Bob and Linda should also find ways to minimize unnecessary demands upon their time and energy, to relax whatever standards they can, to "fill their buckets." They need to pamper themselves a little. Establishing a normal and anticipated routine seems to give both old and new children a sense of safety and order, and to make parents feel that they are managing to retain some control over their days. It is important to maintain clearly defined limits on acceptable behavior and to consistently enforce these limits; this will help Gena and Tommy to behave in ways that make them likable to have around.

Problem Solving

It would probably be helpful for Bob and Linda to keep some written records in an effort to find answers to some of their questions. Such records are reassuring because they help parents remember what has happened and see from past episodes how mistakes can be avoided; and they help point out over a period of time what bothers the people involved so that they can work on getting along better. There are several useful things to look for:

1. What keeps happening again and again?
2. How does it begin?
3. When does it happen? Does there seem to be a connection with some part of the routine — bedtime, mealtime, in school, at recess, after failure or success? Does the problem occur because the child is hungry, or not quite awake, or overtired?
4. At whom is the behavior directed? Is it the "old kids" doing something to the "new kids" or vice versa? Is it an older child picking on a younger one or a little one

annoying an older sibling until a fight ensues?
5. What kind of behavior is involved? Is it verbal or physical?
6. How does the episode end? What kinds of feelings result?
7. What kind of modification is desired?

Parents should explore how a bridge can be built between the old pattern and the new one to help the child change gradually. Substitution and invention can often be used to this end.

Substitution consists of teaching an alternate action that the child already knows but does not use in the problem situation. For example, a child can be taught to pound clay or hammer nails or stamp his feet instead of hitting. A child can be shown how to greet people by shaking hands instead of pounding them on the back or punching them on the arm. Invention is the teaching of alternative behavior that is not already a part of the child's repertory of actions.

Sometimes parents can give permission to continue the behavior in a modified form ("You may kick the table, but you may not kick me." "You may tear or wad up newspapers, but you may not break toys.") (Trieschman, Whittaker, and Brendtro 1969, p. 13). And it is often possible to use humor as a light-handed way to suggest change, to add to the reminder the closeness of a shared joke. Table manners, for example, are often an ongoing irritation. The child who eats with elbows askew or both forearms resting on the table can be told lightly, "You look like an airplane about to land." Then the word "airport" or "airplane" becomes a catch phrase that takes on the good-naturedness of a freely shared family joke. "Napkins," said without more discussion, can remind children that napkins belong in the lap.

It is interesting to note that often the same qualities that were initially appealing to parents are the ones that wear their patience thin after a time and become a source of difficulty. The confident child becomes arrogant; the shy one becomes withdrawn; the affectionate one becomes smothering; the helpless one becomes lazy. The difference is the degree and the length of time in which the trait is experienced.

Often when a child makes an effort to control himself in one area, his effort may yield a problem somewhere else — low frustration tolerance, throwing or breaking things, temper tantrums that come out of his accumulated fatigue and the newness of his actions.

By Thanksgiving the Allen family has regained some of its sense of rightness. And Christmas is a busy, joyful time. Linda knits two more stockings with fuzzy Santa faces to hang from the massive fireplace mantel. Bob keeps the boys busy with a secret project in the barn that involves much whispering and vague hinting. The girls have something going on in their bedroom and a big sign taped to the door: "Do not enter. This means you."

Gena and Tommy are now definitely a part of the family, though some problems remain. Tommy is still overly sensitive to being away from his mother, but he goes off to school willingly now and is developing a case of puppy love for his first-grade teacher. Gena still is quite competitive with her brothers and sister, but she is showing more willingness to share. Bob and Linda feel that the progress the children have made is remarkable. More and more, the problems that arise are just the normal, everyday pitfalls of living together and not so much the results of past hurts and deprivations.

Close to the anniversary of Gena's and Tommy's arrival, the day comes for making the adoption final in court. Everyone is excited. The day is a combination of solemn commitment — with unspoken echoes of the marriage vows, "for better, for worse; for richer, for poorer; in sickness and in health" — and festiveness, including a trip for ice cream with Mrs. Gardner, who has driven out for the occasion. Over massive hot fudge sundaes Linda and Bob agree that, while they have been convinced that there was no way Gena and Tommy could seem more truly theirs, somehow going to court has deepened those feelings. Frequently children feel the same way, and they may show a remarkable settling down and positive change once they are legally adopted. But with other children, anxiety may flare up at the finality of the break with the biological family, and sometimes difficult behavior will recur.

Mrs. Gardner also reminds the Allens to check the wording of their insurance policies to be sure the benefits apply to "children born to or adopted by" their family.

The court date does not seem to affect Gena and Tommy visibly. But things take a significant turn for each of the children as a result of two totally unrelated events: an antiques buying trip, and the birth of the spring lambs.

In late winter, Bob and Linda usually make a final trip to other dealers and suppliers to fill in their stock of antiques before the demands of spring planting make such a trip impossible. In other years, Bob's younger unmarried sister has come in for the week to look after Mark and Julie and to feed the stock. But this year the Allens feel it would set Tommy back seriously to leave him for so long. Instead they decide to go for a shorter period and to take all four children. If they pack much of their food and stay in motels that don't charge extra for children, they figure, they can just swing the trip financially.

Over the course of the few days they are away, there is a sudden marked change in Tommy. Instead of clinging tightly to Bob and Linda because of all the strangeness — new people, new beds, new places — he and Mark go off eagerly at the motels, exploring the lobbies, checking out the pools, playing with the ice machines. Tommy, who has always been shy with new people, is outgoing — greeting other dealers freely and making conversation with them. Bob and Linda are astounded. It is as if someone has flipped a switch inside Tommy's head. They talk about it as they head for home, with the children asleep in the back of the van. "You know what else I noticed?" Linda says. "I think that Tommy has been too busy to suck his thumb while we've been gone." Sure enough, watching him at home for the next several days proves her right. The thumbsucking that has been diminishing has now all but disappeared. And the fuss and clinging at separation seem to be completely gone, too.

One frequently reported phenomenon in older child adoptions is the signs of decreased anxiety and growing trust in a child who is taken on a trip or vacation for the first time by his new family. Instead of being set back by another change, the child makes strides forward. There seems to be something about going away with the family, being included, that communicates to the child that he is truly one of them. This is also sometimes seen if the family has to move during the first year. Whether it is the actual going away together; or being out with strangers who automatically accept him as one of the family and know nothing of his past and the adoption; or everyone coming home together as part of a family whole—somehow the child is more sure that he belongs.

Additionally, if the child's new grandparents willingly accept him, even if this takes time; and as the other children at school stop asking questions ("Why didn't your parents keep you—didn't they want you?" "What happened to your *real* parents?" "Do you like it here?"), as they eventually do; the child seems to take strength from public acceptance of him as part of this family, and his new identity is reinforced.

With Gena the change is more gradual, but equally striking. In early March one of the Allens' ewes has a difficult, lengthy labor. Although she is delivered of twin lambs, the vet is unable to save her and the Allens are left with two tiny bundles of fur, hooves, and greedy mouth to care for. Bob brings the young orphans into the kitchen where they can be kept warm, and he and Linda take turns getting up during the night to check on the babies.

In the morning the children are enchanted. The little lambs are so cute. It is hard to get breakfast with four young-sters underfoot, enticed by the surprisingly loud bleats and the wobbling, wiggling activity in the kitchen. During the day, the smaller of the lambs, a ram, grows weaker and dies. But the little ewe becomes noticeably stronger and more active.

As soon as the children come home they are in the kitchen, wanting to know what will happen to the surviving lamb. Will it die? Can they name it? Who will feed it? But before too long, some of the excitement wears off. Mark and Tommy disappear to the swings that Bob has hung from the rafters in the barn. Julie, snatching one more cookie from the plate on the table, is off to find her dad. But Gena sits on the floor, patting and crooning to the lamb through the afternoon and into the evening. When the lamb grows tired, Gena accepts Linda's explanation that new babies need lots of sleep and is content just to sit and watch it nap. Although she has never been much interested in the other sheep, now she is filled with questions. At dusk, as Linda is making supper, the lamb wakes, loudly demanding food. Linda shows Gena how to fill the big nursing bottle, hands her the lamb, and lets her feed it. Later she tells Bob, "There was a whole new side to Gena I'd never seen before. You know how her lovingness always shows itself as just one step away from havoc, how she grabs for a hug as she dashes past or gives you a smack for a kiss? Well, today she sat quietly holding that lamb and she was so tender, so caring. I'll never forget how she looked. We've got to encourage that softness to come out, Bob. Let's give her the lamb."

Gena is momentarily subdued by the news that the lamb is to be hers to raise. But her effervescence quickly returns and there is lively discussion about what to call the little ewe, who eventually becomes "Honey." Even after Honey is large enough to be tethered in the yard and to sleep in the shed, Gena does not lose interest. She plays with her, brushes her, feeds her, cleans the shed—all willingly and without reminder. Bob is impressed by the length of her involvement. Linda knows that she will always remember the picture of a graceful, blonde, long-legged child running through the fresh spring grass with a lamb at her heels. It is like something out of a fairy tale or a nursery rhyme.

Honey proves helpful to Gena's development in a number of unexpected ways. Because of her fierce competitiveness and her tendency to make caustic remarks, Gena has had a lot of difficulty making friends at school. But working with Honey involves Gena in the local 4-H club, where her enthusiasm about the ewe and her evident desire to learn more about sheep help her make friends; she eventually becomes a popular leader in the group.

Her desire to use Honey as a 4-H project turns Gena's strong aversion to reading into demands for reading help so she can get the information she wants from publications on sheep tending. Her academic performance takes a sudden turn upward, which helps her take pride in herself and in her growing ability to succeed.

By the end of the spring term, Gena has become less a problem in almost every area. She is no longer so overly concerned about Tommy, although she is interested in him like everyone else. She and Julie seem to have worked out their adjustment and rivalry problems and now spend much time together, as well as being involved in their own separate interests. The quarreling, siding with Tommy, and "dumping" of bad feelings have given way to genuine lovingness for each member of the family and a working with, rather than against, the whole.

By summer vacation there is no doubt that the work and worry the Allens have put in have paid off richly. The constant problem solving, refereeing, and chaos have subsided, giving way to a closely knit, smooth-running family. Bob and Linda have met the task, followed their dream. Their years to come will be enriched because they opened themselves up to their adoption experience.

9
Danny

Although the matching process has long been completed for Gena and Tommy and for Maggie, the state agency has found making plans for Danny to be more difficult. Thirteen years old, in a foster home with a large number of other children and very little parental supervision, Danny's increasing toughness is viewed with growing concern.

His foster care worker senses that if Danny continues to spend most of his time with his current gang of friends he will almost surely become involved in some sort of delinquency. It seems to her that Danny's foster mother has essentially washed her hands of any responsibility for the boy's behavior. She threatens to throw him out if he continues to be a problem. It is felt that Danny's previous moves have contributed to his difficulty, and the department feels both a sense of responsibility for him and a reluctance to move him again. In spite of Danny's troubles he is an attractive, intelligent young man, and his foster care worker believes that under the bravado there is a needful, receptive child who could still be reached by committed parents and helped to have a more satisfying, valuable life. Adoption seems to be the best answer for Danny; but the staff workers reviewing his case are unsure that parents can be found for a black teen-age boy with Danny's problems.

In order to find an appropriate adoptive home for Danny, Mrs. Gardner has been trying to get to know him better and to talk with him about a possible placement. She is finding this difficult for a number of reasons in addition to the fact that they are of different races. Denied parental closeness, Danny acts as if he has taught himself not to miss it, thereby protecting himself from the fear and loneliness of a boy without a family. Now he just wants to be left alone and not be bothered by having to risk another parent-child relationship.

His genuine closeness to his friends suggests that Danny has made them into a substitute family — where he is trusting, where he can give of himself and receive from others. Danny refuses to believe that he will ever have to leave his present foster home. He adamantly insists that he will not be separated from his friends. Sometimes Mrs. Gardner arrives at his foster home to find that Danny has gone off with his gang, no one knows where. Each time Mrs. Gardner brings up the subject of a new home, Danny becomes very defensive, hiding himself behind a comic book, or changing the subject so skillfully that Leah Gardner somehow finds herself involved in an unrelated conversation. When she confronts him with his obvious lack of cooperation, he just reassures her that she doesn't need to worry about him, that things will be fine because he is staying put.

Danny's attitude is certainly understandable, and it is not atypical of teen-agers approached with the idea of being adopted. Although some are eager to have a permanent place where they will belong, many resist the thought of being moved. Workers often think that the way to deal with this problem is by seduction, making the teen-ager so enamored of the benefits to be gained that he changes his mind. But because teen-agers are so remarkably able to discount any adult argument, especially those of social workers, this is not usually very successful. Rather than focusing on reducing the child's reluctance to move or worrying about how much of the decision should be left to him, the worker should attack those identifiable fears that prevent the teen-ager from looking at the move positively. There may be fears of being adopted (a process foggy to many); of being strange or different; of starting at a new school; of losing friends and the identity that comes from that group; of having to explain himself; of the unknown authority in the new home; of not meeting the demands; of replacing others from the past to whom there is still loyalty; of getting close to people and therefore being vulnerable. Once the social worker is able to identify the things that frighten a particular teen-ager, she can begin to try to make those fears more manageable. Perhaps misinformation can be corrected. Perhaps a bridging process can take place at the time of the move so that the new school and the new peer group can be tackled according to the child's own speed and style. Perhaps there is a need for closing off unfinished relationships from the past.

Interestingly enough, the same fears that make a particular teen-ager fight being moved will motivate him to work at making the new family last once he is placed; he has already been through whatever fears made him unable to see the benefits of adoption. If the problem was fear of starting at a new school and having to make friends with a strange group of kids, the teen-ager is now in that new school and knows some of the members of his class. If the adoption doesn't work out now, the youngster, unable to return to his former home, will have to go through the process of starting out with new people again, so he has a real reason to try to hold the placement together.

While Danny is insisting that he will never move, Mrs. Gardner is hearing more from Danny's foster mother that his placement in this home is becoming increasingly marginal. Each visit to the home means listening again to the growing list of complaints about the boy's behavior. The neighbors have begun to talk, it seems, and they are labeling the members of Danny's gang as "bad ones." Mrs. Gardner senses that the foster mother is becoming more positive about an adoptive home for Danny because she sees it as a way out of dealing with her help-lessness about him. In an attempt to keep him in line, the foster mother has started to threaten that she will "kick him out." This misguided attempt at discipline only reinforces Danny's conviction that the idea of another family is just talk.

Leah Gardner would like to try a three-way conversation among Danny, the foster mother, and herself about the problems in this home and the plans being made; but the foster mother is very ambivalent, one minute saying that Danny will have to get out because she can't handle him, the next excusing his behavior and saying, "Boys will be boys," as if to imply that he can stay indefinitely. A three-way conversation, Mrs. Gardner decides, might only result in strengthening Danny's conviction that he need not deal with thoughts of another move, supported by his foster mother's inconsistency and lack of action.

Mrs. Gardner also has her own mixed feelings about the move. Will Danny sabotage an adoptive family because he resents being displaced? Is it wrong to think of adoption for him? How much should he be involved in the decisions being made about his future? She would like to make him more a part of the process, but his fears get in the way. The decisions will have to be made for him.

Leah Gardner continues to see Danny regularly, deciding that her present task with him is to establish a nonthreatening relationship. She uses available agency funds to take him out to eat, to an occasional ball game, or for a drive in the car. During this time she forms a strong belief that adoption is the best plan for Danny, and she continues her attempts to find an adoptive home for him. She feels that when she can talk to him about an actual family he may ease up in his defense against the move and profit more from her attempts to prepare him for another separation.

During her visits with Danny she talks with him about past moves in order to clear up any confusion he feels about why he has had to leave other families. Danny seems interested in talking about himself. He brings out his anger at his first parents for their alcoholism and lack of care. He remembers them as drunk all the time. Mrs. Gardner agrees straightforwardly that they did have problems that made them unable to care for him. She and Danny talk about some of the reasons that adults are sometimes unable to cope with the pressures in their lives. There are members of Danny's gang who are the same age that his first parents were when he was conceived and when their marriage took place. Danny can easily imagine how difficult it would be for these friends suddenly to be tied down to the responsibility of a wife and new baby, how hard it would be for them to find some kind of a job to provide for a family, and how much they would hate having to do it. He can understand that the girls he knows would not be ready to care for the needs of a baby or to build a good marital relationship.

As Danny talks about his first home he speaks fondly of his grandmother, who obviously loved him a great deal and may have been the source of much of the strength and ability to love that are evident in this young man. Danny confides that shortly before he was taken into care his grandmother was upset at the way his parents' problems were preventing them from being able to look after him. There was talk that maybe Danny would go to live with her, and he had been very excited about it. But then the grandmother had a heart attack and died. Struggling to keep his control, Danny tells how scared and lost he felt after her death, with no one left in the family to take care of him. It was a terrible time. Danny returns over and over to the fact that he never told his grandmother how much he loved her, that he never had the chance to tell her good-bye. No amount of reassurance seems to comfort him.

With a bit of detective work, piecing together the information from Danny's record and the newspaper obituary in the files of the public library, Mrs. Gardner is able to find out where Danny's grandmother is buried. After talking it over with her supervisor, she decides to ask Danny if he would like her to take him to visit his grandmother's grave. At his request, she takes him to the cemetery and helps him find the modest stone. Taking her cue from Danny, who seems to want to be alone, she walks away and sits on a granite bench where she can be seen, but out of earshot. She gives the boy a chance to come to peace with this person he has loved and missed so much.

On the ride home, Danny is quiet, lost in thought. Usually taut, his body is more relaxed and his moves more fluid. From this time on, although still unwilling to talk about a move, Danny is more open with Leah Gardner, counting her among his friends. She begins to get a good sense of Danny's other side, of the tenderness and caring that are there and that could make him receptive to the give and take of a family relationship.

As Danny seems to have dealt with some of the unfinished business in his past, Leah Gardner feels he is ready for placement. She sees to it that he is featured in a newspaper article about children waiting for adoption. She hopes to find a two-parent black family that will be just right for him.

Mrs. Gardner has other criteria for Danny's new family. It is important to her that he be placed in a home with people who are already parents. She is looking for parents who have worked with adolescents and have an understanding of the special needs they are likely to have, the skills they are working on, and the ways in which they may act out their frustrations in growing up. She feels that Danny needs a strong father, whose strength he can respect and admire as he works on his own self-control. She wants Danny's parents to be able to accept and nurture a boy/man who is resisting their family, without feeling personally rejected. They should feel comfortable with his loyalty to past relatives and past friends, and with his swaggering, streetwise attitude; and they should be able to see the tenderness inside. They will have to be secure enough to set firm limits and loving enough to do so in an accepting manner.

When the DeSandos complete their home study and are referred to Mrs. Gardner, she has still not found the right family for Danny. As she reads through the report, she becomes more and more hopeful. Maybe this is it—maybe this is the place for Danny. The DeSandos have voiced ongoing interest in him. They seem to have the desire and the ability to defer their own needs in order to help him. They have had considerable experience with children Danny's age and are not likely to be surprised or appalled by some of the less attractive aspects of adolescence. It looks as if they have carefully thought through the possible effects of Danny's entry into their family—both on them and on their children. With other children to gratify their needs as parents, they may be able to give Danny time to feel at home.

Leah Gardner calls the DeSandos' worker, who has no doubts about going on to the next step in the adoption process — making arrangements for the DeSandos to find out more about Danny. This worker calls Beth DeSando to suggest that they get in touch with Danny's worker and set up an appointment to talk about him.

The call comes as Beth hurries in from the car, her arms full of groceries. Setting the bags down, she grabs the phone, a little out of breath. She listens as her worker explains that she has ‘heard from Danny's social worker, who is interested in meeting the DeSandos to talk with them about adopting Danny. Beth calls Mrs. Gardner immediately and sets up the appointment. The two women have a short, pleasant conversation and both hang up feeling positive. Beth stands in her kitchen, a surge of anticipation welling up inside her. She dials Tony's number at work. He too is excited. What did the worker say? How did she sound? When are they meeting with her? Beth realizes that she hasn't gotten much new information about Danny, but she doesn't care. Somehow, she feels as if he were already her son.

Sam, Gillian, and Adam get home from school and hear the news. They are caught up in the excitement of having a new brother. The conversation flows fast and furious. When can they meet him? Where will he sleep? They talk about what it will be like to have four children in the family and about the things they will do together. Suddenly Beth looks up. Somehow it is five o'clock, dinner isn't started, and the ice cream in the forgotten grocery bag is melting down the counter. It has been an afternoon that Beth knows she will remember clearly for the rest of her life.

The placement process is quite different for Danny and the DeSandos than for Maggie, or Gena and Tommy. Mrs. Gardner has expected that it would become much more difficult for Danny to refuse to consider his impending move after a suitable family was presented to him. After her meeting with the DeSandos she feels that if any family can work out for Danny, this one can.

Her next session, in which she talks to Danny about them,

is a stormy one. Showing him their pictures, she tries to tell him a little about the DeSandos, but he says he's not interested because he is not moving. She tells him that he is. He says he'll get one of his friends' families to take him; she tells him that would not be approved. Mrs. Gardner keeps assuring Danny that this move can be good for him, that it can work out well. But he sits, tipped back in his chair, rolling his eyes to the ceiling and saying, "Sure, sure." Mrs. Gardner is frustrated. Here she has found a good family for this difficult-to-place youngster and he refuses to cooperate. Well, she thinks, maybe he'll come around after he meets them. At any rate, she is going ahead with the placement; the only other option is to move him to yet another foster home.

When Beth and Tony DeSando meet Danny for the first time he is obviously still resistant. They try to draw him out in conversation. He does seem very concerned about seeing their house and meeting their other children, so the DeSandos pick up on his lead and arrange to take him home for a short visit. As they ride in the car, Danny monopolizes the conversation, talking about the wild exploits of his gang. He gets carried away with himself, and talks about the powerful motorcycle he absolutely must have if he moves in with them, to cut down the time it would take him to commute to his old hangouts. When Tony points out that Danny at thirteen is nowhere near old enough to get a license for a motorcycle, Danny assures him that it will be okay. He'll just ride it carefully and not get himself picked up. The DeSandos have a terrible time trying to figure out how much of this talk is for real and how much is just to make an impression. They stall the motorcycle issue by explaining to Danny that if he needs a motorcycle, they can talk about it later. They say that Danny would be expected to earn half the money to pay for such an expensive item, hoping that by the time Danny could earn the money his ideas about needing a motorcycle would have changed.

At home the introductions to Sam, Gillian, and Adam seem to go fairly well. There is a quick tour of the house, and then Mrs. Gardner gets everyone together to go over the whys, hows, and whens of the proposed move. It is agreed that Danny will visit overnight the coming weekend and then spend the several remaining weekends here until the closing of school, when he will move in for good.

The following Friday, the DeSandos arrive in Danny's city early enough to have a conference with his schoolteachers in an attempt to get a better feel for this aspect of their new son's life. It seems that Danny is well known at school. He is not really a troublemaker, but he hangs around with a group who are, and seems to find much pleasure in their antics. He kids around in class a lot, paying little attention to the academic work; and he is notorious for the inventiveness of his stories about why he never hands in any homework.

Beth is very discouraged after this meeting. Next year Sam will be going to junior high school and it is important that he get off to a good start. What will be the effect of an older unmotivated brother on Sam? Is he likely to "catch" Danny's attitude?

Beth's fears about Danny's effect on the other children are amplified by Friday evening's visit. Danny the tough gang member has vanished, to be replaced by a slaphappy youngster who is extremely giddy and silly—more like an eight-year-old than a teen-ager. As Danny performs, Sam and Gillian get higher and higher. Dinner is a disaster. Not only are Danny's table manners terrible, but he soon has the other three children so wound up that finally Sam has to be sent from the table to finish his meal in the kitchen. Later, when Adam is told that it is time for him to be in bed, Danny coaxes Beth and Tony to let the little boy stay up longer, and he does it in such a way that six-year-old Adam is finally incited to a tearful protest and an ugly scene about his bedtime. The entire situation seems out of control. Beth and Tony begin to see that this adoption is not going to be as simple as they hoped.

Unexpectedly at breakfast the next morning, Danny informs them that he has to be back to his foster home right after lunch. It seems he has made plans that are not changeable. Cutting the planned visit short, the DeSandos pile everyone into the car. Again Danny takes over the conversation. He explores what his ground rules are to be. What will happen if he "forgets" and uses bad language? What will the DeSandos do if he comes in late? What are they going to do when he loses his temper and "goes mental"? It seems that when he is out of control he has been known to tear up the place and is likely to take on anybody. Beth feels the tension knotting up her stomach and the panic rising. What have they gotten themselves into? Sam, Gillian, and Adam sit wide-eyed, taking in the conversation. But Tony refuses to be shaken, in spite of the effect Danny is having on the rest of the family. Surely, he thinks, Danny must be exaggerating. "Danny," Tony says firmly, "if there is a problem in this family, we sit down and try to work it out. If you break rules, and you undoubtedly will in the beginning, we'll point out to you where you went wrong and we'll work something out."

As Danny gets out of the car at his foster home, several of his friends are waiting. They look the DeSandos over and snicker among themselves, making loud remarks about the family's personal appearance, their choice of clothing, and their automobile. Beth and Tony barely have a chance to calm the younger children down after this incident before Danny's foster mother comes to the door, saying, "Are you back so soon? Too bad — it was so nice without you." There is a heated exchange between the boy and his foster mother. No one seems even to notice when the DeSandos get into their car and drive away.

All the way home, Beth and Tony try to piece together what has happened. Danny is not going to be easy to deal with. There will have to be some quick changes in how they handle him. Next time, for example, they will not be so easily intimidated. *They* will be in charge. Part of what happened with the younger children was the result of letting Danny take over so completely. Sam has already taken a strong dislike to Danny — he thinks that he is "weird." Gillian and Adam are afraid of him. Beth and Tony reassure their children (and themselves) that next time things will be different. The rules do not change when Danny comes, and there is no reason for him to upset things so badly.

The DeSandos ought to get in touch with Mrs. Gardner quickly. Part of their trouble right now is in sorting out fact from fantasy. It is often hard to tell when a child like Danny is exaggerating, deliberately lying, kidding himself about his own toughness or importance, or trying to talk the prospective parents into giving up and going away. Mrs. Gardner will have a better idea of how much of what Danny says is real.

Two things come through clearly to Mrs. Gardner when she next talks to the DeSandos: Beth is obviously frightened by the potential problems Danny presents; and the DeSandos are still very much interested in adopting the child. The social worker talks to Beth at length. Is she having second thoughts? Does she want a little time to think about the adoption? Would it be a good idea to postpone next weekend's visit? Beth says that her concern is primarily about her own reactions to Danny. Much as she had wanted him to come, it was a great relief to get home after Danny's visit and to have things back to normal. What will it be like when he is there permanently and there is no relief from the upsets he causes? She is just as drawn as ever to the idea of having him; her hesitation is over her ability to solve the problems he brings with him. What if they can't do it?

Mrs. Gardner shares several reassuring pieces of information having to do with the lovingness locked up inside this young man and his conflicts about leaving the dependable companionship of his friends for the unknown strangeness of a new family. She tells them that Danny needs strong parents to help him feel less alone, more protected. He is clearly demonstrating that control is going to be a primary issue in this placement. "Take a firm stand," she tells them. "Being out of control is undoubtedly as frightening to Danny as it is to you." Beth and Tony talk about several things they want to try to make the next visit go more smoothly. Together the three adults begin to work out a plan to deal with Danny's behavior. Leah Gardner hangs up the phone relieved to have found a family so willing to give the placement a try. They are showing real commitment to Danny. For his sake, Mrs. Gardner hopes they will continue to respond this way.

Later Mrs. Gardner talks with Danny about how his initial visit went. When confronted with her opinion that he was out-of-bounds in an attempt to scare the DeSandos off, the boy laughs uneasily, denying that he did anything out of the ordinary. He thought that the DeSandos were nice people, he says, but he wouldn't be interested in a family with all those little kids. He suggests that maybe Mrs. Gardner has somebody else who really needs a home and could go to the DeSandos.

Unable to sway his worker, Danny calls Beth from school the next morning. "Hey," he says, "something has come up and I can't make it to your house on Saturday." Beth has a momentary sinking feeling — "Here we go again." But this time she is more ready for Danny. Determined to go ahead, she is just not going to let him casually call things off. Firmly Beth tells Danny that she is really sorry to hear he has a problem about the weekend, but that they have made arrangements with Mrs. Gardner to pick Danny up on Friday. If he wants to change the plan he will have to call his social worker and work something out with her.

After she hangs up, Beth calls Leah Gardner to alert her to Danny's intentions. Soon the boy calls in. He is insistent that he doesn't want to miss out on the weekend with his friends. Mrs. Gardner schedules a meeting with him the following day to talk things over. For the rest of the day she has a hard time concentrating on her work. What is she going to do? How should she handle Danny? How much should she force him?

She nabs a bit of her supervisor's time to talk things out with her. While the two women are talking, Danny's foster mother calls. She has been visited by a police officer wanting information about one of Danny's friends. "I've had it! Get this kid out of here," she demands. "If you don't pick Danny and his junk up by Friday afternoon, I'll put him in a cab and send him to you."

"Look," says Mrs. Gardner reasonably, "that gives us only two days to make plans for him. Surely you can hang on a little longer." But no appeal works; the foster mother refuses to change her mind.

Now Mrs. Gardner anxiously considers her problem with the supervisor. Can another foster home be found on such short notice? Both women keep coming back to the same possibility — maybe the DeSandos would be willing to take Danny. Would that be a bad idea? It would be rushing things, but it would also save Danny from having to be moved twice. On the other hand, he is so agitated already. Is it fair to the DeSandos to push it? Maybe Danny needs a cooling-off period before he joins an adoptive family. Finally, they call the DeSandos to involve them in making the decision.

Beth answers Mrs. Gardner's call with a laugh. "I thought I might be hearing from you — did Danny call?" "I wish that were my only problem," the social worker replies. "Danny called this morning. His foster mother called early this afternoon — she is throwing him out. He has to leave on Friday."

A seldom used expletive bursts from Beth. Mrs. Gardner listens while Beth thinks out loud. "I suppose he could go to another foster family . . . no, that's dumb. What would that do? . . . What if . . . maybe we should . . . no, we're nowhere near ready for him . . . but . . . Look," Beth finally says, "let me get in touch with Tony and get back to you, okay?" Knowing how crowded Beth must feel, Mrs. Gardner encourages her to take all the time she needs. She says that it will be perfectly understandable if the DeSandos decide to proceed with the end-of-school date agreed on before.

While she waits to hear from Beth and Tony, Mrs. Gardner begins to look into what other arrangements can be made on such short notice. No one is eager to take Danny, but there is a possible opening in one of the foster homes she gets in touch with. She has visions of Friday evening arriving with no choice available. Who will provide a bed for Danny? Must she?

Meanwhile Beth has driven down to talk with Tony at work. They are both very angry at Danny's foster mother for being so unconcerned about what happens to him. They weigh the pros and cons. Eventually they call Mrs. Gardner with the decision that, although this is not how they would have chosen to move Danny, it seems foolish to think that a temporary foster home would have any advantage for anyone. The best way to find out how things are going to work with this adoption, they say, is just to go ahead and try it. Their concern for and emotional investment in Danny come across clearly.

Everyone is hurting for Danny. The adults talk about how they might help this proud teen-ager save face and feel more in control of his life. Mrs. Gardner suggests that they negotiate a contract with Danny, with everyone agreeing to the terms of the arrangement. The DeSandos realize that Danny will have to adopt them as much as they will be adopting him. It is important that he not feel the relationship as just an imposition on him, without his having any say in the matter. If at the end of the contracted time Danny wants out, the DeSandos will agree to let him go.

This kind of contract is a very useful tool in placing teenagers. In it the concerns of the youngster are given equal weight with the concerns of the adopting parents. The contract is drawn up following open discussion. It states how long the trial period will be; who is to be responsible for deciding bedtime, curfew, hair style, rules, and chores; what the rules will be about smoking or drinking; how disputes will be settled; and anything else of importance to the teen-ager and his new parents. As for the length of the trial period, six months seems to be the absolute minimum, with one year being a more logical choice. Steps for renegotiating any other part of the contract (such as the changing of a rule) should be spelled out in detail. Frequently, small parts of the contract are set up for shorter time periods. For example, the contracting parties may agree to try a particular set of rules and expectations for a month, with the stipulation that these items will be renegotiated at the end of that time. One of the items often included as a renegotiable part of such a contract is what the youngster is to call his new parents —Mom and Dad, first names, or some other title. Spelling this out takes away some of the tension inherent in this somewhat awkward part of adding a teen-ager to the family.

Things settled with the DeSandos, Leah Gardner drives to the foster home to tell Danny that he is moving. Danny does not take the news easily. Jumping up from his chair at the kitchen table and knocking it into a cabinet, he begins to shout at his foster mother. "I never did anything to you—why are you doing this to me?" He pounds his fist on the counter. "Why are you kicking me out? What did I do? I don't want to move." Mrs. Gardner and the foster mother try to calm him down and assure him that the DeSandos want him and that they will be a good family for him. "Oh yeah, tell me more," is his angry reply. Danny stomps around, shoving furniture, kicking the refrigerator. He continues to shout, drowning out any attempts at reason. Finally he storms up the stairs and slams his bedroom door, sobbing loudly with tears of anger and frustration. The women in the kitchen are shaken by the confrontation. Mrs. Gardner tries one more time to get the foster mother to reconsider and give Danny a little more time, but it is no use. Plans are made for Mrs. Gardner to be at the foster home to pick Danny up after school on Friday.

Tony DeSando stays home from work on Thursday. He and Beth spend the day fixing up a bedroom and emptying out a chest and closet for Danny. Both of them are exhausted; neither slept well last night. There is a sense of resignation — things have been set in motion and no one knows how fate will respond. Later in the day Beth bakes her special devil's food cake and spreads it with thick fudge frosting to make things seem more festive. The children make signs that say "Welcome Home, Danny" and hang them in the front hall.

At four-thirty on Friday Danny arrives with Mrs. Gardner. He seems quiet, and a little unfocused. The contract is discussed, rules negotiated. Surprisingly, Danny voices little opposition to any of the suggestions. When it comes to deciding what he will call his parents, he astounds them by saying that he feels perfectly comfortable about calling them Mom and Dad. He also wants to use DeSando as his last name at school. Beth and Tony don't know why he is so willing to assume the outer trappings of being one of them, but it makes them feel some relief. Maybe he will try to fit in. Maybe it won't be as uphill a struggle as they had feared.

After arranging to visit the family regularly through the adjustment period, Mrs. Gardner leaves. Danny seems thoughtful and emotionally spent. Nobody quite knows what to do. A celebration would seem forced and unnatural. Danny listens quietly to the expressions of welcome from the other children and dutifully admires their signs. After dinner he watches television a little; then he goes up to bed, explaining that he is tired because he hasn't slept too well for the past couple of nights.

Tony and Beth are not far behind him. The house settles into darkness. Danny is home.

For the next few days Danny seems numb, as if there has been too much change. Assaulted by the barrage of events, he seems to have walled the world out, letting reality in a bit at a time. He is subdued, while Beth finds herself to be the one who is acting anxious. Intellectually she knows that she should give Danny some space and not crowd him emotionally, but she has difficulty pacing herself. She wants to jump in, buttonhole Danny, and explain herself and the family to him immediately. Surely, if he just gets to know them he will trust them and feel that this is a good place to be.

Part of Beth's anxiety is the fear that something may happen to destroy this placement before it has taken hold. She runs at Danny full tilt, her fears of becoming overinvolved and getting hurt fluctuating with the fear that she may not get involved soon enough.

Beth knows that she is acting as if she could cram a year or two of living into a week or two, and that what she is doing doesn't make sense. But she wants to know everything about Danny right now. What makes him tick? Who is he, really? Partly she is just trying to get over the newness so that everything can get back to normal. She has to work hard at controlling herself, to keep focused on what is best for Danny.

This is not an uncommon beginning in older child adoption. One person needs a lot of space, while another needs closeness. One person forms relationships by circling around cautiously, while the other needs instant intimacy. In this case it is the parent who will probably have to adjust her speed to match the child's need. Already bombarded with newness, the child is less able to change his personal tempo.

Beth and Tony have decided to start off with Danny by working on his school performance. For him to make no effort at school, they feel, would be a bad choice. It involves him for most of the day in an environment where he doesn't measure up, and to graduate with a poor school record will limit his options as a black adult. So Danny's new parents take a stand from the beginning, making it clear that while there will be no punish-

ment for low grades, Danny will be expected to try. He is to do
his homework and to prepare himself for tests; and he is to pay
attention in school. They will help him any time he asks. They
expect that once Danny begins to work at school he will succeed.
His success will help him feel better about himself, and his cycle
of failure should stop. They don't expect him to do a lot of
catching up during these last six weeks of school, but they do
hope to help him establish a pattern of study habits that will
be useful next year. This will be his first experience that they
mean what they say, and will follow through on it.

It is unrealistic for parents to think they can make their
children succeed. But there are ways that they can try to structure the environment and the events surrounding their new
child to make success more likely. Bruno Bettelheim (1950) has
shown that there is a readiness to move that occurs at the beginning and ending of the school year and also at Christmas recess,
because these mark off logical, calendar-supported changes to
children. But it is interesting that some workers and families
find benefits in moving a child just before the ending of school.
It is not a time of academic pressure in many schools; often the
staff and students are just marking time. And it gives the child a
chance to meet other children while school is in session, a much
easier time to do so than over summer vacation. It takes away
the strangeness that makes some children spend summer in
dread of the unknown new school. And it provides the school
staff with a chance to become familiar with the child so that
good plans can be made for the coming year.

Beth and Tony give Danny a little time to take on his new
academic responsibilities. During this period he does very little
homework, explaining that "the teacher didn't assign anything"
or that he "did it in school." Beth and Tony are not convinced.
They realize that they will have to stay on top of the situation if
they hope to modify Danny's longstanding aversion to schoolwork. At the end of two weeks, they call the school and schedule
a group conference with all of Danny's teachers in the guidance
office.

The conference is very interesting. The teachers all like
Danny and are not intimidated by his rough appearance and

speech. But in their desire to help him adjust to his new situation, they have responded to him with too much pity; and Danny has taken advantage of this, milking their sympathy to avoid handing in expected assignments. There have been weekly tests both in Danny's math and his social studies classes, and his scores have been all "D"s and "F"s. In addition, Danny has begun to hang around with the "troublemakers" at school, and is beginning to be very flippant when he talks in class.

Beth and Tony share some of their concerns with the teachers. They try to enlist their cooperation in setting consistent expectations of effort. They point out that it is important to prevent Danny from getting behind or out of control at school. If the teachers treat Danny as a basket case, they say, he will become one. If they just feel sorry for him they are likely to teach him that he has the right to give up and to feel sorry for himself, that life owes him something and he has the right to demand more and more. The teachers agree to keep the DeSandos posted. If Danny is not doing his homework, they will let his parents know.

Beth and Tony also talk to their new son. "What's the idea of telling us you didn't have work to do? What are you trying to pull? From now on your teachers are going to be clueing us in about what is going on at school, so you'd better get to it, Danny."

The following week Beth gets a call from Danny's science teacher. Yesterday, it seems, the teacher took the class out onto the school grounds to do some field work. Danny was a problem the whole period, clowning around and acting foolish. Twenty minutes before the class was over he and another boy disappeared. They were spotted by another teacher and sent to the principal's office, a fact that Danny had neglected to mention at home as he assured his parents that it had been a good day.

Today the teacher gave a test on the previous day's work and Danny cut class. When the teacher noticed him getting on the school bus and asked where he had been, Danny said he hadn't been feeling well and that he had spent the period in the nurse's office. A subsequent check with the nurse revealed that

Danny had looked in at the nurse's door, muttered something about trying to find a friend, and then disappeared.

Lying

When Beth and Tony confront Danny, he is extremely slippery. It is hard to pin him down as he switches stories.

"Where were you last period today, Danny?"

"At school. How come you're asking?"

"You may have been at school, but your science teacher says you weren't in your science class where you belonged."

"Oh, that."

"Danny, where were you?"

"In the nurse's office."

"Come on, Danny, the nurse says you were only there for a minute."

"Yeah, then I felt sick and went to the bathroom."

"Then what did you do?"

"When?"

"After you went to the bathroom."

"I don't know. I guess I was there a long time."

"You spent the whole period in the bathroom?"

"Yeah, I guess so."

"What about yesterday. Your science teacher says you took off and cut the end of class."

"She is such a nerd. I didn't do anything wrong—I thought we were dismissed."

"How come you thought so? The bell didn't ring."

"We weren't doing anything but looking at some dumb stuff and I thought we were through."

"The other kids didn't seem to think so."

"Well, a bunch of us did."

"Your teacher says it was just you and Robert."

"Oh, I thought some other kids were coming."

"Then you ended up in the principal's office, huh?"

"No."

"You *didn't?*"

"Well, not exactly. I saw him in the hall."

"Was he mad?"

"I dunno. I guess so."

"How come you didn't say anything to us about this yesterday?"

"I forgot."

"You *forgot?*"

"Well, I guess I didn't think it was very important."

As Danny talks he changes his story several times. In trying to give the "right" answer, he seems to make no critical evaluation of what he is saying. He is just concentrating on figuring out what his parents want him to say. What can he get by with? What will they believe? What will get them off his back? The things he says appear to have bypassed his reason altogether. It is as if he will say anything, whether it makes sense or not, to establish that he is blameless. Talking to the DeSandos about this problem, Mrs. Gardner confirms their feeling that it is wise to keep trying to make Danny accountable for what he says, and to do so in a way that clearly conveys their disbelief without attacking him as a "liar." Sometimes parents are so angered by their child's dishonesty, and so engrossed in teaching him to be trustworthy, that they give the child the impression that he will always be a "liar" or a "thief" or a "dishonest person."

Stealing and lying are just behavioral failures in learning, or misguided learning. Perhaps the child has not realized that such behavior is unacceptable. Many times older adopted children have consistently been lied to by adults. There may have been a biological parent who promised, "Someday you will come back home and everything will be fine. We'll all be together again"—or who promised visits but never came, or said a present was on the way that never arrived. Sometimes a foster parent will have promised wrongly that the child could always stay; or will have said that an injection wouldn't hurt when it did; or will have promised treats, parties, outings that never happened. Perhaps adults have made these statements to soothe the child, to alleviate feelings of guilt, or to get the child to stop bothering them. But the child "layers" unreliability and dishonesty from past parents onto his new parents. When they promise him something, he hears all the unkept promises from the past and expects nothing to come of what they say. Some children do not allow themselves to anticipate pleasures. Others nag: "When are we going? You said you'd take me. Why can't we go now?"—leaving the new parents defensively wondering what they have done to earn such distrust.

Children like this frequently have no scruples about breaking promises themselves. They casually promise another child a gift, a toy, a turn, and then explain their failure to follow through by insisting that they only said "maybe." The other children, feeling they have been set up, tend to respond angrily; they try zealously to correct a fault that they may have only recently overcome themselves.

To combat this kind of "layering" a parent can point out times when the child is inappropriately carrying something over from the past. The parent may say, "I think you are confusing me with someone else who let you down. I do what I say." In dealing with the child's own lack of followthrough on what he says, the parent can explain, "Different families have different rules. In this family when we tell someone we are going to do something, we do it." In time the parent's reliability becomes established and accepted by the child.

Another way that newly adopted older children bend the truth is by exaggerating or bragging. Sometimes they do it to save face ("I knew how to do that—I just didn't want to"). Sometimes they do it to impress ("My other father let me fly his airplane all the time"). Sometimes they do it out of loyalty ("My first father was the president of a big company and the tallest man in the world"), or they do it to avoid being pitied ("In my first family we had ice cream whenever we wanted it, any flavor, three times a day"). Sometimes they do it to manipulate ("My foster mother always let me stay up to watch the late show"). This bragging tends to bring the wrath of other children down upon them. And the new parents are liable to get stuck on the comparisons, fearing that the child is saying that he doesn't like his new family very well, instead of seeing the behavior for what it is—an outgrowth of low self-esteem. They may make the mistake of trying to set the child straight about how much better this family is than any other place he has lived, encouraging him to make comparisons instead of focusing on the child's need to learn to value himself, to feel safe and loved. When the child's sense of self becomes more positive, this kind of "lying" disappears.

Many times the child is dishonest not by what he actually says, but by what he implies. It is common for children to be selective about which grades and what parts of the school day are reported to their parents—the good is relayed, the bad forgotten. That is part of the problem that the DeSandos are having with Danny. But Danny takes it a step further, using omission to slip out of things.

When Tony gets home one day, for example, Beth is furious at Danny. She and Danny have been having words lately about the state of his room. Each day Beth has reminded him that he is expected to make his bed and to pick up his dirty clothing. This afternoon as Danny left to play baseball with some friends, the last thing that she asked him was if he had done his room. "Yeah," he had called over his shoulder as he zipped out the door. Later, when Beth took up some clean laundry to put it away, Danny's room was a mess. The bed was not made and there was at least two days worth of clothing accumulated on the floor.

When Danny comes in for supper, his parents are on him. "How come you told your mother you did your room when you left today?"

"I did my room."

"Danny, come up with us and take a look at it. Does this look done to you?"

"Oh, I didn't know she meant did I do my room *today*. I just thought . . . "

"You just thought what?"

"Well, you know."

Every single detail has to be spelled out or Danny finds a loophole and uses it. Having once given himself an excuse, even an impossibly flimsy one, Danny adheres to what he has said as if it were gospel truth.

Children like Danny are likely to use strategies to manipulate their parents by putting the guilt onto the adult. "You don't trust me," they may say in an attempt to activate the adult's sympathy. The parent must resist assuming the blame, and be able to reply without guilt, "No, I don't, but I would like to," thus sending an accurate message about his own feelings and including the expectation that the distrust can be defeated by the child's own future actions. Children also will imply that their parents are glad the child is in trouble, or that they are accused "just because I made one mistake today," or that the parent is "trying to pin it on" the child.

Parents can best help a child stop lying by minimizing the gain realized from a lie and making it difficult for him to get by with an untruth. If the child finds that he stands to lose from dishonesty he becomes convinced in time that more honest behavior is in his best interest. The parents have to be willing to keep a close check on what is actually happening in their child's life until he is able to be truthful; they should confront him when he denies known fact, pointing it out when he changes his story.

It is vital to helping a child become more honest for the parents to be absolutely trustworthy themselves. A promise made must be kept. Any plans that are conditional should be spelled out that way ("Tomorrow, if it doesn't rain, we'll go to the beach"). It is wise for parents to refrain, at least in the beginning, from making promises that can't be fulfilled within twenty-four hours.

Parents must scrupulously practice "congruency." What they say and do must match how they feel one-hundred percent of the time. They should refrain from hugging the child they want to smack. If they are hesitant to let their child do something they should say so, rather than just giving reluctant permission and leaving the child aware of their conflicting messages. A parent who is irritated by the child who stalls about going to bed should say so, instead of smiling with pretended patience.

Does This Child Have a Conscience?

Dishonesty is one kind of behavior that is most likely to cause new parents of an older child to overreact. Usually their response comes from an inner fear that the child will grow up without a conscience, unable to tell right from wrong.

> A conscience, in the proper sense of the word, consists of standards and prohibitions which have been taken over by the personality and which govern behavior from within. Such an internal system of standards will usually not require outside controls to support it. When one has a conscience he forbids himself to do certain things, checks his impulses, experiences guilt reactions for transgressions, without the need for a "policeman" outside (Fraiberg 1959, p. 147).

Parents who worry about the morality of their child need to know that conscience development is a continuing process.

Conscience comes about as the child understands and accepts his parents' standards. Part of the process can be clearly seen in the toddler who is confronted by his parent's displeasure when he overturns the full ashtray on the coffee table. "No, no, don't touch," says the mother as she taps the child's hand and removes the ashtray. If she consistently prohibits the child from playing in the ashes, he begins to understand the connection. The time comes when the child can be heard telling himself "No, no" as he grabs the forbidden ashtray; he has the idea but he still lacks the control to carry it through. In time, this same child may be seen to slow his hand as he reaches for the ashtray, or to slap his own hand as if he were his mother. Finally, the child is able to stop himself before he touches the ashtray at all.

The development of a healthy and adequate conscience is a complicated job. Unlike physical development, the ability to control one's impulses does not come to the child unless he is required to learn it. The child has no inherited tendencies to be good or bad, selfish or unselfish, to control himself or his temper. The incentive comes from his parents through a process called "attachment."

Attachment grows out of the child's anxiety and discomfort when he needs food or physical attention. Noticing the child's need, his parent satisfies it and the child's anxiety and discomfort disappear. The child feels safe. In time, the child comes to identify his feelings of security with his loving caretaker. This attachment process is intensified because the parent not only relieves distress but also initiates positive interaction with the child, making him feel even more safe and content. Because the child is anxious when there is emotional distance between him and the adult, he is motivated to behave in ways that minimize the chances that the adult will be angry or displeased with him. Eventually the child goes a step further and incorporates the parental standards within himself, trying to become the kind of person the loved adult would like him to be.

Many older adopted children, for several reasons, have areas of delayed conscience development. Maybe there was not enough affection and attention from the adults in the child's past for him to become properly attached. Maybe the child had formed a stable attachment to an adult only to lose that person, and has abandoned his own attachment to the one he feels has abandoned him; therefore the child denies previously learned values and prohibitions. Maybe several moves have caused continual interruptions in the attachment process. Maybe the child has lived with adults who confused him with inconsistent standards, permitting an action some of the time, and forbidding it at others.

Some of these children are like the toddler who knew it was wrong to play with the ashtray but whose conscience was not yet strong enough to help him resist temptation. Others have developed a "post-action" conscience that does not raise its voice at the moment of temptation but envelops the child after he transgresses — just like the parent who is too uninterested or rejecting to help the child keep out of trouble, but then descends upon him in fury for the discomfort he has caused (Redl and Wineman 1951, p. 239).

Normally the close link between feelings of being loved and approved of by the parents and the child's personal self-esteem makes the child feel guilty when he does something the parents think wrong. But until the new child knows what this family considers unacceptable, and until he trusts in the love and approval of his new parents, his behavior is controlled by fear — fear of punishment, or of moving again.

> If fear of punishment from the outside, instead of the child's own guilt feelings, sets off the danger signal, there are a number of subterfuges open to the child. He may only need to assure himself that he will not be found out in order to pursue his mischief. Or, calculating the pleasure-pain risks, he may decide to have his fun even if he has to pay for it later. . . . Some children have an elaborate accounting system which permits them to go into debt on the "sin" side of the ledger up to a certain amount and pay off periodically on the punishment side by getting themselves spanked. With the ledger balanced, such a child can make a fresh start and go into debt again (Fraiberg 1959, pp. 253-54).

Moved children frequently have learned to make excuses to their consciences that make their forbidden actions permissible and prevent them from feeling guilty or anxious. "He did it first," they say, and "Everybody else does it"; or, "Somebody else did it to me before"; "He had it coming"; "I made up for it afterwards"; "It doesn't matter because he's a no-good so-and-so himself"; "Everybody is against me, nobody likes me, they are always picking on me."

Reputable child psychologists tell us that "although the strength of conscience may vary from child to child we have never seen a child in whom it is totally absent" (Redl and Wineman 1952, p. 19). Even severely delinquent children understand "making a deal" or "not ratting," or have an idea of what constitutes "playing fair" in their group. Overseas adopted children, many of whom have been taught that it is all right or even necessary to steal, frequently have deep convictions that it is wrong to reveal the transgressions of another. Most children have some loopholes where they have rescued memories of some relationship from the past; parents should look for these values and build upon them.

Because conscience development depends upon attachment, there are some things that have to happen before the child begins to show signs of improved self-control in his new home. Attachments take time to develop; the same person must be involved in relieving the child's discomfort and anxiety over a prolonged period. The length of time varies considerably. Some children display an "attachment readiness" — if there has been a stretch of happy childhood, the child is just waiting for the right person to enter his life and give him affection; and he doesn't hesitate long before he identifies with some of the adult's values. Other children, who have had a frequent turnover of uninterested or hostile adults in their lives, hardly know how to like new people anymore. They have to start learning what it means to like, and especially what it means to be attached, all over again (Redl and Wineman 1951, p. 240).

The child's fear of letting himself become vulnerable and dependent sometimes gets in the way of the attachment process. Some children attempt to resolve this dilemma by denying that the new adults in their lives actually do offer them love and security. These children refuse to acknowledge acts of affection or gratification, focusing instead on privation, real or imagined. The child who has just been outfitted with new sneakers, new jeans, a hand-knit sweater, and a new windbreaker of his own choosing dissolves when refused a piece of penny bubble gum, insisting, "You never give me anything" — to which his parent wisely responds, "How can you say that when . . . ."

Sometimes the child has built his whole value system upon what Erik Erikson terms "basic distrust." Unlike the normal child, he has not learned to associate adults with pleasant experiences; he has not found that adults meet his needs in predictable ways, nor that they can be counted on in times of trouble. More likely, he has learned that adults are connected with unpleasant experiences, fail to provide what he needs, and can even be dangerous to him. The behavior of such children suggests that they view others with uncertainty and suspicion. Their distrust has often served them well when faced with a threatening or unpredictable adult, and it is understandable that they act the same way towards new parents. From the child's point of view, it is likely that he is being deceived, that beneath the friendly facade of the adult is a person who is not to be trusted. When the new adult tries to convince the child otherwise, the child is apt to become even more suspicious or frightened, and may develop strategies to prove that he is right.

> Threatened by an adult attitude of acceptance and friendliness which might force them to admit our fairness and make them feel ashamed or guilty, they try to make us angry, make us act in a way which they can easily interpret as being hostile (Redl and Wineman 1951, p. 218).

> The same ego which knows just how "mad" the adult is at any given moment and when it is safe to goad and provoke just a little more, is not able to tell when the adult loves, when he is fair and reasonable (Redl and Wineman 1952, p. 20).

These children may try to get the upper hand, to render the adult harmless so that they need not fear the adult so much. They develop an amazing repertory of behaviors that serve to neutralize the effectiveness of the adult, putting *him* on the defensive. They sometimes strip the adult of his composure and competence, hoping that he will retreat in fear; and frequently they try to prove the adult untrustworthy by catching him in a lie (Trieschman, Whittaker, and Brendtro 1969, p. 68). Ner Littner (1956) describes how sometimes the child's behavior develops an edge to it, and the new parents start feeling rejected, frustrated, or angry. Or perhaps the child begins to step on his parents' emotional corns, causing them to withdraw, to reject him and thereby provide him with an excuse to be angry at them. When this happens the parents may need assistance in resisting the child's efforts at manipulating them. They can be helped to understand and accept what is happening, and not to withdraw, reject, or retaliate even though they are angry at the child.

Sometimes the child's need for distance from his new parents stems from the fear that loving them implies disloyalty to other parents. This is particularly so in children whose early experiences forced them to take sides and to love only one adult at a time.

In attempting to become attractive to a new child and to encourage the attachment process, parents should avoid the following three things in particular:

1. Building oneself up by criticizing other adults the child has known. This tends to make him dislike past pieces of himself and to assume the implied inferiority. Many adopted children already have "bad seed" feelings about themselves stemming from weaknesses they feel they have inherited, and they do not need to have these feelings reinforced.
2. Being too lenient. Most of these children need external controls; they may even ask for them. They need the fear of punishment or the outside control of an attentive adult before their attachment can form and their conscience can catch up in its development.
3. Being one of the gang. The biggest lesson that many of these children need to learn is how to relate to adult authority figures (Trieschman, Whittaker, and Brendtro 1969, p. 89).

A growing body of research suggests that children may be more susceptible to becoming attached at times of stress, anxiety, fear, illness, or fatigue (Rutter 1972, p. 19). Certainly a move to a new family involves several of these states. First, there is the point of entry, a significant change in the child's life containing elements of fear, stress, and fatigue; second, there is the letting go of those good things that did exist in his previous life, involving anxiety; and third, there is the reestablishment of himself in his new life. All these things tend to cause a period of disruption in his personality and to add to a lack of inner stability. New parents should remember that there is a potential for growth present in this stressful situation. Even though they may fight it, children are particularly vulnerable to attachment after a move. The child has a drive to reorient himself, to get started up again, to take on new modes and standards. If an adult is present who provides comfort and helps the child through a trying situation, attachment is fostered.

Rutter also points out that "attachments probably develop most readily to persons who can adapt their behavior to the specific requirements of the individual child, taking into consideration his individuality and by learning to recognize his particular signals. It may be the intensity rather than the duration of the interaction which is the crucial factor" (Rutter 1972, pp. 18-19).

Placement of teen-agers involves both special problems and special advantages when it comes to reactivating the attachment process. On the one hand, the need for members of the family to become close comes at the same time that the child's developmental task is to become independent, to prepare himself to leave the family. Those teen-agers who have already been on their own, who have never known or long ago forgotten the pleasures of family closeness, are particularly hard to reach. Many of these youths seemingly could not care less about adult approval or belonging. Instead they tend to exaggerate their differences from the adult by behavior, dress, or language that is directly opposite to the adult standard. Indeed they may reject the family so totally that placement is not appropriate for them because they refuse to let it work. But on the other hand, adolescence is a time when a great many teen-agers look about them for adults to pattern themselves after, and they are open to choosing their new parents as models. Some teen-agers who have been without a secure place in a family harbor a deep hunger to belong, to have parents to fill their ungratified dependency needs. The "age swings" seen in most displaced older children, the crisis of the move, and the need for a role model all tend to make the positive values in the teen-ager's personality retrievable, and placement an excellent opportunity for both child and family.

Because conscience development is a continuing process, and not completely independent of outside authority until the child leaves his parents in late adolescence, parents need not fear that there is no hope that the child who lies, steals, is selfish, or carelessly or deliberately damages things, can become more reliable as he matures.

Sexuality

Sometimes the family's concern about a newly added teen-age child centers on a very special issue—the new youngster's obvious and vital sexuality. This can shake families deeply. The normal triangulation that occurs whenever a new member enters a family may develop thorny complications if the new person is a physically maturing teen-ager. Sometimes the problem arises because the youngster has witnessed "love" only in its sexual side and lacks the ability to display affection in other ways, or because the teen-ager does not perceive that he or she can get affection and attention in other ways than sex. Such a child can be frankly seductive, setting off warning signals in one or both of the new parents.

Sometimes the emerging sexuality of a teen-age youngster poses a psychological threat to a parent whose own sexuality is on the wane, who sees himself as aging and less attractive, and who feels jealous that the youngster will soon have experiences that are not available to the parent. Sometimes the arrival of the maturing teen-ager reveals areas in the parents' relationship where there are past problems or anxieties in their sexual adjustment. Areas of sexual vulnerability in both child and adoptive parents should be carefully considered at the time of placement.

Workers sometimes quietly express the concern that placing a teen-ager in a family with other maturing youngsters may encourage incestual relationships in the children who have not been raised together long enough to have absorbed some of society's strongly communicated taboo. Somehow this rarely turns out to be a problem. By the time the new member of the family has settled in enough for intimacy he or she is viewed as a brother or sister; in much the same way, colleges have found that coeducational dormitories where meals are shared tend to discourage sexual relationships among the men and women who live under the same roof.

Good judgment should be exercised in the kinds of physical affection dished out by the parent of the opposite sex to the teen-ager, to avoid confusing or inappropriately stimulating the youngster. And it is important to remember that it is not the amount of sexual information a youngster has that causes problems, but how she or he chooses to use it. It is never a good idea to withhold facts about sex and reproduction from a teen-ager.

Beth and Tony DeSando have not had any particular worries about Danny sexually; their hardest problem has been the everyday rule-making and permission-giving, and the conscious thought and effort this takes. Even though both adults have had experience with teen-agers, they have never before been parents to one. Now they have to decide all at once how they feel about what freedoms Danny should be allowed and where he should be restricted. It is hard for them to decide what is reasonable.

Danny has spent most of his life being his own boss. Now he has parents who want to know where he is when he is not at home, whom he is with, what he is doing, and when to expect him. They expect that if his plans change, Danny will call in and let somebody know. Danny agreed to do this when they signed the contract, but it is obvious that he thinks it is an unnecessary infringement of his rights. The DeSandos are having little luck helping him see that they are not just trying to check up on him. This rule holds for everyone in the family — Tony and Beth never leave without telling the children where they will be and when to expect them. But Danny doesn't understand that in this family people worry about one another and that it bothers them if they don't know how to get in touch with each other.

Danny is also quick to make plans that take him away from home all the time. He would like to leave for school, spend the afternoon hanging around with his friends, slip in for dinner, and then be gone until bedtime. Beth and Tony feel strongly that Danny is not to be a boarder in their home; eventually he has to become one of the family. As far as they are concerned, this means he has to spend time with the family so everyone can begin to build up relationships with one another. So far, the DeSandos have stuck to the arrangement that Danny can either be away during the afternoon and spend the evening at home, or put in some time with the family after school and make plans with his friends for after dinner. They have explained this expectation to him, but still he pushes them about it. Time after time he asks if he can be away during the periods he is supposed to be at home, and he is amazed when the answer is "No." His response is usually that he must have heard wrong—they can't be serious. Staring at them challengingly, he rewords the question three or four times: "You mean I can't . . . ? Well, what if . . . ? Well, how come . . . ?" It is hard for Beth not to back down, and she is the one Danny usually tackles first.

The issue is still not settled when permission is denied. Danny huffs, sulks, shuts himself off, avoids conversation. When his parents confront his unreasonableness, he has nothing to say.

Many older adopted children have very refined abilities to manipulate. They use a number of techniques in trying to get around their parents:

1. They sulk, hanging on to their resentments, grudgingly doing what is asked of them and then blaming their moodiness on the parent ("You made me be that way," or "I did it because you wouldn't let me [or you made me] do . . . ").
2. They storm out, refusing to discuss the situation by removing themselves.
3. They storm in, refusing to talk at all, even in response to direct questions.
4. They change the subject, bringing up past injustices or disagreements, frequently using "You always . . . " or "You never . . . " as the point of departure.

The Parents' Right to Make Rules

Beth and Tony are especially vulnerable to Danny's behavior; he is their first teen-age child and they have not had time to resolve clearly their own feelings about what kinds of rules are necessary, normal, and enforceable. In addition, they are in an unusual situation. They know that their rules for Sam at age thirteen will probably be different from their rules for Danny, because they have had more chance to help Sam develop good judgment and work within family expectations and standards. It is hard to find the balance between restricting Danny enough that he draws strength from being one of them, and irritating him so much that he is driven to define himself as a separate individual and reject their values and support. There is constant pressure from the feeling that time is running out as Danny gets older. There is so much he needs to learn, and so limited a time.

Not only is there a problem with forbidding Danny to do some things, but there is also the problem of telling him he has to do others. What if he refuses, saying, "You can't make me — you're not my real parents"? Although most parents of older adopted children feel in retrospect that they should have been firm sooner in disciplining their child, they are often slow to do so because of their own mixed feelings about their right to enforce rules — an ambivalence often shared by the new child. Alfred Kadushin points out that "the less ambivalence there is about such entitlement the more limited is the conflict in application of discipline" (Kadushin 1971, p. 201).

Beth eventually has a run-in with Danny that makes her conscious of her own anxiety in this area. Last Friday Danny brought home a math pre-test on decimals. It was obvious that he was confused about what he was supposed to do and how he was supposed to do it. Tony worked with him over the weekend to try to figure out where Danny's confusion lay. This morning the boy's father reminded him to bring home his math book so that they could work on the homework assignment together.

But today has been very hot and muggy, one of those still, late June days when no one has much ambition. Danny comes in after school and fixes himself a cold drink. He plans to bicycle up to the local Y.M.C.A. for a cool swim. As he talks to Beth about his day, something nudges her memory uncomfortably. "Hey, Danny," she says, "where's your math book?" Danny sits quietly. "I guess I forgot it," he says.

"Danny, you have math last period on Mondays. You had to make a trip to your locker to put your book away in order to 'forget' it. I can understand why doing math is no treat on such a hot day, but Dad has a meeting tomorrow and tonight's the time he can help."

Danny just shrugs his shoulders, as if to say, "Well, what do you want me to do about it?" Beth would like to let it go, but this kind of thing has been happening too often lately. She decides she has to take a stand.

"Look, Danny," she says, "I'm sorry, but you're just going to have to hop on your bike and go back to school for the book. Then you can go swimming."

Danny has ten reasons why that is a rotten plan—it's too hot, he'll get the book tomorrow, Dad won't mind, and so forth. He calls to the friend who has appeared at the screen door, "I'll be there in a minute." But Beth stands firm. There is no reason that Danny can't go swimming, but he'll have to go get his book first. She leaves the kitchen and sits down in the living room with the newspaper, feeling slightly sick. What is she going to do if Danny ignores her and goes to the pool? She hears the boy saying something to his friend, but she can't make out what it is. Then Danny stomps up the stairs to his room. Beth leans her head back on the couch, her eyes closed and her mind churning. After what seems like hours, Danny comes downstairs in his swimsuit, his towel rolled under his arm.

"I'm going straight to the pool after I get the book, okay?" he says challengingly. Relief pouring through her, Beth replies, "Sure, have a good time." She listens to him take off on his bicycle, thinking, "He did it. He did it. We're going to make it." Later, when she tells Leah Gardner about the episode, she notes that Danny's accepting her right to tell him what to do made him seem like her son as much as anything ever had.

It is likely that Danny also will feel more like one of the DeSandos as he deals with their reasonable and fair limit setting. It is normal for moved children, particularly newly placed teen-agers, to try to figure out what are the "real" limits, whether the adult can control him, and how the adult exercises his control. If the resulting behavior can be handled in a straightforward, firm, but unemotional manner, the adult not only weathers this stage of the child's adjustment, but also achieves greater status in the eyes of the child. If the adult is rattled, unduly upset, or frightened, the youngster tends to devalue the adult's competence and may even escalate the misbehavior until he finds out just where the limits really are. Particularly with the older youngster, the fact that the adult is able to "see through" and successfully handle testing behavior can have a positive effect on their developing relationship

(Trieschman, Whittaker, and Brendtro 1969, p. 63). If the youngster believes he can outwit or outfight his parents, he tends to feel unprotected and afraid. He needs the security of being cared for and protected by strong, effective adults. It makes him able to feel that his new parents can be counted on to maintain control so that he is not hurt by outside forces.

Bad Influences in the Peer Group

Leah Gardner was in regular contact with the DeSandos and Danny during the beginnings of their adjustment period. After the first few weeks, she left it up to them whether they would join one of the post-placement support groups or just continue as they were, using her as their support service. Beth and Tony have found Mrs. Gardner very helpful and understanding, and see nothing to be gained by joining the group. They have arranged that each month they will fill out an evaluation sheet for Mrs. Gardner, with a brief paragraph describing Danny's general progress and school adjustment, and another describing his relations within the family including areas of success, areas that need improvement, and any problems of particular concern.

This month one of Beth's and Tony's concerns is Danny's selection of friends in his new school. He has taken up with a group similar to his old gang; they are constantly courting trouble and seem to pride themselves on their tough, sophisticated rejection of adult goals and standards. The DeSandos worry about where this group may lead Danny. Mrs. Gardner shares their concern, but all three adults recognize the value of the youngster's friendships for him, and they are reluctant to interfere. Instead Beth and Tony wisely encourage Danny to bring his friends home so that they can get to know the other boys personally rather than by their reputations, and so that they can keep an eye on what the group is up to. Danny seems to enjoy having someplace to bring his group. Every afternoon Beth feeds what seems like an army of voracious kids, and lives with the jarring sounds of loudly amplified music, the noise of the banging air hockey puck, and the rhythmic bounce of the

Ping-Pong ball. But she finds the racket less of a problem than worrying about what mischief might be going on when the group gets together somewhere else.

Many times moved children involve themselves with other children before they develop much of a relationship to their new families. The child does this because he has to define his public place at school — where he sits at lunch, what he does at recess, who he hangs around with — and also because he may well have a better idea of how to make friends than of how to fit into a family. All children are inclined to answer the question "Who am I?" by aligning themselves with a particular group; it gives them status, reinforces their feelings of power, and becomes the source of their values. Knowing the importance of this alignment to the youngster's own feelings of self-worth and his development of positive values, new parents of moved children are often seriously worried by their child's choice of friends. The child who has a poor self image, or who sees himself as having difficulty attracting friends, succumbs to the first group willing to have him; and this group is usually made up of other children who have social difficulties. The child who has been a problem seems to have a knack for ferreting out other children with the same tendencies, whose actions he can then use to support his own. In either case, the old patterns are reinforced, to the consternation of the new parents.

Parents of a younger child can subtly encourage his participation in activities that cut across school groupings, such as Scouting, church activities, 4-H clubs, or sports programs. By doing so they keep their child from becoming so entrenched in one group that it is difficult for him to select another should he choose to as he changes.

In adolescence, when there is an even stronger drive to identify oneself as an individual apart from the family, membership in a gang, a club, a team, or even the armed services is the usual way for the youth to begin to define himself. In later adolescence there is often a shift to or an inclusion of close identification with a person of the opposite sex ("You and me against the world"), which serves many of the same functions. Parents of teen-agers usually know that it is important to avoid a struggle that makes their youngster answer the questions "Who am I?" and "Where can I find security and acceptance?" either by rejecting his current group or date or by totally excluding his family.

Overdressing

Beth and Tony have observed with interest how Danny has taken on the trappings of his new circle of friends. When he first came, he dressed like his old friends — boots, patched army khakis, tight T-shirt, and a large denim vest that he wore with everything, everywhere. Now he has traded his heeled black boots and khakis for the locally favored sneakers and jeans. He looks much more like the other children in his school and does not have such a "delinquent" air, much to his parents' relief.

But Danny does a curious thing: he wears several shirts at once. It is not unusual for him to come to breakfast in a colored T-shirt under a long-sleeved shirt, and with his vest or a sweatshirt of his dad's over it all. Beth has no luck pointing out to him that he is going to swelter before the day's end and that he is making lots of unnecessary laundry.

If Beth were to ask a child psychologist about Danny's frequent overdressing, chances are she would learn that all children use their clothing symbolically — a fact that is apparent to anyone who has watched young children playing "dress-up." Many newly adopted children share Danny's habit of wearing layers of clothing almost like defensive armor, which not only protects them physically but also makes them feel bigger than they are. Many such children often top these layers with a garment that conveys strength, like Danny's vest, or borrow strength by wearing a borrowed piece of clothing from a larger, stronger person — just as Danny has latched onto his father's sweatshirt. The garment becomes like a security blanket and is frequently worn in utterly disreputable condition; but it should be tolerated by the parent until it is no longer needed.

This behavior will probably go away when Danny feels safer, but he may go through other changes with his clothing before he settles down. He may go through a stage of relishing attractive, lovingly selected garments, changing his clothes several times a day as if it is important to wear them all in a short period. Maybe there will be marked swings from day to day in the style of clothing, one time dressing like a tough dude, another like an African prince in his dashiki, another like an all-American boy. He may love a piece of clothing he has chosen for purchase one day, and refuse to wear it the next. Eventually, he will find his style and settle into it.

During the next several weeks Beth and Tony begin to see some changes in Danny's relationship to their family. It is as if he has stopped just marking time, as if he is no longer waiting until he is eighteen and able to move on. He seeks Beth out for conversation, often sitting in the kitchen to talk while she fixes dinner or asking her a question that leads to a late-night conversation after the other members of the family have gone to bed. She begins to get a better feeling for what her son is like inside. Although Danny continues to see a lot of his school cronies, it is now summer vacation and the group is not as structured by time or place as it had been. Danny spends more time just being at home. He seems to be enjoying family outings, no longer walking far ahead of or behind the family group as if to disclaim any relationship to them.

Things are also improving between Tony and Danny, although the boy is still uncertain how to take his dad. He seems slow to be able to tell when Tony is serious and when he is joking. But he is not as defensive as he once was, and seems more able to join in when the laugh is on him.

Fears about the Future

Tony is concerned about Danny's lack of followthrough on jobs. Several times he has been hired to haul trash or groceries, agreeing to do it for a certain sum of money. He comes home excited about how he is going to spend the money, going on about how much he will have in his pocket; but he peters out on the job. He understands being paid, it seems, but doesn't understand what is entailed in earning money. Tony doesn't know what to do about his son's aversion to work.

One of the questions that hangs over the teen-ager's head is "What will I become?" Though his drive to find an answer is healthy, the teen-ager is often discouraged from trying to grow beyond the place where he is. He or she is beset by a society that says, "Work is dull, playing is great"; surrounded by adult entertainment media that say, "Youth is golden; adulthood means disillusionment, ugly aging, futility, and pressures"; and often allowed the adult pleasures of drinking, smoking, and sex. Many teen-agers in such circumstances are hard pressed to see any reason why they should take on the hard work and care of a family or a job, or why they should look forward to the pleasures of adult life. The moved youngster may have been surrounded by adults who presented poor models of how to cope with life. The teen-ager fears turning out to be "just like his folks" — unemployed, overburdened, poor. This problem is intensified by parents who respond to their children's questions with "You are too young to know," or "You wouldn't understand," implying that a sudden age of enlightenment will clear up the confusions and insecurities that the teen-ager knows he feels.

It is important for the parents of these children to convey their own personal satisfactions, their pleasure in life, and their sense of achievement for a job well done. They should work alongside the youngster, so he understands the camaraderie that comes with shared striving. They should make the child follow through on what he says, and then help him take pleasure in his accomplishments. They can point out clearly that his opportunity to achieve a satisfying life is his own choice, not predetermined by other family life styles he has known.

Changes in the Family Balance

Surprisingly, the member of the family who has captured Danny most completely is six-year-old Adam. The same teen-ager who has attached himself to the most provocative group at school, who baits and goads Sam, and who usually ignores Gillian, is proving to be a sensitive, protective brother to Adam. Unlike the other children in the family who casually and fondly tolerate the youngest, Danny is fiercely protective and openly tender with him. Danny's toughness is a source of pride to Adam, who has a distinct case of hero worship where his oldest brother is concerned. It is to Danny that Adam goes for help with a stubborn shoelace or a problem with shirt buttoning, Danny who pitches in to help Adam tidy up his room before dinner, Danny who has taken it upon himself to teach his little brother to swim. And it is not unusual to see Danny in the shallow end of the local pool playing "baby" games with Adam, or to find the two of them sitting on the floor engrossed in a complicated game of cars or soldiers. Beth and Tony feel their ties to Danny being strengthened as he shows his caring for Adam.

The presence of a much younger child in the family seems to encourage the older new child to form a parent-like relationship as he begins to feel more at home. He frequently models his own behavior with the young child after the nurturing he is receiving from his new parents, and almost seems to be "reparenting" himself as he gives the care, interest, and protection he has missed to the little one. Not only does this add positive things to the family "bucket," but it also provides an acceptable way for the adopted child to go back and fill in missing areas in his own development. The older child, who would feel conspicuous playing with dolls or blocks or soldiers alone, can use the acceptable means of entertaining the younger family member to act his chronological age on the outside while catching up developmentally on the inside.

In spite of the growing closeness among Danny, his parents, and Adam, friction is increasing between Danny and Sam. They seem to be constantly at odds, fighting and bickering over small issues most of the day, with major flare-ups not infrequent. Beth and Tony are coming to realize that Sam has had a number of difficult adjustments to make, too. Although he has not moved into a new family, his own family has changed significantly. He is no longer the oldest child, and that requires some adjusting. The biggest problem, though, seems to be that Sam now has a brother who outshines him in many of the areas that he has always placed importance on. Sam, though a good student, has never been particularly good at sports, and Danny is a natural athlete. Sam could handle that by becoming one of Danny's boosters if Danny didn't make things so complicated between them. But Danny, feeling the pressure of a younger brother who crowds him intellectually, uses his own physical prowess to gain leverage. He sets Sam up time and time again to look like a loser. Although Sam is more mature than Danny is many ways, Danny considers him inexperienced and a sissy. He ridicules Sam about the areas where Sam can't compete with him — sports, girls, physical build.

Tony and Beth have an absolute rule that there is to be no physical fighting in their family, and they have enforced this rule so strictly that Danny no longer settles his arguments with Sam by pounding him out. But the fighting has not gone away; it has turned into a constant shouting match, each boy convinced that the other is totally wrong.

Today the DeSandos are up early for a planned outing to the beach. They are in the midst of confusion, trying to pack a lunch and to remember towels, the radio, the beach blanket, and all the other paraphernalia to take along. While Tony is carrying things to the car and Beth is trying to hurry the children, the two older boys, instead of helping out, are in the bathroom arguing. The volume increases until Beth, who normally would have tried to help them find a compromise, yells, "Hey, you guys, knock it off! We're never going to get out of here at this rate!"

Suddenly Sam shouts, "I hate you, Danny! I hate you! I wish you had never come here! Why don't you just get out and leave us alone!" There is a rush of running feet, a door slams, and then abrupt silence. Tony, who has just returned from a trip to the car, stands dead still. Beth is stunned.

Both parents react the same way. They take quick stock of Danny, who seems to be fine, and then head for Sam's room. Their son is packing, his open gym bag on the bed. "I'm getting out of here," he says. "There isn't room enough in this family for the two of us."

Parents who add a demanding older child to their home sometimes expect their other children, who have not been so deprived and unsettled, to draw on their own strengths for too long a time. The resentments build up and are likely to explode at some point. These children may show remarkable compassion for their new brother or sister. Often they will go out of their way to help the other child adjust to the family, mustering their own reserves of lovingness and generosity to share with the needful one. But instead of noticing what a fine job they are doing, their parents are liable to take their efforts and emotional strengths for granted. In the rush of constant problem solving that goes on around the new child, they sometimes expect their other children to take care of themselves. Many times the "old" children begin to wonder if their parents like the newly adopted child better, because he gets away with more things and the parents spend so much time paying attention to him.

Sam DeSando is now demanding that his parents recognize and do something about the pressures on him. This kind of crisis can be agonizing, but chances are things will be better now that some basic issues are out in the open.

Later, the DeSandos will mark this incident as a family turning point. First, it focused their attention on communicating their love for Sam more clearly. As they worked at convincing him that they loved him and needed him in the family, and that they appreciated the way he had handled the changes that had taken place, he regained his feeling of inner stability and began to see some positive things in Danny. Second, the DeSandos made it clear that no one was leaving — Danny was staying and Sam was staying. This helped convince Danny that he was not going to be kicked out, and Sam that the addition to the family was a permanent fact. The boys stopped wasting time complaining and wishing each other out of the picture and began to deal with each other as brothers. Finally, Beth and Tony demonstrated their own conviction that the family must be a good place for everyone, that the boys' problems could and would be solved. They sat down with the boys regularly to try to figure out what the problems really were and what could be done about them. Danny began to understand his effect on Sam more clearly and to believe that his parents expected him to do something about it. He knew them well enough to believe that they were going to make sure he followed through. Sam began to relax; he could see that his parents were in control and were looking out for him.

Beth and Tony intensified their own efforts to help each of their sons feel like a unique and valuable person, and to help them find common ground where they could relate to each other. They spent time with just the two older boys, doing things that brought them together, building up some pleasant memories of shared interests. At the same time, they provided the boys with time away from each other, making opportunities for each son to pursue his own interests and to have some time alone with one or both parents.

Gradually, over a period of months, the relationship between Danny and Sam changed. They developed some mutual respect and understanding. Although they remained very different personalities, they eventually surprised their parents by not only finding room in the family for one another but actually becoming close friends.

10
Joey

The waiting period for the Lamberts has dragged on and on. As their worker explains it, they are in a large pool of parents waiting for similar types of children at the Adoption Resource Exchange; it is going to be some time before their "turn" coincides with the registration of a suitable child. Dick and Ellen lapse into what Dick calls "a holding pattern," trying to control their eagerness for a child by keeping busy with other aspects of their lives.

At long last the worker calls; a referral has come through. The available child is a ten-year-old boy named Joey who lives several states away. Over the telephone the worker says that Joey has an early history of slow physical and intellectual development but seems to have narrowed the gap and now attends a regular class, though he is a grade behind in placement. He has been getting extra help with reading and math. Joey's mother, with whom he lived until he was fifteen months old, has been described as immature and erratic in her handling of the child, which may have contributed to his developmental problems.

Joey is an enthusiastic youngster, interested in everything—especially cowboys. He can be quite loving, and has a good relationship with his foster mother. He does have a short temper and has tantrums when frustrated.

During their subsequent meeting the Lamberts' worker expresses her concern about the sketchiness of the information on Joey. She is surprised, for example, that in spite of the fact that Joey was considered to be slow in his development no testing has been done on him. Dick and Ellen think Joey sounds fine to them. Ellen secretly has the feeling that they have waited so long that she would take any child at all, even an ugly blue one with green horns.

Joey's worker is contacted and a visit is arranged; if things go well the Lamberts will bring Joey home with them. Now that there is an actual child involved Dick and Ellen find the waiting even more difficult. Eventually the arrangements are completed, and the airplane tickets purchased. The big day so carefully circled on the calendar is only one day away.

Ellen has taken this Thursday off from work to finish preparations before the trip to Williamstown. She carefully selects what she and Dick will pack. Dick, she thinks, should wear his turtleneck sweater with his sports coat; a shirt and tie would be too formal, too distant. She knows what one wears to create a good image at her job, but what do little boys expect a good mother to look like? Maybe she should get her hair done. Oh dear—what if he doesn't like them? Finally she decides on her red dress—it looks motherly and it is a warm and cheerful color. She would laugh at herself for being so concerned about making a good impression, if it weren't so terribly important to her.

Ellen spends the afternoon cleaning house, polishing furniture, arranging flowers. She checks Joey's room with the checkered bedspread and the carefully chosen furnishings. Everything must be ready, she thinks. By Monday, this house will shelter a new family—mother, father, and son. Tonight is partly the celebration of an ending as well as a beginning. Ellen is very conscious of the fact that this is the last time Dick will come home to just her. This is the last time that the two of them will sit on the floor in front of the fireplace, eating their dinner from the coffee table, alone. When next they have dinner in this house, there will be three Lamberts.

By six o'clock everything is ready. The wine is chilled, the candles are lit, Dick's favorite boeuf bourguignon is ready, the salad waits only to be tossed. The air, filled with soft music and the scent of flowers, also holds the hint of cinnamon and nutmeg from the cookies baked to take to Joey. After their dinner, Dick and Ellen lie on the soft carpet watching the glowing embers of the fire. They talk about the richness of their marriage and of this moment, and of their hopes for the future. It is a time of change, a ritual moment.

The next afternoon finds Dick and Ellen sitting on kindergarten chairs in a child's playroom at the agency in Williamstown. Dick looks so funny perched on the little yellow chair, his knees sticking up almost to his shoulders, that Ellen has to struggle to keep from giggling. Did the agency think the Lamberts would be midgets? "Oh my goodness," thinks Ellen, "I have got to get a grip on myself. I'm getting hysterical." Soon the Lamberts hear voices and Mrs. Greene, Joey's worker, comes into the room leading a small child by the hand. This is Joey, for better or worse.

Parents who adopt children from a distance often make a commitment to the child before meeting him. Particularly in overseas adoptions, there is an instant placement. The new child steps off the plane to become a member of his adoptive family. There is no visiting, no transition, just a sudden change. Parents who adopt in this way report several reactions: sometimes there is an immediate sense of identification and recognition; other times, although the child resembles his picture, there is a moment of panic as the imagined child slips from memory and the actual child materializes; sometimes the emotions are so overwhelming that the new parent numbly goes through all the proper motions as if in a dream.

Ellen Lambert feasts her eyes on the boy poised at the doorway. He looks so much scruffier than his picture; what an awful haircut! Before she has a chance to complete her first impression, the young man bounds into the room, taking charge of the situation. Sweeping the small toy cars from a shelf, he asks, "Do you guys want to play?" He begins a game that involves scooting the little cars along the floor. Wanting to be included, Dick joins Joey on the floor. They begin to talk. Dick is surprised at how small Joey is, not nearly the size of the neighbors' nine-year-old son. Joey's face looks like that of an old man, pinched and with thin, tightly stretched skin.

The game is short-lived. Joey's attention is obviously distracted by the other tempting toys in the playroom. Leaving the cars, he takes out some plastic soldiers which he dumps on the table and begins to arrange in teams. Ellen helps him set things up, asking him questions. The army game becomes wild, with lots of shooting and bombing going on. When it seems just about to get out of hand, Dick suggests that they share the cookies Ellen has brought and then go to the zoo.

Joey grabs several cookies. Stuffing the largest into his mouth, he begins to ask questions about the zoo and about the Lamberts' other plans for the visit, spraying cookie crumbs all the while. Ellen and Dick try to return the playroom to some semblance of its original order as Joey gets more and more impatient. His cookies finished, he is ready to be off and away. The worker tells them to go ahead, and that she will pick things up; and gratefully they head for the car.

At the zoo, Joey is entranced. He loves watching the monkeys, and laughs a surprisingly deep, throaty laugh. He throws peanuts to the bears and shudders over the snakes. Inside the lion house he becomes somewhat more subdued, talking about how some boys are afraid of big cats but not him — he isn't afraid of anything. Would they like to see how strong he is? One of the lions growls unexpectedly and Joey, already tense, gives a start and takes Dick's hand, pulling him towards the exit and asking to see the elephants. Ellen's and Dick's hearts go out to this little boy, obviously frightened but determined to make a brave impression. They see that he may be as nervous as they are. Ellen begins to relax, concentrating on giving Joey a good time, feeling protective of him. The lion house behind them, Joey is off again, running ahead while they follow and call to him to slow down and wait.

By evening, when it is time to return Joey to the agency,

Ellen and Dick are exhausted. It has been quite a day. When the worker meets them in the office, Joey throws his arms around Ellen's waist and asks why he can't go with them. Aren't they going to be his family? Ellen bends down and hugs him. "Tomorrow, Joey," she says. "That's when we'll see you again. On Sunday we'll go home." Joey is not convinced; he seems hesitant to leave them for fear they will disappear for good. Dick hands him the package they have brought from home. "Here," he says, "you take this to help you remember we'll see you in the morning." The box contains a set of cap guns with holsters and a cowboy hat. Joey is unbelieving. "These are for me? You got these for me?" With Ellen's help he buckles on the holster and guns. The hat sits a little large on his head. He looks so cute that Ellen grabs another quick hug. There is a sudden change in him. "So long, pardner," Joey says, and then he is off at a gallop with his worker.

Two days later, Ellen and Dick, having just survived a three-hour airplane trip with Joey, pull up in front of their house. Their new son has needed constant supervision since they picked him up at his foster home early this morning. Eager for his first trip on a plane, he had darted out into the busy traffic of the parking garage at the international airport, oblivious to the oncoming cars. Rescued from a near accident, he was content to hold Dick's hand as they entered the terminal. Later they almost lost him on the down escalator as they checked their bags. Buckled into his seat belt, Joey was a jumble of questions about the various buttons and dials around his chair. He spent some time reclining and adjusting his seat and more time working the folding tray and the air vent. He said the takeoff was "terrific," but Dick noticed that there was a tight white ring around Joey's mouth and that he held onto the arms of his chair until the plane leveled off. He was fascinated by the rest room on the plane and could have spent much of the trip investigating the gadgets available there. It has been hard to keep him confined to a seat. Wearied by the steady stream of questions that has occupied most of her attention during the trip, Ellen would like to have a light supper and a soothing bath, and to go to bed early to unwind.

But it is Joey's first night in the Lambert family, and bedtime is still a long way off. He loves the house. After a quick tour with his parents he runs from room to room, investigating everything. Flipping on light switches, working the remote control of the color television, he is everywhere. The house seems so small all of a sudden, assaulted by the noise and motion of an active, curious boy. By the time dinner is eaten and Joey is into his new pajamas, Dick's patience is wearing thin and Ellen is worn out. Having settled their new son in bed, the Lamberts sit in their kitchen surveying the shambles of dinner and the unpacked suitcases in the hall. They are home, instant parents to an instant kid.

Newness Panic

Although Joey's behavior might be the result of neurological damage, his intense need to touch, manipulate, and explore everything in such a jumpy, nervous, incomplete manner may be an outgrowth of his overwhelming anxiety about new situations, his "newness panic." He may not really be exploring or trying to understand the new environment; he does not ask questions; in fact, the desire to fend off fear of the unknown is so strong that any attempt to explain the new situation will probably increase his panic and intensify his irrationality. Other children respond to this same encroaching panic through the "delusion of familiarity," in which they superimpose on the unfamiliar situation an imagined memory of an object, a place, or a person ("I know this gas station; I used to come here all the time," or "I saw someone that looked just like you before," or "Look, that is my uncle driving that truck."). Many times this delusion of familiarity comes across as bragging—the child has been everywhere, done everything, knows all—but it is actually another way to deny newness and to deal with overwhelmingly strange situations. Still other children try to break down the strangeness and to cope with their newness panic through buffoonery and ridicule—the strange new thing or person is simply silly, funny, ridiculous beyond words. This behavior may include grimaces and jerky, disjointed movements, a type of goofing off and clowning that is clearly meant to be funny even though it does not provide any clue as to what is supposed to be so ridiculous (Redl and Wineman 1951, pp. 118-121).

Sleep Problems

This first night with Joey is far from over. It seems to Dick as if he has just fallen asleep when he is startled awake by terrified screaming. On his feet instantly, his heart pounding, Dick races toward Joey's room, with Ellen in close pursuit. Ellen settles on the edge of Joey's bed and wraps her arms around the tense, trembling body. "What is it? What's the matter?" she says over and over. Joey pushes her away. "I want to go home. I want my mommy," he says, sobbing. Ellen looks at Dick helplessly.

"Hey, fellow, settle down. It's okay," Dick says. "This is your home, remember? This is your mommy."

"No, no." Joey huddles up, his arms around his knees, rocking back and forth. "I want my *real* mommy." Can this be the little boy who only yesterday begged to be taken home, frightened that the Lamberts might not want him?

Although Dick and Ellen are able eventually to get Joey calmed down, nighttime is to be difficult for some time. Joey has trouble falling asleep and needs to have Ellen sit with him each evening. He wakes calling his mother almost every night. Ellen comes to dread bedtime; she sleeps poorly, lying awake for Joey's call. She wonders how long it will be before she can really rest and wake refreshed after an uninterrupted night.

Sleep patterns differ greatly in newly moved children. Many youngsters seem to need unusual amounts of sleep — they go to bed early, sleep soundly, and wake after the other members of the family are up and about their business. Children far too old to take naps fall asleep in the daytime hours, lulled off by quiet play or while reading or listening to the radio. It is as if sleep is part of the healing process for the pain of separation from the past family and the demands of assimilation into the new family. Other children, like Joey, find the quiet time before sleeping, when there is nothing going on to dilute their homesickness, to be filled with pain and grief. Many children have dreams that awaken them suddenly—alone, afraid, disorganized in their thinking.

Even if the child has come from a home that seemed neglectful, or even harmful, it was familiar to him. Being taken from it means a collapse of everything the child has known, the death of all he has accepted and trusted. He is plunged headlong into what Sigmund Freud calls "the work of mourning."

Mourning

Frequently the first reaction to the loss is numbness and sadness. It is almost as if the child is in shock. He may be apathetic and uninterested and may show a marked inability to get started and to follow through on anything. Often the child seems to go through his day mechanically, doing what he is told in an absentminded, out-of-touch manner. Locked up in his grieving, the child is preoccupied and lonely. If he smiles, it is only on the outside. Sometimes the reaction is denial—the child is contantly on the go, subconsciously running away from his loss.

In time this initial reaction gives way to angry protest. Rage and resentment work their way up to the surface as the child deals with his pain and feelings of guilt, loss, and grief. The youngster may become easily frustrated, quick to cry, yell, or lash out.

As acceptance of the finality of their loss comes, some children lapse into obvious depression. They don't seem to care about themselves or about anything at all. Frequently they neglect to eat, wash, and groom themselves.

Though painful, the work of mourning is necessary before the child can come to love his new parents. If grief is not expressed and worked through, it goes underground and may leave a lasting inability to be involved except at very superficial levels. Sometimes the normal energies of loving are turned back in upon the child; they may be released physically by excessive sucking, rocking, or masturbation. Incomplete mourning causes other children to withdraw into a fantasy world.

No matter how well the child has been prepared for his

move, there do not seem to be any effective rituals or "letting go" skills that might help him with his pain when the separation comes. The child may also feel guilty; sometimes everyone tells him how happy he will be in his new family, and instead he feels miserable. It is important for the adults around him to realize that the child needs the same support in his grief as if his previous parents had suddenly died.

The period of mourning can be difficult for the new parent. Unable to help the child in his pain, jealous of the love the child shows for his previous family, the parent finds it hard to hang onto his own early feelings of excitement and joy about the child's arrival. The child may add to the problem by behaving like an adult who has lost a mate—clinging to his memories of the past, treasuring letters, pictures, and toys or clothing given him by his previous family. He may talk about them a great deal and ask how they are. If the new parents can keep down their feelings of rivalry and rejection, and instead be glad that their child shows the ability to be attached, the child will eventually work through his loss. In time the strength of the new relationship will begin to take precedence and the past will be less frequently mentioned or remembered.

Eating Problems

Dick and Ellen have been worried not only about Joey's emotional state but also by his physical condition. The boy is *very* small for his age. Although he has a voracious appetite he seems to have trouble digesting his food, and frequently throws up soon after eating. At first the Lamberts thought he had picked up some kind of intestinal virus, then maybe that he was so upset that he vomited; but the problem has gone on long enough that they are worried that there may be something seriously wrong with him. Not wanting to seem like an over-reacting new mother, Ellen has delayed calling a doctor. But she finally becomes concerned enough to make an appointment with the pediatrician that most of her neighbors use. The doctor doesn't find anything wrong; he suggests that the vomiting is just part of Joey's adjustment process. He tells Ellen to keep her eye on the condition and to get back to him if it doesn't improve.

It is not unusual for older adopted children to be quite small for their ages. Usually when they come to feel permanently at home in their new families they go through a period of accelerated growth, eventually catching up. This growth spurt is so common to undersized children that experienced workers watch for it as a sign that the child's adjustment is well under way.

A great many moved children share Joey's problem with vomiting. If the Lamberts are observant they will probably notice that their son is overeating, gorging himself to the point of nausea. Some children who overeat do not lose the food, and thus become obese. Sometimes this is an outgrowth of having gone hungry in the past. Perhaps the child has been moved so much that he is no longer confident about where his next meal is coming from, and so he eats as much as he can while he can. Sometimes the child overeats because he desires a particular food that is not available; unfulfilled desire leaves him feeling unsatisfied by what he does eat. When people are unhappy they often want the same foods — tea, milk toast, custard, or chicken soup — with which they have been soothed when they were ill. It can be helpful to ask the previous foster parents what they have given the child to eat when he was sick. Some children overeat because they feel uncomfortable, lonely, and hollow inside; they try to fill themselves up with food.

What works best with children who display these types of eating problems is to encourage them to eat slowly and to chew their food. It helps if, instead of passing food at the table, the parent serves the plates, giving the child a little more than he asks for to help him feel secure about the amount of food his parents are willing to provide for him. Parents should then refrain from urging more food on the child; many who overeat don't actually ask for more food than they can handle, but eat it because it is offered.

Impulsiveness

By the end of their first month as parents, Dick and Ellen have a number of the pieces to the puzzle that is Joey. They share them with their post-placement support group at the monthly meeting sponsored by their agency. First, there is Joey's impulsiveness. He seems to have no hesitations about anything physical; he just plunges in. Dick tells the group what happened the first time the Lamberts took their new son sailing. Dashing to the end of the dock, Joey dropped his prized new life jacket over the side as he was getting onto the boat. Before anyone knew what was happening he had jumped into the water after it. Apparently he "forgot" he couldn't swim, and he had to be fished out, coughing and sputtering but triumphantly waving the very wet garment. They have had to restrict his use of his new bicycle because Ellen fears for his life every time he rides it, he is so oblivious to traffic. The Lamberts' yard is littered with things that Joey has broken through inappropriate use and then rendered totally irreparable by his attempts to force them back together, hammering or bending pieces "to make them fit."

Ellen finds it difficult to take Joey shopping or visiting because he is likely to just pick up and pocket anything that takes his fancy; he "fiddles" with everything, regardless of whose it is. He seems to be totally at the mercy of his impulses and the temptations around him, and utterly unable to think things through.

Although such behavior may be indicative of neurological damage, John Bowlby has found it in many deprived children. He describes them this way:

> Their behavior is impulsive and uncontrolled and they are unable to pursue long-term goals because they are the victims of the momentary whim. For them, all wishes are born equal and equally to be acted upon. Their power of checking themselves is absent or feeble; and without this people cannot find their way efficiently about the world—they are swayed this way and that by every impulse. They are thus ineffective personalities, unable to learn from experience, and consequently their own worst enemies (Bowlby 1965, p. 62).

Many impulsive children have trouble in school, where they have to be able to postpone immediate pleasures and work for more long-term goals. They have difficulty comprehending the relationship of cause and effect; their own impulsiveness precludes the experience of making choices with an awareness of consequences. Instead of sizing up the problem, they rush to give the answer. They have trouble with reading; they don't stop to figure out a difficult word, but just blurt out a guess. When this approach fails they are likely to give up on the whole process.

Correcting this impulsiveness takes a good deal of time and some readiness on the part of the child. The child has to be taught to oppose his own wish, to postpone gratification or to accept a part of or substitute for it; and to take the time to figure out what the appropriate way to get a particular gratification is. Learning this may involve substitution or invention of behavior (such as teaching the child to take a deep breath, think, and then act before he answers a question or endangers himself). As his control develops, Joey will become less at the mercy of his immediate surroundings and more able to plan ahead. The Lamberts will probably find that Joey masters small pieces of his environment and its temptations at a time. They may be in for periods of real discouragement when the unfamiliarity of a change of routine, such as a vacation to some new place, causes a recurrence of impulsiveness long after they think Joey has the problem licked. Joey's self-control will develop in much the same way that conscience does, through an effort to act in ways that both please and copy the loved parent.

Temper Tantrums

Hand in hand with Joey's impulsiveness is his low tolerance for frustration. "Anything can set him off," Dick tells the parents' group. "We had three major episodes over the weekend. The first one happened Saturday morning, out of nowhere. Ellen and I were lingering over a big breakfast. We could hear Joey banging around in his room — drawers and closets, that kind of thing. But he makes this kind of racket all the time and neither of us thought much about it. Then he storms down the stairs, accusing Ellen of having 'lost' his cowboy shirt. It turns out the shirt is in the laundry and wham, he's off, screaming and pounding his feet and fists on the floor, rolling and thrashing around. When he's like that you can't reach him. It's as if he can't hear or respond to what you say to him. After a while he calmed down, but of course by then neither of us felt much like eating.

"So then, on Saturday afternoon, we're in the yard. I'm making like the involved parent, you know, and putting together a new jungle gym with my son. I hand him the wrench and ask him to tighten up a bolt so he'll feel part of the action, but he doesn't get it square over the bolt and it keeps slipping. Before I can get to him to show him what to do, he's thrown the wrench, heaven only knows where, and he's off again. After a while you begin to feel like you're walking on egg shells or juggling a hand grenade. Then on Sunday he can't get his shoe to stay tied so he heaves it out the car window and there we go again."

The group is full of well-meaning advice about the tantrums. "He just wants attention; walk away and remove his audience." "I disagree. I think he's frustrated and frightened. Comfort him and hold him so that he knows that you are there and that you care." "I think he's just trying to manipulate you so he can get his own way. Don't give in to him."

In an excellent discussion of temper tantrums, Trieschman, Whittaker, and Brendtro point out that parts of each of these statements about the tantrum are true. The tantrum is at once a power struggle, an attention-getting device, and the expression of childhood frustration and terror; but there is no quick and easy cure, like "isolate him." The tantrum is a series of attempts by the child to signal his rising anxiety that some internal sense of danger and helplessness will overwhelm him, and a last-ditch attempt to maintain his self-esteem, which is threatened by his inability to help himself. The three authors break tantrum behavior into six stages: Rumbling and Grumbling, Help-Help, Either-Or, No-No, Leave Me Alone, and Hangover—though not all are present in every tantrum.

Nevertheless, their analysis does provide good ideas on how to help the youngster.

Rumbling and Grumbling. At first the child walks around scowling and looking grouchy, uncomfortable in his own skin. He may whack at things as he passes. Nothing seems to satisfy him; he complains about anything offered and is equally displeased with his own choices. Something is brewing. Eventually the child picks a specific concrete issue to which he can attach importance as a focus for his vague feelings. Occasionally the issue represents feelings that are overwhelming to that particular child. The child who has a deep sense of loss may focus on some toy, now gone, which he remembers in great detail. The child from a broken family may search out an impossibly broken toy and then demand that it be repaired. Sometimes it is the time or place—such as bedtime, mealtime, or a trip in a car—that reminds the child of an especially difficult memory or emotion and sets him off.

Observation over a period of time can help the parent see the child's particular vulnerabilities and characteristically difficult issues, times, and places. Then the parent can try to help the child verbalize his growing discomfort to a supportive adult before he explodes. Sometimes phrases like "You have that throw-something, break-something feeling" can help establish the point that the child has some feelings he is trying to defend against.

Help-Help. Once the issue is settled upon, the child usually signals for help—often by a very visible and deliberate rule-breaking act, which he knows will alarm the adult. His activity usually causes the adult to move very close to him in order to stop the forbidden act. Feeling his own inability to hold back his impulses, the child signals the adult so that the adult's hands, voice, and closeness can give him the safety and control he can no longer provide for himself. At this point some children need to be held for their own safety.

In this stage the adult can help the child by avoiding a discussion of the broken rule, by refusing to talk about punishment, and by getting the youngster if possible to a comfortable place like a couch or bed. Any directions to the child should be given in a loud, clear, repetitive manner. If it is possible to safely postpone or avoid it, the child should not be restrained. If it is necessary to hold the youngster, it should be done no more firmly than is necessary, and from behind so that no one gets hurt. The adult should tell the child what he is doing: "I am not trying to hurt you. You are having trouble keeping your body from hurting yourself and others. I am going to hold you until you can control yourself."

Either-Or. At this point the major theme of the child's behavior is most often a combination of impossible alternatives, which he shouts or mutters through gritted teeth. "Either you do this or . . . ." Often this stage includes verbal abuse directed at the adult ("You're fat," or "You're dumb"). It is the way the child's inner being struggles to control the environment, as compensation for his loss of personal control. This is not the time to be drawn into an argument over the insults, threats, or impossible alternatives; nor the time to return aggression to the child, tempting though that may be. What the adult can do is to maintain time and place boundaries—this is very important in this stage of the tantrum. "You and I are staying right here . . . I am going to hold you until you can hold yourself . . . We'll get this all straightened out by suppertime [or some other time the child knows] . . . This won't last forever." It helps if the adult is able to offer more appropriate ways to handle the situation by seeking alternatives to the either-or choice. ("That may be the only choice you have, but there are other things to do." "I can give you some other choices to make.") Another helpful adult reaction at this stage is to show the child a more reasonable way of expressing anger—tell him that you are angry at what he is doing, sounding and looking angry as you say it, but not losing control.

If seeking legitimate "either-ors," broadening alternatives, limiting the situation in time and place, and demonstrating reasonable anger all fail to stem the tantrum, it proceeds to the next stage.

No-No. Much like the toddler who defines himself by negating the wish of his parent, the child in this stage of the tantrum frequently functions by opposing the adult. Trieschman, Whittaker, and Brendtro point out that if the adult pulls the youngster's arm slightly in one direction, the child pulls in the opposite direction. If the adult says to lie down, he tries to get up, or vice versa. If the adult suggests quiet or calm, the child yells or produces a flurry of movements. If the adult talks about help, the child twists his body to promote hurt. This stage is not a good time to tell the child how much you want to help him ("You want to hurt me," is the response), how much you still like him ("You hate me"), or how he will feel better soon ("I'm never gonna stop hating you"). Probably the safest position for the adult to take is that he hopes the child will regain more self-direction. ("You can be your own boss again when you say no to all this silliness, craziness, thrashing around.")

Leave Me Alone. Gradually the child begins to quiet down, seeming more placid or sad. Although there may still be occasional bursts of negativism, the child may allow the adult to help him get more comfortable. The crying and yelling are replaced by a rather hollow, distant voice, and there often are pursing or sucking motions of the mouth or licking or biting of the lips. The child often checks himself out—feeling his arm or leg, wiping his eyes, straightening his clothing. The adult who has stayed with the child gets a breather. The offer of a drink of water or a cool cloth may be welcomed by the red-faced, red-eyed participant in the battle.

The child usually talks and moves in ways that convey a desire to avoid or curtail interaction with the adult. He puts his head under the covers, blocks his ears, or acts in other ways to avoid contact, occasionally even getting under the bed or in the closet. He is clearly not ready to be involved in a warm, friendly conversation or to resume normal activity. If pushed to do so, it is likely that he will fall apart again.

It is important that the adult respect the child's withdrawal during this stage. It is usually sensible to allow the child to block out the world by hiding under a blanket or covering his ears. Any conversation should be brief, quiet, and calm, communicating concern, availability, and recognition of the child's sadness. The adult may want to move away a little and to focus his attention on something else without really leaving. An acknowledgment that the tantrum is over is often useful.

This period may last only briefly or may extend for several hours. Sometimes the child falls asleep.

Hangover. Although some children look and act as if nothing had happened following a tantrum, many children look "hung over" and feel guilt, annoyance with themselves, and some self-reproach. There is clearly a memory of the tantrum and some distress over its having happened. Now is the time for the adult to help the child develop his awareness of the cues that preceded the tantrum. The adult can talk to the child about what might have led to the blowup, helping him become more aware of the period when he missed alternative ways of dealing with his feelings. Not only are moved children like jigsaw puzzles to their parents, who are mystified by blank or missing pieces; but they are frequently puzzles to themselves. Conversations after troubled times can sometimes help the child fit together his own pattern, filling in the blank spaces in his understanding of himself as the adult shares his observations and notes connections.

It is useful to develop a mutually understood reference to the lead-in behavior, so that the child comes to recognize that his "something lost" or "black mood" or "wild" feelings are a signal of distress and anxiety for which he can seek help from an adult (Trieschman, Whittaker, and Brendtro 1969, pp. 172-91).

For some children temper tantrums are unavoidable; neither parent nor child need feel guilt when they occur. The child is faced with three things at the same time: a great need or fear, the inability to satisfy or alleviate the pangs of the feeling, and the lack of an appropriate way to express his frustration. Children are more prone to tantrums at certain ages simply because those ages have more frustrations than others.

Among the factors that contribute to frequent temper tantrums is the severe underdevelopment of the child's ability to use language to express emotion; this leaves him only physical actions through which to vent his feelings. In addition to giving the child verbal handles for the patterns that usually mark the beginnings of his tantrums, the parent should focus on his need to use language as a better means of expressing himself. During the hangover stage the adult, without "dumping" on the child, can say, "I'll be glad when you can tell me in words." As the child becomes more able to express himself, the adult can sometimes avert another exhausting episode by gently touching the child and saying, "You are rumbling and grumbling [or any other phrase familiar to the child from post-tantrum discussions]. Tell me in words"; or "I know you feel frightened [or sad]. Let it out with words, not with your body." Sometimes tantrums can be headed off in an overstimulated or manipulative child by temporarily isolating him, giving him a chance to catch his breath and regain perspective. The adult may find that saying to the child, "When you are back in control you may come back," will give him the sense that he is in charge of himself. The impersonal use of the kitchen timer to mark the limit of isolation time can be a good device.

Although with some children it would be impossible and unwise to avert all tantrums, parents should help their child find more appropriate ways of handling their rushes of feelings. Children have a deep fear of losing control; they are relieved to have parents step in and put on the brakes when they can't stop themselves (Fraiberg 1959, p. 228). It is also important to the child's developing sense of self-esteem that he eventually give up tantrum behavior. Just as the child comes to view himself as competent through mastery of physical skills, he learns to view himself as one who has control through handling his emotions. The child who succumbs to tantrums often begins to see himself as "bad," "different," or "weak." It helps the child if his parent notices with him the increasing length of time between tantrums without pressuring him to prove that he will never have another. When the child becomes able to resist a feeling's rush and not fall back upon the body language of a tantrum, the parent can point out that the child is learning to stop himself. Although Joey's impulsiveness and his short temper tend to wear out his parents, it is important that Dick and Ellen continue to lavish love and affection upon him without making him "earn" it through good behavior. At this point their positive attention is like healing medicine to Joey; to make him perform in a certain way to get it would be like promising penicillin to a sick patient if he kept his fever down for twenty-four hours.

Shadows of Past Parents

Joey is showing an unusual reaction to his father. If Dick reaches out to touch him, Joey cringes and tenses up. A sudden move from Dick is enough to send Joey sinking to the floor, protecting his head with his arms as if to ward off blows. He seems to expect attack from even a friendly hand on his shoulder. And it can be most embarrassing. Several times Dick has caught neighbors looking at him, obviously wondering what he has done to cause his son to be so afraid of him. If it happens in public, in a store or at a ball game, perfect strangers sometimes come right up to him and tell him he should be ashamed of himself. What makes it worse is that he has never, not even once, struck Joey. Although there is nothing in Joey's record that confirms it, the Lamberts and their social worker share a growing conviction that somewhere, sometime Joey has been abused. Dick jokingly talks about having cards printed up saying, "No, not me," which he could present to accusing observers. But it is gallows humor; inside, Dick is deeply hurt.

Even if Joey has not been abused, he certainly has been raised by different standards. His personal habits are appalling. He has had to be taught, at age ten, how to wash his hands and clean his nails, brush his teeth, shampoo his hair, and take a shower. Even now he doesn't understand why Ellen gets so annoyed when he hops out of the tub and back into the same underwear he has been wearing all week. His grammar is not only earthy, but also filled with "ain'ts" and double negatives.

This "disjoint" between child and family seems to come about as children are moved from what are often lower-income foster families into the more common middle-class adopting homes. Kadushin remarks that as parents speak of the details of helping the child fit into his adopted family, "the transition seems to be not so much from one home to another, but rather from one class culture to another" (Kadushin 1971, p. 149). The necessary adjustments and incorporation of more demanding expectations sometimes make the children long for their former families. They have been "rescued," but they do not always see that as an unmixed blessing. Sometimes they perceive the attempts of the new family to change them as a criticism not only of them, but also of past parents to whom they feel loyalty.

> It is a problem for the child because he is confused by the different patterns of doing the same thing which he has to learn and unlearn. It is an emotional difficulty for the child because the different behavioral responses are tied, affectively, to the different parent-teachers with whom he has identified in learning such responses and whom he now has to deny in giving up such responses. It is a problem for the parents because initially they have to tolerate and accept what is, in terms of their own standards, the unacceptable behavior which the stranger has brought into their family circle. . . . The parents further face the difficult problem of showing acceptance of the child but rejecting his behavior in initiating the process of changing it (Kadushin 1971, p. 149).

New parents are often taken by surprise by the loyalty and protectiveness their child shows for past parents who have obviously neglected or even abused him.

> The attachment of children to parents who, by all ordinary standards, are very bad is a never-ending source of wonder to those who seek to help them. Even when they are with kindly foster parents these children feel their roots to be in the homes where, perhaps, they have been neglected and ill-treated, and keenly resent criticism directed against their parents. . . . These sentiments are not surprising when it is remembered that, despite much neglect, one or the other parent has almost always and in countless ways been kind to him from the day of his birth onwards, and however much the outsider sees to criticize, the child sees much to be grateful for. At least his mother has cared for him after a fashion all his life, and not until someone else has shown herself equally or more dependable has he reason to trust her (Bowlby 1965, p. 80).

It must never be forgotten that even a bad parent who neglects her child is nonetheless providing much for him. Except in the worst cases, she is giving him food and shelter, comforting him in distress, teaching him simple skills, and above all is providing him with that continuity of human care on which his sense of security rests. He may be ill-fed and ill-sheltered, he may be very dirty and suffering from disease, he may be ill-treated, but, unless his parents have wholly rejected him, he is secure in the knowledge that there is someone to whom he is of value and who will strive, even though inadequately, to provide for him until such time as he can fend for himself (Bowlby 1965, p. 78).

It is against this background that we can understand why children with bad parents are, apparently unreasonably, so attached to them.

The "Good–Bad" Parent Split

One of the underlying problems of many adopted children and their families is a mechanism called "splitting." The ordinary child, who lives until adulthood with his biological parents, understands and accepts as he matures that the "good" parent who gives pleasure and satisfaction is the same person as the "bad" parent who frustrates, denies, and punishes. In coming to deal with the contradictory love-hate response the child grows to understand that no one is all good or all bad, and to accept the wholeness of himself and his parents.

But the adopted child has more than one mother and more than one father. If he projects the contradictory feelings of love and hate onto them in such a way that one parent is seen as totally good and the other totally bad, his adjustment is impeded. Adoptive parents who feel competitive with past parents aggravate this problem by sending subconscious messages that, of course, they are the "good" parents and that previous parents are "bad."

This split leaves the child and his adoptive parents open to even more serious problems, because the child identifies himself with his biological parents. If they are bad, so is he — the child fears or expects that he is fated to "turn out just like his dad or his mom." His self-esteem and confidence are dependent on his being able to think well of his parents. If the adoptive parents allow themselves to be aware only of the good they have done the child by taking him into their home, if they remain unable to acknowledge their part in his behavior or unhappiness, and place all the blame on the child and his past parents, the results can be devastating to the youngster.

Adoptive parents must make room in their lives for the goodness of their child's previous parents as well as their bad traits. Their child needs the freedom to love where he will, to hold on to loyalties, to see his other parents realistically and compassionately. Their acceptance of their child's previous parents is perceived by the child as acceptance of himself; and so despite their own anger at these past events, they should make serious attempts to see the strengths these adults have imparted as well as the problems they have created.

> Unlike adults, who are generally capable of maintaining positive emotional ties with a number of different individuals, unrelated or even hostile to each other, children lack the capacity to do so. They will freely love more than one adult only if the individuals in question feel positively to one another. Failing this, children become prey to severe and crippling loyalty conflicts (Goldstein, Freud, and Solnit 1973, p. 13).

Provocativeness

Ellen is running into some real difficulties with Joey. Although he is obviously fearful of being beaten, Joey seems almost to invite attacks, goading his parents to be angry at him. He makes everything into a battle. The combination of Joey's impulsiveness, which requires much physical restriction, and his provocative behavior means that Ellen spends a large part of her day being "mean" to her son. Against her own intention, she ends up screaming at Joey time and again, sounding like a shrew. She feels like a rotten mother most of the time.

It is hard for Ellen to keep from overreacting because she is usually so terribly tired. Caring for Joey is like living on a seesaw; everything is up and down, up and down. She hates it when people ask her, "How's it going?" Those endless nights when Joey's terrors kept her from sleeping stopped about the time her own inner problems began. Now, instead of getting the rest she has longed for, she finds it hard to sleep at all. Her restless nights are filled with thoughts of guilt and anxiety.

Ellen's initial anger at the unknown person who has made Joey afraid of his dad is turning into more compassionate understanding. Before she had a child of her own she felt horrified that anyone could physically abuse or batter a child. But Joey can be so impossible, and his tantrums so provocative, that Ellen is now frightened at how hard it sometimes is to keep from pounding or slapping him, or pulling his hair when he is out of control. Yesterday, during his second temper tantrum of the day, she found herself kicking him to get his attention as he lay on the floor screaming. Her loss of control frightens her, but the memory that at the time it seemed like the right thing to do and that it even felt good frightens her even more. She worries that sometimes she denies Joey something just to "get back at him." What is happening to her? Is she losing her mind? What kind of a monster is she turning into?

A child who has lived with an adult who gave the child attention primarily when driven to anger may unconsciously decide that an angry mother is better than no mother at all. He doesn't know how to get the positive attention he needs to quiet his fears of being a bad, unlovable child; but negative attention is easy to get. The child finds that triggering his parent's irritation, anger, or even active hatred gives him the complete, intense, highly personal attention he wants. He comes to believe that his parents prefer him in the state of being punished, so he sets up that situation time and again.

There are other aspects to this kind of interaction. Negative attention is simultaneously its own punishment and license. The child may endlessly seek to punish himself for his inner guilt. Some develop a "bookkeeping approach" to misbehavior, going into debt on one side of the ledger and then balancing it off with the spankings provoked by egging his parents on. Then the child is in position to repeat the forbidden act; at the same time he uses the parent's anger as license to continue to punish the parent.

Punishment doesn't help much with provocative children; the very threats that the parents shout are what the child is after. Instead, parents must figure out ways to set strong, non-punitive limits without anger or blame. They may want to involve the youngster in deciding what the consequences are to be when he exceeds limits. Parents need to avoid direct commands ("Sit down this instant"), which encourage the child's defiance. Likewise they should avoid hurling challenges ("You do that just one more time . . . ").

It is helpful to structure the day so as to avoid run-ins. If the child has a short attention span, plan his day accordingly. If the child explodes whenever he has to do a certain thing, try to establish a routine that avoids a direct clash. Providing an alarm clock to wake him, for example, may be helpful if that is a tense time between parent and child.

Parents should avoid taking the bait of the child who says, "I'm not going to . . . ." Frequently, children refuse to do something while they are actually in the process of complying. The parent who "permits" such verbal resistance finds that it eventually loses its attraction because it doesn't irritate or antagonize the adult.

Almost all negative children have mixed feelings about their behavior. It often helps to verbalize their confusion for them ("You want to mind and you don't want to"), and to acknowledge their feelings ("You feel quite upset and you are not sure what you want to do").

The only reliable criterion of improvement in this kind of child is the frequency of his negative episodes. Progress is definitely under way when the daily temper tantrums are seen only twice a week. This is one reason why keeping records is often reassuring to parents who wonder if any progress is being made.

Aggressive Behavior

A lot of Joey's problems seem to be tied up with hitting or aggression. He is physically fearful with his father; extremely provocative with his mother, almost determined to seduce her into hitting him; and he is continually involved in fights with the other children in the neighborhood. At first, Dick felt amused that tiny Joey was turning out to be such a "scrapper"; but the amusement has faded with the complaining calls from the neighbors, Joey's scrapes, bruises, and torn clothing, and the recognition that Joey is usually alone because no one will play with him. He has made himself so disliked that he is the target of taunting and bullying by the other children. Always defensive and quick to pick a fight, he has become worse and worse, seeing persecution in everything.

This pattern of aggression and fighting is not uncommon in displaced children. Many times the child behaves as if he were threatened on all sides and is always on guard and ready for attack. His personality is marked by defiance and over-aggressiveness (Fraiberg 1959, p. 6). If the child has had real cause for fear — such as parental rage accompanied by threats or violent physical attack — he forms a view of the world in which he must ceaselessly defend himself against dangerous persons. The child who indiscriminately attacks other children in his neighborhood or in school often feels impelled to attack before he is attacked. He may interpret the slightest gesture or harmlessly derogatory remark by another child as a signal of hostile intentions. He is often so certain of the danger that he will insist afterward with conviction that the other guy was going to beat him up and he *had* to do it (Fraiberg 1959, pp. 20-21). Fearful of injury to his self-esteem, he is also quick to put other children down, to discount or reject them first.

These children frequently complain that a teacher, a parent, or some other adult has hit them. Their expectation of attack is so strong that they can come to believe it has occurred even when it has not. So ingrained is this basic distrust that it is sometimes a long-term problem. It can be overcome eventually, but this requires much help for the child from supportive people — his parents, his teachers, and perhaps a counselor.

The last lazy days of summer simmer to an end at the Lamberts'. Ellen is looking forward to having her own "vacation" over. She has been on a leave of absence from work over the summer, a wise and necessary decision. Now she is eager to leave the demands of full-time housekeeping and the drain of dealing with Joey all day, and get back to the routine of her job. She hopes her work will provide some tangible successes to bolster her ego.

School Problems

On the other hand, Ellen is really dreading the beginning of school, fearful of what it will bring for Joey. In spite of the fact that he can drive her crazy, he can also be a loving youngster, full of fun and quick to hug. If Joey has the same need to provoke his teacher that marks his relationship with his parents, if he continues to be unable to get along with other children, if his impulsiveness doesn't abate and his frustration tolerance doesn't improve, Dick and Ellen can't see anything ahead for Joey but a school year of disaster.

Ellen shares her worries with the guidance department at Joey's school when she takes his transcript in and enrolls him. She explains some of the problems he has been having over the summer and his early years of neglect and deprivation. The people at school are reassuring. Joey's grades from his previous school seem to indicate that he is properly placed in the third grade. It is decided to put him in Mrs. Snow's class.

Joey's defensiveness and impulsiveness attend his third-grade class with him. At first they give him the most trouble when it is time to line up. If someone pushes or bumps or accidentally nudges Joey in the confusion of lining up, a fight ensues. Usually it happens so quickly that Mrs. Snow misses the beginning and is left with having to sort out, "He hit me." "He pushed me." "He hit me first." "I did not." When the class is told to line up, Joey hustles and jockeys to be first. Frequently he is in such a rush that he forgets to get his jacket or leaves his books on his desk. While he attends to those matters, someone else takes the lead position or moves up to where he had been standing, and there is a scuffle as Joey indignantly tries to push into the line and reclaim his place.

Joey also has trouble in the classroom settling down to work. Each morning he is up wandering around, fiddling with the equipment in the science corner display, giving the globe a spin, sharpening pencil after pencil. Mrs. Snow has to speak to him repeatedly, stopping her instructions to the rest of the class. And getting Joey seated at his desk in no way assures that the class can continue, for he is incessantly blurting things out, talking to and bothering the people around him, and just fooling around.

It takes some time for the teacher to notice how much work Joey is able to avoid. As soon as Mrs. Snow says, "Take out your workbooks," there is a disgusted groan from Joey. The other children usually have to wait for directions while Joey paws through his desk muttering and dropping things to the floor as he searches for his text. During math time Joey is usually up and out of the room on another trip to the bathroom. Indeed, it seems to the teacher that Joey spends a great deal of his day going to and from the boys' bathroom or getting a drink, and very little time participating in the class. He always leaves or returns in a way that causes the other children to shift their attention to him, and Mrs. Snow has to call them back to their work.

When it is time for Joey's group to gather at the reading table, he frequently complains of a headache and asks to go to the nurse for an aspirin. If granted permission, he manages to stretch the trip out and miss most of his reading. If denied permission, he fidgets and mutters, "It's not fair. Won't even let me go for an aspirin. Who needs this dumb stuff"—making it difficult for the other children to proceed. He never seems to know the place when it is his turn to read, and he reads very slowly, with much hesitation and guessing. It is hard to integrate him into the group because his abilities are so far below the other children's.

It is obvious that Joey needs tutorial help; arrangements are made for him to do much of his reading and math with the special needs teacher. It is hoped that this will take Joey out of the class at the times when he seems most under pressure, and put him in a one-to-one learning situation where he can begin to catch up without the competition or distraction of the other children.

Even with the extra help, things do not improve much for Joey at school. He is apt to start his day off badly with a scuffle on the bus, followed by a dash up the hall to be first into the classroom only to be stopped by some adult for a lecture on not running. This, of course, makes Joey late to class, and the day goes downhill from there.

Unable to avoid displaying his difficulties in the individualized tutorial classes, Joey is found to be even more seriously behind the other children in his grade than was originally suspected; there is already discussion about his placement in school. Joey is convinced that reading and math are too hard for him to master. He sees them as enemies out to "get" him, who make themselves deliberately hard and who hate him as much as he hates them.

Mrs. Snow is finding it hard to keep a fresh outlook and to remain patient with Joey. At first she could give him the benefit of the doubt, encouraging and cajoling him to try; but now her temper is growing shorter. She begins the day sensitized to his disruptions from the days gone by. As the weeks pass, Joey becomes more able to irritate her and she less able to tolerate him. He is thoughtless, restless, and distractable. His blurting out, his bothering the other students, and his volatile temper harass her; and it is hard not to respond to him negatively. More and more the only solution that works is to evict Joey from the classroom and send him to the principal's office.

Unfortunately, when a child's problems are not easily understood or corrected they act as a threat and a challenge to his parents and teachers. Because the adults feel incompetent in dealing with the child, they often react by increasing the pressures upon him. Mrs. Snow has been much more willing to try than many teachers are. But she has made a common error: she has not called his parents to involve them in the solution. Because so many teachers feel that they should be able to handle difficult children at school without parental help, and because even more teachers are reluctant to let parents know that they are unable to teach their child, things often deteriorate drastically at school before the parents have a clue that there is trouble. With older adopted children, teachers and school officials sometimes feel that the new parents must be "protect-ed" from knowledge about their child; the parents already have their hands full, they reason, or "they will kick the child out if they know" how low his I.Q. is, how far behind he is, how much of a discipline problem he is. Especially parents like the Lamberts, who know that their child comes to school with numerous problems, are wise to set up a standing biweekly conference in the beginning, assuring contact with the school, making their availability to the teacher a reality, and demon-strating their willingness to be involved. When the time comes for the appointment, the teacher is more likely to bring up the little problems, which are often solvable but about which the parents might not have heard until the situation had worsened. As time passes, the parents may want to arrange for the teacher to call them on the day of the biweekly meeting if there is nothing needing discussion. Eventually, the meetings can taper off into monthly, then quarterly conferences. This time spent working with the classroom teacher is often well invested.

Unless the parents use the information they receive from the teacher to criticize, punish, or frighten their child, it also points out clearly to him their intent to help him find school a good experience.

At home, Ellen is relaxing and getting her second wind. Going back to the job she enjoys and having some other things to think about besides Joey have helped her gain a little distance and perspective. But she is concerned about the growing tension she senses in her son. Joey has started to rock himself in bed at night, singing to himself in a monotone. Over the noises that the bed makes, she and Dick can sometimes catch snatches of "dumb school" or "dumb teacher" in Joey's chant; but when asked how things are going at school Joey doesn't say much, except to complain that the kids are always picking on him at recess. Dick and Ellen talk about whether they should call the school, but they don't want to appear pushy.

In early October Joey's school holds an open house. Dick can remember how excited he used to be at Joey's age on parents' night. The classroom, clean and decked out for the event, always took on a festive atmosphere. The kids he hung around with would arrive, their hair combed and their shirts tucked in, showing little resemblance to the playground champions they were. It had been fun to help his folks find his papers among the ones hung on the chalkboard, and to see his dad trying to fit himself into his seat. Joey, however, seems nonchalant about going.

The corridor outside the third-grade classroom is covered with samples of artwork. Joey has a good number of his drawings displayed. Both Dick and Ellen are surprised at how well he draws. Their son has a side they haven't seen. They talk to him about his work, getting him to point out the picture he likes best.

Joey's classroom is a far cry from the classrooms his parents remember. There is a great deal more interesting equipment — a typewriter, a large terrarium, a cage of gerbils. It could be really fun to be in the third grade here, Ellen and Dick think.

The Lamberts stand in the line waiting to meet Mrs. Snow, Joey actively running around and bumping in and out of place. When Dick casually asks, "How's it going?", Mrs. Snow suggests that it would be a good idea for them to make an appointment to talk about it at another time. The way she says it leaves Dick and Ellen feeling, "Uh oh, we've got trouble."

Mrs. Snow's conference with the Lamberts is very discouraging to Joey's parents. Their son is in serious trouble academically, especially in reading and math. He is starting to be labeled a "troublemaker," and they have no idea what to do about that. His teacher is obviously at her wits' end over his behavior and just plain dislikes Joey. How can he ever overcome his problems shut in a classroom with an unsympathetic teacher or spending most of the day in the principal's office? The Lamberts are at a loss.

Because their worker has kept in close touch with them, and because the parents' post-placement group at the agency has given them a number of people whom they can talk to when they need a sympathetic ear, Dick's and Ellen's first thought is to call their agency. They meet with their worker and pour out their frustration and worry.

Ellen sits in the worker's office, tears coursing down her

cheeks. "I never thought it would be this hard. What if Joey is like this for the rest of his life? What will happen to him? To us? There is something the matter with him, really the matter, and I just don't know what to do or how to help him. Maybe we are the wrong parents for him; maybe we should just let him go."

It can be very difficult for parents to accept a child with Joey's problems, whether the child is born to them or adopted. They may openly reject the child or they may outwardly assume responsibility for him but inwardly blame him for a great deal of their own hurt and disappointment. If they harbor the wish to give up on their child they face the guilt of having rejected a vulnerable and damaged youngster who really needs them. If the parent comes to decide that he can never meet the child's needs, the situation usually deteriorates; instead of trying to solve the problems that besiege him, the parent gives up and makes his expectation come true.

The Lamberts' worker talks with them at length, trying to help Dick and Ellen get their feelings out openly, listening to and supporting them without judgment. She finds their anger reasonable, both at the amount Joey has changed their lives and at the lengths they have gone to trying to adjust to him, and she tells them so. She thinks they have reason to be concerned about how Joey will function as an adult and about whether they will be able to find the strength and the time to help him. If they decide to hang on, she says, there will be no easy answers.

Sometimes parents who are not in such close touch with their agency run into real trouble with their child and do not feel able to reach out for help until it is time for the adoption to be made final; then their ambivalence about the child as a permanent member of the family finally surfaces. Joey's worker, though, is in a much better position to try to help salvage this placement, if that seems the best plan; she has established a good enough relationship with this family that they are including her as they seek an answer.

Sometimes just talking about the situation helps it to resolve itself. Joey's parents may see some good qualities in him that will make their situation look less bleak and will balance things out. Maybe his parents will stretch their tolerances, have a change of attitude, and decide that they can deal with Joey, that they can accept the problems he brings into their family. Maybe they will make a new commitment to try harder, to try differently.

Disrupted Adoptions

If this is not the outcome and the Lamberts decide to "disrupt" or end their adoption process, several things will occur, most of them revolving around deep feelings of failure. The worker will most likely feel that she has failed both family and child. The parents will feel that they have failed themselves, their child, and their adoption agency. And the child will feel that he has failed everyone, has not measured up, and has been rejected again. These feelings make it difficult for the people involved to work with one another so that good plans can be made.

In 1975, ninety people met at St. Paul's Church in Chelsea, Michigan to discuss disrupted adoptions. In the course of that two-hour open forum, several important points were made:

1. Disruptions normally occur at a higher rate when agencies are placing children who have had very damaging experiences. Some disruptions, therefore, must occur if the children who need placement most are to be served.
2. A solid, reliable relationship between the adoptive family and the placement worker is essential. Workers must be prepared with more accurate information about the child before placement. Families must antici- pate adjustment problems. The possibility of disruption must be explored with families and children even before placement.
3. Not all placements should be "saved." Placements are usually supported until it is clear that more bad than good is resulting from the relationship between parents and child, and that the situation is not reversible in the foreseeable future.
4. Workers must have their own feelings of guilt and grief well in hand, and must be prepared to help the family

and child better cope with their problems and deal openly with the changes in their relationship. A worker involved in a disruption will need help and support from coworkers, supervisors, other adoptive families, and resources in the broader community.

5. Assigning blame does not help the family or the child with their problems.

6. The situation *will* prod·ıce pain for those concerned.

7. Families can get help from other families who have lived through a disruption as well as from the worker who has a grasp of the complexities of disruption. They will be under enormous social pressure from within their own family group and from the community. The fact of a disruption should not mean that the family could never be considered for another adoptive placement, especially if the reasons for the disruption are known and understood.

8. The disruption follows the predictable pattern of a separation and grief experience.

9. The disruption may well be the occasion for the worker to learn more about the child, from both the family and the youngster, in order to make another adoptive placement possible. A disrupted placement often spurs the worker to a renewed commitment to placing the child with another family at the earliest possible date.

(A videotape of the actual two-hour workshop is available on loan from the North American Center on Adoption, 67 Irving Place, New York, New York 10003. Another videotape, one hour in length and especially suited to training purposes, is available through the Michigan Department of Social Services, 300 South Capitol Avenue, Lansing, Michigan 48926.)

Any worker who has gone through the disruption of an adoption is likely to become overly cautious for a while in her placements of other children in other families. The worker needs the support and help of others on the agency staff to help her keep her own perspective.

Many times arrangements are made for the child to receive

professional counseling as he deals with his loss and his feelings about himself. Perhaps if this counseling had happened before the adoption, things would have worked out differently. But with help from a trained professional or a good social worker, the child is often able to face up to his problems squarely and enter another family successfully.

From the Michigan disruption workshop also came some suggestions about how to talk to a child who is involved in a disruption. Over several conversations, in conjunction with lots of listening and reassuring, the worker might say:

- Things between you and your mom and dad are not working out.
- It is not your fault that it isn't working out. It is not really anyone's fault. I don't know exactly why it did not work out. We all tried our best.
- What we all need to do is talk with each other so we can figure out why it didn't work. Maybe we can learn from each other so that the next time we have a better chance of making it work.
- You can help a lot by talking with me about the things you liked and didn't like. I will try to help you and your mom and dad understand how each of you feels about the things that happened.
- You must be feeling very sad and very angry. That's okay. I feel some of those feelings, too. So do your mom and dad. It's really hard when something you want very much doesn't work out.
- You aren't the only one whose adoption didn't work out.
- It doesn't always work the first time. That doesn't mean that anyone is bad. It usually means that we didn't have the right combination of parents and children.
- Lots of times it works out the second time. We will just keep trying until it does.
- Whatever happens, I'll make sure that you have someone to take care of you. You won't be alone. It's my job to find the mom and dad who will be best for you.
- Even though you feel really scared and sad now, I think

things will be okay after you get settled in your new family.

The family that has experienced the arrival of a greatly desired child, fought through the decision to have him removed, and then must deal with his "death" as a member of the family and with the loss of their dreams, is too often left holding the bag. It is too often cut off from the support of "successful" adopting friends, because of its own feelings of inadequacy and failure or because of insensitivity in the support group. The family is wide open to charges of "I told you so" from unfeeling friends or relatives. And the agency is often unavailable because of the anger and blame felt either by parents or staff. Too often, the parents themselves are temporarily in so much pain that they are even unable or unwilling to support one another.

The other children in the home that experiences a disrupted adoption are vulnerable to both guilt and fear — guilt because when things were rough they wished the adopted child would be sent away; and fear that sooner or later the same fate may befall them.

Agencies ought to provide services for families that experience disruption. If help cannot be provided by in-house staff, other counseling facilities should be suggested. It is helpful if there are other couples who have been through a similar experience and are willing to be used as a resource for the just disrupted adopters. It is totally unfair and unwarranted for no support to be provided.

Dick and Ellen Lambert deeply desire to work things out with Joey. But they need some answers. What is the matter with their son? How serious is it? Can anything be done to help him that they haven't yet tried?

It is time for Dick and Ellen to seek a child psychologist who can do some diagnostic testing of Joey, to help pin down his trouble more clearly and to find ways to work with him and solve his problems. His difficulties may be behavioral, intellectual, or due to a malfunction in the way his body processes visual and auditory information.

The agency should be prepared to guide the Lamberts in

their selection, so that whoever does this testing will have had some experience with older adopted or moved children. Families of these kinds of children too often turn to mental health professionals who automatically assume that the child's problems are due completely to either his age at entry into the family or the personal inadequacies of the adopting parents. Unfortunately, such professionals are quick to suggest that the only solution to the problem is to terminate the placement.

It is also important to find a therapist who will work with the child's parents and his school in finding ways to solve the problems the child presents. All the adults involved can benefit from such skills. Parents' groups, the school guidance office, and the child's pediatrician can be other sources of valuable information in locating a qualified person to test, diagnose, and treat the troubled youngster.

Testing

The battery of tests administered by a trained psychologist helps to answer questions about the source or sources of a child's difficulty, whether the problem is intellectual, emotional, the result of some organic dysfunction, or a combination of these factors. Among the tests commonly used for diagnosis are the following:

The Wechsler Intelligence Scale for Children—Revised (WISC—R) has two sections—verbal and performance. The verbal section tests

1. General information. Does the child understand basic factual information such as the number of days in a week?
2. Comprehension. Can the child use what he knows and apply it with judgment in everyday situations?
3. Mental arithmetic. Is the child able to solve problems ranging in complexity from one step to several steps?
4. Similarities. Is the child able to categorize and group?
5. Vocabulary. Can the child think of things in terms of the abstract and conceptual as well as the functional and descriptive?

6. Digit span. Is the child able to remember several numbers and to repeat them correctly in both identical and reverse order?

These tests are useful because they not only point up areas of difficulty but also begin to establish whether problems stem from educational or cultural deprivation or from retardation. The performance section tests

1. Picture completion. Can the child point out missing details in pictures?
2. Picture arrangement. Can the child unscramble pictures and rearrange them in sequence to tell a story?
3. Block design. Can the child reproduce a block pattern with colored blocks?
4. Object assembly. Does the child have the organizational skills to assemble puzzle pieces?
5. Coding. How fast can the child pick up assigned symbols and use them?
6. Mazes. Can the child correctly solve a maze?

The Stanford Achievement Test is basically a reading test of increasing difficulty in which the child reads a paragraph and answers questions about it within a time limit.

The Jastak Wide Range Achievement Test (*WRAT*) provides a quick, initial rough screening to determine the child's decoding skills (such as reading and spelling) and what kinds of academic material he does not comprehend. It compares the child's intellectual performance range with the average range for his age and grade, and is frequently used as an indicator of the kinds of additional testing that should be conducted.

The Thematic Apperception Test (*TAT*) contains pictures of various situations and asks the child to describe what is happening in the picture to provide a sense of how he views his environment.

The Rorschach Test asks the child to describe ink blots in order to diagnose brain damage or personality dysfunction.

The Bender Visual Motor Gestalt Test; the Benton Visual Retention Test; and the Graham Kendall Test ask the child to reproduce special geometric figures to test for eye-hand coordination and neurological damage.

Drawing exercises are often used — for example, drawing a man, or a house-tree-person series, or pictures of members of the child's family — to gain additional information about the child's coordination, body image, and social perceptions.

During testing the psychologist will watch how the child approaches the testing tasks in order to draw some conclusions about how self-confident the youngster is, how he tolerates frustration, and how much his impulsiveness or distractability contributes to his problems.

Dick and Ellen make an appointment with the psychologist recommended by their agency. But during the three weeks they have to wait before the doctor can see Joey, his relations at school deteriorate further. He is becoming more aggressive in his run-ins with the other children. Several times he has become so upset that he has bitten or scratched another child seriously. When disciplined he now fights back, refusing to do as he is told, crying and shouting, "I don't care what you do to me."

Getting him up and dressed in the morning becomes harder and harder. Joey has little to look forward to each day to help him overcome his lethargy and give up the security and comfort of his nice warm bed. His father wisely mirrors Joey's feeling, saying, "I know you'd rather stay home in bed," and pointing out that sometimes he feels the same way. Once Joey is up he is irritable and full of hostility; all too frequently he begins his day with a tantrum and gets on the bus already worn out.

Finally the testing begins. Even before there are any answers, Dick and Ellen begin to feel some relief. The pyschologist does not seem to feel overwhelmed at the difficulties Joey has. He seems to think there are things that can be done.

Joey's tests show that he functions at the lower limits of the average range of intelligence. He will be able to learn, but he will learn slowly and may need to be exposed to the same information over and over before he grasps it. Because Joey reads so poorly and has trouble understanding and remembering parts of what is said to him, very little of the intellectual content of his classes at school has been available to him. This has undoubtedly fed his frustration and has not helped him curb his impulsiveness. The psychologist believes that Joey is inappropriately placed at school.

Several options are discussed for Joey: a smaller class with less background noise and confusion; moving Joey down another grade level; or placing him in a private school. In the end, the psychologist, the Lamberts, and Joey's school decide to keep him in a tutorial program for reading, writing, and arithmetic, and to leave him in his present class for the rest of the program — art, gym, science, and social studies. The psychologist has a conference with Mrs. Snow and the guidance counselors at Joey's school, explaining how special projects may be used to tailor a more individualized program for Joey — to catch his interest and to allow him to succeed in learning material during the time it will take him to catch up academically. He also suggests that Mrs. Snow take the pressure off Joey in testing situations as much as possible, by testing him individually aloud so that his lack of writing ability does not prevent him from being able to demonstrate what he has learned from listening. Together, the adults come up with ways to constructively channel Joey's energy — sending him on an errand or asking him to wash the blackboard when he gets fidgety.

The special needs teacher is to continue tutoring Joey, and the psychologist draws up some suggestions to help her teach to Joey's strengths and master his weaknesses. He explains that children like Joey are often not aware that their minds have wandered off the subject, or that they have understood only part of what was said to them. It is helpful if Joey is not overwhelmed with words. He can be given what he needs to know in smaller pieces, with the teacher stopping and asking him to repeat what she has just said so she can correct any omissions or misinterpretations. This technique may help parents, too.

Dick and Ellen get a boost from their new understanding of what is going on with Joey. They no longer have the tension that came from thinking his problems were unsolvable. Undoubtedly they will begin to feel increasingly competent as they can more easily decode Joey's behavior — where it begins, how it progresses to its final results, and how the interactions fall into place. The psychologist will be seeing Joey for some time to try to help him modify his behavior. The Lamberts' problems will not go away immediately, but a beginning has been made.

You don't have to be a superwoman or a superman to raise a child like Joey, or any other child with special needs. But you do have to be willing to spend more time at it. Sometimes progress can be very slow.

There is another bright spot for the Lamberts. Dick and Ellen have started taking Joey to the pool to teach him to swim in preparation for the coming summer on their boat. Joey has shown considerable talent and strength as a swimmer. The pool seems to quiet him down. He can learn with his whole body, not just through listening and decoding information. Swimming provides an acceptable outlet for his energy without many distractions. The Lamberts enjoy watching their son develop confidence in his swimming ability; it gives them real satisfaction to find an activity where Joey can earn genuine praise.

One of the most painful parts of raising a child like Joey is watching him spend most of his time at school, where he continually fails to measure up. The intellectually slow, the culturally deprived, the emotionally neglected or disturbed children have little opportunity for praise or recognition. In spite of the fact that their successes invariably take more effort and persistence, they get fewer rewards because what they have achieved falls short of the other children's accomplishments. Some of them are almost totally deprived of satisfaction of their need for significance. It is important for parents and teachers to reward these children for improvement, even if they haven't mastered a task; they must not take their hard-won progress for granted. It helps if parents point out their own strengths and weaknesses to their child, and help him see the virtues in himself — a sense of humor, energy, a willingness to try.

The Lamberts can use Joey's swimming talent as the starting point for helping him understand and accept that people have different things they do well. Some children have a lot of trouble learning to swim or to ride a bicycle, they can point out. Those children have to practice and practice. Others master such skills easily. Likewise, it is very difficult for some children to learn to read or to calculate. They have to practice and practice. No one can choose what he will be good at. But most people, with practice, can master the things they want to learn.

At home and in school Joey is responding to the new regimen. Ellen, who now works only until school gets out in the afternoon, picks him up right after school, gives him a snack, and takes him for a swim. She is working with him on different strokes and dives and he is becoming quite a competent swimmer.

After a few weeks, Joey is doing so much better in his limited class contacts with the other children that he begins to remain in class through more of the day. His sessions of counseling seem to be helping him get along better with the other children, and he begins to talk about one or two of them at home. Ellen accordingly starts to include the boys Joey mentions and some of the children from the neighborhood in their daily swimming trips. Gradually, Joey gains some social leverage from these outings and his swimming prowess, and as he is better able to control himself he begins to make a few friends.

By the end of the school year Joey is finished with his counseling program. It is expected that things will continue to improve for him. The school plans to promote him with the rest of his class, and to continue with a somewhat reduced special-needs program.

Joey and his parents have made it.

11
How Does It
Work Out?

A visit to the DeSandos three years after Danny's placement finds Danny a stable, dependable, well-motivated, and well-liked sixteen-year-old. A junior in high school, he is on both the varsity basketball and the varsity soccer teams, but manages to concentrate enough time on his studies to maintain a solid "B" average. College is his goal.

Danny's interest in rock music and the electric guitar faded at about the same time that his interest in girls blossomed. Lately there has been one girl in particular with whom he spends his time; they sit in the DeSando family kitchen watching television most evenings. Beth jokingly complains that she never realized that teen-age girls eat as much as boys, and she threatens to bill Danny for a "minimum cover charge" if he does all his dating at home. Secretly she is delighted that Danny chooses to spend so much of his time at home.

Danny's interest in girls has deepened his relationship with Gillian. He has discovered that his little sister, now a young lady of twelve, has some pretty good observations to share about dating. Danny is openly proud of his family, affectionate and supportive to Sam, Gillian, and Adam, and good friends with his parents. Tony and Beth are deriving more and more pleasure from their children and occasionally wonder aloud how they "got so lucky."

At the Allens', where there are now two attractive high-school daughters, the phone and the bathroom seem busy all the time. Gena's vivaciousness has earned her the distinction of being the only freshman to make the cheerleading squad, and the house reverberates as she and Julie practice cheers. Gena is still active in the 4-H club and her menagerie of pets continues to grow. She hopes to be a vet.

Tommy and Mark have become inseparable friends, always up to some joint project. Last spring they began building a tree fort deep in the woods; it grew from a simple platform into a two-story affair with windows, a deck, and all the luxuries they have been able to scrounge in various excursions to the town dump. With parental permission (and the understanding that there were to be *absolutely no* matches, fires, or candles) the boys moved themselves into their "castle" for much of the summer, sleeping out there nightly and devising elaborate schemes for getting miscellaneous pieces of furniture up the tree trunk and through the narrow main doorway. Bob and Linda find it hard to remember the insecure, frightened little boy who used to be afraid to be away from his mother.

Lately, as the income from their antiques business has increased, the Allens have begun to think seriously about adding another child or two to their family.

Two years ago, Maureen Reilly was able to get a job working as a secretary at Maggie's school. She and Jack earnestly saved until they had enough money for a down payment on a small ranch house in a nearby development. They love their new home; Jack even enjoys mowing the grass.

Maggie is continuing to be a source of pleasure to her parents. There is no more bedwetting, no trouble finding things to do, no more difficulty with lying or stealing. Although Maggie may never be someone who reads much for entertainment, her grades in school are running slightly above average

for her class. The biggest change in Maggie is her openness —
her face actually seems more candid and alive. She looks people
directly in the eye when she talks with them and there is a
captivating twinkle about her. She has a real way with younger
children, which makes her much in demand as a babysitter. She
has become a responsible, capable youngster.

Currently the Reillys are waiting to hear from their social
worker, who is looking for a brother or sister for Maggie.
Maggie is convinced that her parents have finally given in to her
begging, cajoling, and teasing about getting another child; but
Maureen and Jack know that her chief contribution to their
decision to adopt again has been the happiness she has brought
into their lives. No longer harboring fears about how this kind
of adoption works out, they are prepared for the difficulties of
adjusting to another child, expecting to have some tough times,
but feeling secure in their conviction that they will succeed.
Now if the agency would only hurry a little bit . . . .

Joey Lambert's family has already grown larger. Dick and
Ellen have continued to be active in their adoptive parents'
group, and last fall they heard through the newsletter about an
eleven-year-old youngster named David with many of the same
problems Joey had when he first came to them. It seemed to
them that they had developed a special understanding of these
problems through Joey, and that it would help them reach out
to David. Their chief concern was the possible effect on Joey,
who had been doing so well.

When approached with the idea of adopting David, Joey
was delighted. He took to his new brother enthusiastically, and
maintained a remarkable tolerance for David's problems and
his need for extra nurturing. Somehow, through sharing in his
brother's adoption Joey seems to understand his own better. He
often reminisces about his notorious exploits "when I first
came."

David's entry into the family has been turbulent, as
expected; but things are already beginning to settle down. Dick
and Ellen have found similarities in their sons as well as
problems that are uniquely David's for which new solutions
must be sought. It is especially reassuring, in this second

adoption, that they seem to have increased stamina for coping with David's behavior and that their fears of being unable to work out the problems are markedly reduced.

As for Joey, he has become quite a plugger. Although math and reading are still difficult for him, he digs in and works at them, determined to do his best. He still occasionally misunderstands directions and lacks intellectual flexibility, but he compensates for his disabilities pretty well and earns the respect of most of the adults who work with him. He plans to attend the regional technical high school after he finishes grade school, and to prepare for a career in the field of graphics and commercial design, where he can make good use of his drawing ability. He has become an excellent swimmer, and competes on the local team; and he handles the sailboat almost as well as his father.

There is little doubt that this kind of adoption changes everyone involved. Through the immersion in a twenty-four-hour loving, caring, accepting, value-imparting environment, a "treatment milieu" is created; and demonstrable, lasting healing and change take place in the adopted child. Having found the security of a "forever" family, the children learn that it is worthwhile to truly care for others. They learn that the risk taken and effort made to become part of a new family are offset by what they have gained. They learn that they are worth loving and caring for; that they count; that they can control themselves, affect their environment, and solve problems. They can see themselves as unique, important people, capable of bringing happiness to others.

Their parents often come out of the adjustment period feeling that the older child's adoption has been one of the most significant experiences of their lives. They talk about a sense of enormous personal growth, of satisfaction at having sought a meaningful challenge and met it, and of the privilege of having shared something of lasting value with another human being. Most are convinced that the rewards of their adoptions were well worth the hard times, and that they wouldn't have missed out on their experiences for anything.

These heartfelt parental beliefs that this kind of adoption presents an unparalleled opportunity for personal fulfillment and growth, and the expectation of joy inherent in the promise of one more child to love, explain the fact that so many families who have adopted one older child return to their agencies to do it again.

Their message to others who contemplate adoption and to the children who wait for parents is:

> Listen to the *mustn'ts,* child
> Listen to the *don'ts*
> Listen to the *shouldn'ts*
> The *impossibles,* the *won'ts*
> Listen to the *never haves*
> Then listen close to me —
> Anything can happen, child
> *Anything* can be.

> — *Shel Silverstein*

Directory of State Agencies

The following state agencies maintain listings of licensed adoption agencies within the respective states, or can direct inquirers to the department that currently handles such information. They also can provide information about state adoption exchanges and other adoption and foster care services.

ALABAMA
> State Department of Pensions and Security
> Bureau of Child Welfare
> Administrative Building
> 64 North Union Street
> Montgomery, Alabama 36104

ALASKA
> Department of Health and Welfare
> Division of Public Welfare
> Pouch H
> Juneau, Alaska 99801

ARIZONA
> Department of Public Welfare
> State Office Building
> Phoenix, Arizona 85007

ARKANSAS
Arkansas State Department of Public Welfare
Arkansas Social Services, Child Welfare Services
P. O. Box 1437
Little Rock, Arkansas 72203

CALIFORNIA
State of California—Health and Welfare Agency
Department of Health, Adoption Services Section
714 and 744 P Street
Sacramento, California 95814

COLORADO
Colorado Department of Social Services
Family and Children's Services
Division of Public Welfare
1575 Sherman Street
Denver, Colorado 80203

CONNECTICUT
Department of Children and Youth Services
110 Bartholomew Avenue
Hartford, Connecticut 06115

DELAWARE
Department of Health and Social Services
Division of Social Services
Box 309
Wilmington, Delaware 19899

DISTRICT OF COLUMBIA
Social Services Administration
122 C Street N.W.
Washington, D.C. 20001

FLORIDA
Division of Family Services
P. O. Box 2050
Jacksonville, Florida 32203

GEORGIA
Division for Children and Youth
State Office Building
Capitol Square
Atlanta, Georgia 30334

HAWAII
Family Services
Department of Social Services
P. O. Box 339
Honolulu, Hawaii 96809

IDAHO
Idaho Department of Health and Welfare
State House
Boise, Idaho 83702

ILLINOIS
Illinois Department of Children and Family Services
524 South Second Street
Springfield, Illinois 62704

INDIANA
Indiana State Department of Public Welfare
Division of Social Services — Child Welfare
100 North Senate Avenue
Indianapolis, Indiana 46204

IOWA
Iowa Department of Social Services
Bureau of Family and Children's Services
Lucas State Office Building
Des Moines, Iowa 50319

KANSAS
State Department of Social Welfare
Child Welfare Services
State Office Building
Topeka, Kansas 66612

KENTUCKY
Department of Child Welfare
403 Wapping Street
Frankfort, Kentucky 40601

LOUISIANA
Child Welfare
Department of Public Welfare
P. O. Box 44065
Baton Rouge, Louisiana 70804

MAINE
Department of Health and Welfare
State House
Augusta, Maine 04330

MARYLAND
Social Services Administration
Department of Employment and Social Services
Family and Child Welfare Services
1100 North Eutow Street
Baltimore, Maryland 21201

MASSACHUSETTS
Massachusetts Department of Public Welfare
Social Services, Division of Family and Children's Services
600 Washington Street
Boston, Massachusetts 02111

MICHIGAN
State Department of Social Services
300 South Capitol
Lansing, Michigan 48926

MINNESOTA
Department of Public Welfare
Centennial Building
St. Paul, Minnesota 55755

MISSISSIPPI
State Department of Public Welfare
Division of Family and Children's Services
Box 4321
Fondren Station
Jackson, Mississippi 39216

MISSOURI
Division of Welfare
Family Services
615 East 13th Street
Kansas City, Missouri 64104

MONTANA
Division of Social Services
State Department of Public Welfare
Helena, Montana 59601

NEBRASKA
Nebraska Department of Public Welfare
Division of Social Services
4900 "O"
Lincoln, Nebraska 68503

NEVADA
Department of Human Resources
Welfare Division, Family and Children's Services
251 Jeanell Drive
Capitol Mail Complex
Carson City, Nevada 89701

NEW HAMPSHIRE
State Department of Health and Welfare
Division of Welfare, Bureau of Child and Family Service
8 Loudon Road
Concord, New Hampshire 03301

NEW JERSEY
Department of Institutions and Agencies
Division of Youth and Family Services
Box 510
Trenton, New Jersey 08625

NEW MEXICO
Health and Social Services Department
Social Services Agency, Adoption Services
P. O. Box 2348
Santa Fe, New Mexico 87501

NEW YORK
New York State Department of Social Services
1450 Western Avenue
Albany, New York 12203

NORTH CAROLINA
Department of Human Resources
Department of Social Services, Children's Services Branch
325 North Salisbury Street
Raleigh, North Carolina 27611

NORTH DAKOTA
Social Service Board of North Dakota
Capitol Building
Bismarck, North Dakota 58505

OHIO
Ohio Department of Public Welfare, Division of Social Services
Bureau of Services for Families and Children
30 East Broad Street
Columbus, Ohio 43215

OKLAHOMA
State Department of Institutions
Social and Rehabilitative Services, Division of Social Services
P. O. Box 25352
Oklahoma City, Oklahoma 73125

OREGON
Department of Human Resources
Children's Services Division, Adoption Department
509 Public Service Building
Salem, Oregon 97310

PENNSYLVANIA
State Department of Public Welfare
Bureau of Child Welfare
Health and Welfare Building
Harrisburg, Pennsylvania 17120

PUERTO RICO
Department of Social Services
Services to Families and Children
P. O. Box 11697
Fernandez Juncos Station
Santurce, Puerto Rico 00910

RHODE ISLAND
Rhode Island Child Welfare Service
610 Mount Pleasant Avenue
Providence, Rhode Island 02908

SOUTH CAROLINA
State Department of Public Welfare
Division of Children and Family Services
Box 1520
Columbia, South Carolina 29202

SOUTH DAKOTA
State Department of Public Welfare
Service Administrator
Pierre, South Dakota 57501

TENNESSEE
State Department of Public Welfare
Social Services
410 State Office Building
Nashville, Tennessee 37219

TEXAS
State Department of Public Welfare
John H. Regan Building
Austin, Texas 78701

UTAH
Utah Division of Family Services
333 South Second East
Salt Lake City, Utah 84111

VERMONT
Vermont Department of Social and Rehabilitation Services
Children's Services Division
81 River Street
Montpelier, Vermont 05602

VIRGINIA
Department of Welfare
Division of Social Services
P. O. Box KM623288
Richmond, Virginia 23288

WASHINGTON
Department of Social and Health Services
P. O. Box 1788
Olympia, Washington 98504

WEST VIRGINIA
West Virginia Department of Welfare
Division of Social Services
1900 Washington Street, East
Charleston, West Virginia 25305

WISCONSIN
Department of Health and Social Services
Division of Family Service
State Office Building
Madison, Wisconsin 53702

WYOMING
Department of Health and Social Services
Division of Public Assistance and Social Services
State Office Building West
Cheyenne, Wyoming 82001

A listing of state and regional adoption exchanges in both the United States and Canada is available through:

ARENA: The Adoption Resource Exchange of North America
67 Irving Place
New York, New York 10003
Telephone: (212) 254-7410

Bibliography

Books

Ackerman, Nathan W. 1966. *Treating the troubled family*. New York: Basic Books.

Berkowitz, Leonard. 1964. *The development of motives and values in the child*. New York: Basic Books.

Berne, Eric. 1964. *Games people play*. New York: Grove Press.

Bettelheim, Bruno. 1950. *Love is not enough*. New York: Macmillan.

Blos, Peter. 1962. *On adolescence: a psychoanalytic interpretation*. New York: Free Press.

Bowlby, John. 1965. *Child care and the growth of love*. 2nd ed. New York: Penguin Books.

Bricklin, Barry, and Bricklin, Patricia. 1970. *Strong family, strong child*. New York: Delacorte Press.

Chapman, A. H. 1971. *The games children play*. New York: Berkley Publishing.

Charnley, Jean. 1961. *The art of child placement*. Minneapolis: University of Minnesota Press.

Coopersmith, Stanley. 1967. *The antecedents of self-esteem*. San Francisco: W. H. Freeman.

Coopersmith, Stanley, and Feldman, Ronald. 1974. *The formative years.* San Francisco: Albion Publishing.

de Hartog, Jan. 1969. *The children.* New York: Atheneum.

Despert, J. Louise. 1965. *The emotionally disturbed child: an inquiry into family patterns.* Garden City, N.Y.: Anchor Books.

Donley, Kay. 1975. *Opening new doors.* 4 Southampton Row, London: Association of British Adoption Agencies.

Dreikurs, Rudolf, and Grey, Loren. 1968. *Logical consequences.* New York: Meredith Press.

Dreikurs, Rudolf, et al. 1974. *Family council.* Chicago: Henry Regnery.

Felker, Donald. 1974. *Building positive self-concepts.* Minneapolis: Burgess Press.

Fraiberg, Selma. 1959. *The magic years.* New York: Scribner's.

Gesell, Arnold; Ilg, Frances L.; et al. 1946. *The child from five to ten.* New York: Harper.

Ginott, Haim G. 1965. *Between parent and child.* New York: Macmillan.

Glickman, Esther. 1957. *Child placement through clinically oriented casework.* New York: Columbia University Press.

Goldstein, Joseph; Freud, Anna; and Solnit, Albert. 1973. *Beyond the best interests of the child.* New York: Free Press.

Gordon, Thomas. 1970. *Parent effectiveness training.* New York: Peter H. Wyden.

Harris, Thomas. 1967. *I'm O.K.—you're O.K.* New York: Avon.

Holt, John. 1964. *How children fail.* Belmont, Calif.: Pitman Publishing.

———. 1967. *How children learn.* Belmont, Calif.: Pitman Publishing.

Ilg, Frances L., and Ames, Louise Bates. 1955. *Child behavior.* New York: Harper.

James, Muriel. 1974. *Transactional analysis for moms and dads.* Reading, Mass.: Addison-Wesley.

James, Muriel, and Jongeward, Dorothy. 1975. *Born to win.* Reading, Mass.: Addison-Wesley.

Kadushin, Alfred. 1971. *Adopting older children.* New York: Columbia University Press.

Kravik, Patricia, ed. 1976. *Adopting children with special needs.* Kensington, Maryland: Colophon Press.

Littner, Ner. (n.d.) *The child's need to repeat his past—some implications for placement.* New York: Child Welfare League of America.

————. 1956. *Some traumatic effects of separation and placement.* New York: Child Welfare League of America.

McNamara, Joan. 1975. *The adoption adviser.* New York: Hawthorn Books.

Mogal, Doris P. 1972. *Character in the making.* New York: Parents' Magazine Press.

North American Center on Adoption. 1976. *The plight of the waiting child.* New York: Child Welfare League of America.

Pringle, Mia Kellmen. 1975. *The needs of children.* New York: Schocken Books.

Redl, Fritz, and Wineman, David. 1951. *Children who hate.* New York: Free Press.

————. 1952. *Controls from within.* New York: Free Press.

Rose, Ann Parrott. 1950. *Room for one more.* Boston: Houghton Mifflin.

Rowe, Jane. 1966. *Parents, children, and adoption.* New York: Humanities Press.

Rutter, Michael. 1972. *Maternal deprivation, reassessed.* Middlesex, England: Penguin Science.

Satir, Virginia. 1967. *Conjoint family therapy.* Palo Alto, Calif.: Science and Behavior Books.

————. 1972. *Peoplemaking.* Palo Alto, Calif.: Science and Behavior Books.

————. 1976. *Making contact.* Millbrae, Calif.: Celestial Arts.

Steiner, Claude M. 1974. *Scripts people live.* New York: Grove Press.

Taichert, Louise C. 1972. *Childhood learning, behavior, and the family.* New York: Behavioral Publications.

Trieschman, Albert E.; Whittaker, James K.; and Brendtro, Larry. 1969. *The other 23 hours.* Chicago: Aldine Publishing.

Wahlroos, Sven. 1974. *Family communication.* New York: Macmillan.

Wheelis, Allen. 1973. *How people change.* New York: Harper Colophon.

Winnicott, D. W. 1964. *The child, the family, and the outside world.* Middlesex, England: Penguin.

Wolff, Sula. 1969. *Children under stress.* Middlesex, England: Penguin.

Journals

Bass, C. 1975. "Matchmaker-matchmaker": older child adoption failures. *Child Welfare* 54:505-12.

Bell, Velma. 1959. Special consideration in the adoption of the older child. *Social Casework* 40:327-34.

Bellucci, Matilda T. 1975. Treatment of latency-adopted children and parents. *Social Casework* 56:297-301.

Chema, Regina, et al. 1970. Adoptive placement of the older child. *Child Welfare* 49:450-58.

Fraiberg, Selma. 1962. A therapeutic approach to reactive ego disturbances in children in placement. *American Journal of Orthopsychiatry* 32:18-31.

Gerard, M., and Dukette, R. 1954. Techniques for preventing separation trauma in child placement. *American Journal of Orthopsychiatry* 24:111-27.

Goodridge, Carolyn. 1975. Special techniques in the group adoptive study for children with special needs. *Child Welfare* 54:35-39.

Hammell, Charlotte L. 1949. Helping children move into adoptive homes. *Child Welfare* 28:9-14.

Krugman, D. C. 1971. Working with separation. *Child Welfare* 50:528-31.

Lawder, E. A. 1958. A limited number of older children in adoption —a brief survey. *Child Welfare* 37:1-5.

Leatherman, Anne. 1957. Placing the older child in adoption. *Children* 4:107-12.

McEwen, Margaret T. 1973. Readoption with a minimum of pain. *Social Casework* 54:350-53.

McCoy, J. 1961. Identity as a factor in the adoptive placement of the older child. *Child Welfare* 40:14-18.

Neilson, J. 1972. Placing older children in adoptive homes. *Children Today* 1:7-13.

Sharrar, Mary Lou. 1970. Some helpful techniques when placing older children for adoption. *Child Welfare* 49:459-63.

Welter, Marianne. 1965. Comparison of adopted older foreign and American children. *Social Service Review* 39:355-56.

Young, L. 1950. Placement from the child's viewpoint. *Social Casework* 31:250-55.

Index